WORLD-CLASS ACCOUNTING AND FINANCE

THE BUSINESS ONE IRWIN/APICS LIBRARY OF INTEGRATED RESOURCE MANAGEMENT

Customers and Products

Marketing for the Manufacturer   *J. Paul Peter*
Field Service Management: An Integrated Approach to Increasing
    Customer Satisfaction   *Arthur V. Hill*
Effective Product Design and Development: How to Cut Lead Time and
    Increase Customer Satisfaction   *Stephen R. Rosenthal*

Logistics

Integrated Production and Inventory Management: Revitalizing the
    Manufacturing Enterprise   *Thomas E. Vollmann, William L. Berry,
    and D. Clay Whybark*
Purchasing: Continued Improvement through Integration
    Joseph Carter
Integrated Distribution Management: Competing on Customer Service,
    Time and Cost   *Christopher Gopal and Harold Cypress*

Manufacturing Processes

Integrative Facilities Management   *John M. Burnham*
Integrated Process Design and Development   *Dan L. Shunk*
Integrative Manufacturing: Transforming the Organization through
    People, Process and Technology   *Scott Flaig*

Support Functions

Managing Information: How Information Systems Impact Organizational
    Strategy   *Gordon B. Davis and Thomas R. Hoffmann*
Managing Human Resources: Integrating People and Business Strategy
    Lloyd Baird
Managing for Quality: Integrating Quality and Business Strategy
    V. Daniel Hunt
World-Class Accounting and Finance   *C. J. McNair*

WORLD-CLASS ACCOUNTING AND FINANCE

C. J. McNair

BUSINESS ONE IRWIN
Homewood, Illinois 60430

This publication is designed to provide accurate and authoritative information in regard to the subject matter covered. It is sold with the understanding that neither the author nor the publisher is engaged in rendering legal, accounting, or other professional service. If legal advice or other expert assistance is required, the services of a competent professional person should be sought.

From a Declaration of Principles jointly adopted by a Committee of the American Bar Association and a Committee of Publishers.

Editor-in-chief: Jeffrey A. Krames
Project editor: Jean Roberts
Production manager: Mary Jo Parke
Designer: Mercedes Santos
Compositor: Publication Services
Typeface: 11/13 Times Roman
Printer: Book Press, Inc.

Library of Congress Cataloging-in-Publication Data

McNair, Carol Jean.
World-class accounting and finance / Carol J. McNair.
    p.   cm.—(The Business One Irwin/APICS library of integrated resource management)
    Includes index.
    ISBN 1-55623-550-X
    1. Information storage and retrieval systems—Managerial accounting. 2. Corporations—Finance. 3. Business enterprises–Finance. I. Title. II. Series.
HF5657.4..M39 1993
658.15'11'0285—dc20   92-33940

Printed in the United States of America
2 3 4 5 6 7 8 9 0 BP 9 8 7 6 5 4

To George and Jason, who once again supported the "team" effort, listened to the outpourings of writer's frustration, and cheered loudly when the final words were written.

PREFACE

This is a book for managers who want to understand their financial management information system (FMIS) and want to put it to work in support of World-Class performance goals. Starting with a review of the basic concepts of the FMIS, the discussion moves beyond existing practice to detail the ways in which modern management techniques are changing traditional FMIS methods. The message carried throughout the text is quite clear: The FMIS must begin to serve its internal customers.

Before this change can occur, the "customer" has to understand exactly what is currently being done by the financial function, and why. Only an informed consumer can ask the right questions. But the challenge for the nonfinancial manager is even greater than becoming an informed consumer: The new forms of accounting *build from* the knowledge held by managers inside the organization. World-Class financial management, then, involves every individual throughout the organization in the quest for new numbers and new analyses that support learning and the attainment of a sustainable competitive advantage.

For the financial manager, much of the early material in the book will be a review. Other than the topics in chapter 2, though, it is quite likely even an old hand at the financial game will pick up a few insights or be reminded of lessons forgotten long ago. This does not mean that the book is less useful for financial managers; in fact, the opposite may be true because new management techniques, springing from the customer perspective and the lessons of the continuous improvement philosophy, have changed the nature of financial work. In exploring the FMIS in this period of transition, then, this book provides a before-and after-look that will help companies redesign their FMIS.

The author suggests ways that the FMIS can be redesigned to integrate better with other information systems used by the organization in its decision making. Each of the ideas presented has actually been tested, and found to work, in real companies facing the very real challenge of global competition. The text, then, provides a complete review of traditional FMIS material, juxtaposed against the way these practices are changed when a customer perspective and the *continous improvement philosophy* are factored into the equation.

The book reflects the strongly held belief of the author: It is time for value-added accounting. Because they have infinite potential for providing decision-relevant information to internal decision makers, financial managers have to turn their eyes inward. If they do so, the books will still get balanced, and the auditor will still be kept at bay. If they do not, there will probably be fewer organizations to keep the books for. The harsh realities of global competition will continue to consume companies and industries.

As with all books, this effort couldn't have been completed without the help and support of a broad range of individuals. First, there are my mentors, who have helped me learn to see the FMIS in a different light: Richard Vangermeersch (Vang), Gordon Shillinglaw, H. Michael Gleason of Coopers and Lybrand MCS, Lou Jones of Caterpillar, Rich Lynch, Kelvin Cross, Marty Starr of Columbia, Tom Johnson, Robin Cooper, Bob Kaplan, Ken Merchant, and Anthony Hopwood. Second, there are the people who cheer me along: George, Jason, Sandy Texeira, Chris Karas, and Fran Gammell. Finally, there is the professional support provided by Jeffrey Krames (Business One Irwin) and Tom Vollmann (Imede). To each of you, thank you.

Finally, because this book does at times move beyond the bounds of "accepted" knowledge, there may be material that is not quite as comfortable to read, or that perhaps raises questions or blood pressure. The author accepts full responsibility for this discomfort, and hopes that it is only a minor experience in the process of reading the text. Keep in mind that change never quite feels right, but it can't be avoided. The FMIS has to change its orientation, values, and practices if it is to regain its relevance: The customer within is waiting.

C. J. McNair

CONTENTS

PART TWO
NUMBERS TO SUPPORT WORLD-CLASS OPERATIONS

PART THREE
PUTTING NUMBERS TO WORK TO CREATE
LONG-TERM VALUE

PART ONE

BASIC ELEMENTS OF WORLD-CLASS FINANCIAL MANAGEMENT

CHAPTER 1

THE AUDITOR COMETH: UNDERSTANDING THE ACCOUNTING MENTALITY

An accountant is a man hired to explain that you didn't make the money you did.

Anonymous (3)

Customers drive the activities of a company. The ability to meet or exceed customer requirements on an ongoing basis is the defining characteristic of a World-Class organization. Adopting a **customer perspective** means more than selling a product; it sets a demanding baseline for performance of tasks both internal and external to the firm.[1] A customer perspective also shifts attention to the **process**—the horizontal value chain that is used to meet these demands. The result of this change in perspective is that the entire basis of management and the criteria for evaluating performance are being challenged. Only activities that add value to the customer *in the long run* are supported; non-value-added costs and activities are not to be tolerated.

In a customer-driven company, financial performance is viewed (correctly) as the result of doing the right job (e.g., meeting customer requirements) the right way. Costs cannot be managed: Only the activities that cause costs can be managed. Inside a company dedicated to the customer, then, the demand for financial information shifts from scorekeeping to strategic analysis, with a focus on integrating the "financials" with other operational and strategic measurements to provide a balanced view of how well the company is meeting customer-defined objectives. Yet, driven by the concept of the time value of money, as well as the reporting requirements of the financial markets, the financial function often appears to be more

---

[1] Throughout this book the terms *company, corporation, firm*, and *organization* will be used interchangeably. Most of the discussion will reflect the issues facing medium- to large-size corporations or privately held companies, regardless of which word is used. The reason for this is simply to avoid unnecessary and uninspiring repetition of one term within short blocks of text.

concerned with the needs of external users of accounting information than with supporting management decision making.

This is changing. As companies adopt a customer-oriented perspective, as they focus on incorporating continuous-improvement concepts into their daily activities, and as they begin to respond aggressively to the challenges of a global marketplace, the financial reporting systems they rely on are being modified. These changes extend beyond new techniques for dealing with overhead costs, to the core tasks performed and roles played by financial managers within their organizations. Adopting a strategic focus, financial managers are pursuing new ways to support the decision-making needs of managers across the company. The objective is to provide information that supports continuous improvement and integrates with other measurement systems (i.e., the operational control system), in order to become responsive members of the strategic management team. The financial function, like the rest of the organization, is responding to customer requirements.

The objective of this book is to provide insights into how the FMIS developed its existing focus, what types of changes are being made in leading-edge firms today, and how the FMIS can be transformed into a value-adding tool to support management decision making. The basics of the existing FMIS will be presented, focusing in Part I on its more traditional reporting requirements. In Part II the transition is made to a "customer perspective" for the design and use of the FMIS, including issues surrounding short-term decision making and the costing of products and services. Part III examines the strategic, planning, and behavioral aspects of the FMIS, concluding with an analysis of how to design an FMIS that effectively integrates with, and supports, other types of performance measurement systems. At all times the key theme, or purpose, will be to focus on one question: How can the FMIS better serve its internal customers? It is a question that needs to be asked and answered before competitive advantage can be ensured.

A CHANGING ENVIRONMENT

In every part of organizational life, change is occurring at a seemingly increasing pace. Three-letter acronyms (e.g., JIT, MRP, CAD, CIM) are everywhere, reflecting the impact of these programs on management practice. Through all of this turbulence, companies keep producing goods and services, profits and losses continue to accrue to the owners, and managers relentlessly pursue ways to beat the competition and ensure corporate survival and personal success.

The continuous improvement philosophy is one of the forces driving change in modern corporations. It is a philosophy dedicated to learning as well as the continuous elimination of waste wherever it occurs within the organization. Whether pursued under the banner of total quality management (TQM), just-in-time (JIT) manufacturing, or any of the other available techniques, the objective remains consistent: Eliminate waste in order to gain a competitive advantage. Figure 1–1 briefly details the major improvement-based techniques being implemented in companies today and the type of "waste" they target for elimination.

A second major influence on the modern corporation is a heightened concern for the needs of the customer. As so aptly stated by Schonberger in his recent book *Building a Chain of Customers,* a **customer perspective** can spawn improvements across the organization:

> The Great Shakeup that has spread through the business functions one by one has a striking effect on the whole. All functions begin to see several common purposes and tasks, namely:
>
> 1. To serve the customer: the grand goal;
> 2. To localize the grand goal, a new mindset for each individual and small group: that everyone has a customer—the next process;
> 3. To fuse combative organization units into a well-connected business team, a parallel new mind-set for every department, office or shop: that each has a customer—the next department, office or shop;
> 4. Continual, rapid improvement as the single-minded, grand operating goal.[2]

The customer perspective links the various functions of the company together. It establishes the baseline for value-added activities and provides an objective yardstick for eliminating efforts the customer will not pay for.

---

[2]Richard J. Schonberger, *Building a Chain of Customers: Linking Business Functions to Create the World Class Company* (New York: The Free Press, 1990), p. 13.

FIGURE 1-1
Tools for Continuous Improvement

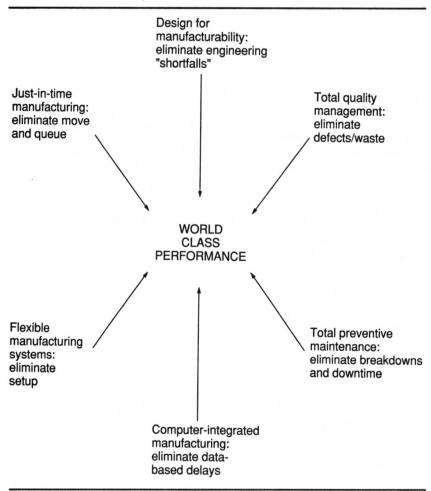

Design for manufacturability: eliminate engineering "shortfalls"

Just-in-time manufacturing: eliminate move and queue

Total quality management: eliminate defects/waste

WORLD CLASS PERFORMANCE

Flexible manufacturing systems: eliminate setup

Total preventive maintenance: eliminate breakdowns and downtime

Computer-integrated manufacturing: eliminate data-based delays

Information in a Customer-Driven Company

Achieving the objectives suggested by Schonberger requires relevant, reliable information. This information has to arrive before a decision is made, be able to support a broad range of strategic and operational analysis, and integrate the financial and nonfinancial results of these decisions. The linkage of activities into customer-defined value chains creates the demand for a flexible data base that is *matched* to the structure, strategy, technologies, and processes of the firm.

The **financial management information system** (FMIS) is a critical part of this integrated information system. It is an umbrella term for the entire range of financial procedures and responsibilities performed in a modern organization.[3] It includes the detailed recording of transactions in the general ledger, the maintenance of accounts receivable and accounts payable records, the issuance of financial statements, the development of management reports, inventory costing, budgeting, and cash management. In fact, the FMIS includes every activity in a company that involves monetary exchange or the use of resources that were purchased with money to create goods or services.

In many companies, though, the FMIS is not serving these needs very well. Chained by external reporting demands and inflexible record-keeping routines, financial managers face a major challenge: the redesign of the FMIS to meet *internal* customers' requirements. Outmoded techniques that are transaction intensive yet value deficient consume most of the working hours of financial managers and their staffs. When change is attempted, the specter of the annual **audit** curtails the efforts. Locked inside the perpetual "do loop" of financial reporting, these managers struggle with the knowledge that they're not serving their organizations as well as they might. In the intensely competitive global arena, this mismatch between the type of information needed by internal customers and that supplied by the FMIS cannot be tolerated. Change is inevitable.

UNDERSTANDING THE FINANCIAL FUNCTION

Finance: *The art or science of managing revenues and resources for the best advantage of the manager.*

Ambrose Bierce, *The Devil's Dictionary*

The traditional role of accounting in both the public and private sector has been one of recording, analyzing, and reporting the results of actions taken by others. The traditional FMIS is an elaborate

---

[3]The acronym FMIS will be used throughout to indicate the broad range of procedures and tools that are developed, maintained, and used by financial managers to support management decision-making needs. If another term is introduced, such as *management accounting,* it will refer to a subsystem of the FMIS and will be clearly defined.

scorekeeping device, often divorced from the decision-making process; it is based on intricate procedures, regulations, and customs that appear to have little bearing on the daily activities of the organizations it is supposed to serve. Today most financial managers are concerned about the relevance of the information they are providing, yet progress toward value-adding financial management is still painfully slow. What roadblocks are inhibiting the transformation of the FMIS?

External Demands: A Relentless Force

> *The perfect bureaucrat everywhere is the man who manages to make no decisions and escape all responsibility.*
>
> J. Brooks Atkinson, *Once Around the Sun* (3)

Financial managers enthusiastically accept the need to create an internal "customer perspective" within the FMIS, but external reporting demands remain unabated. In fact, the external reporting demands on the financial manager appear to grow on a daily basis, as the **Financial Accounting Standards Board** (FASB) and **Securities Exchange Commission** (SEC) continue to develop reporting regulations and disclosure requirements in an ongoing attempt to protect the "informed investor."

Who is this informed investor, and why does he or she need protection? The answer to these questions can be found in the stock market crash of 1929 and the regulatory environment that grew out of its aftermath. In discussing this formative period, Delaney et al. note:

> The widespread growth in the activities of the Exchange had led to expanded ownership and trading activities by an underinformed public. This lack of information, more than the stock market crash of 1929, caused the accounting profession to become involved in the concept of generally accepted accounting principles.[4]

The impact of **generally accepted accounting principles** (GAAP) on modern financial reporting is so profound, it is difficult to believe that there was a time when disclosure was both voluntary and unregulated,

---

[4]P. Delaney, B. Epstein, J. Adler, and M. Foran, *GAAP: Interpretation and Application of Generally Accepted Accounting Principles* (New York: Wiley, 1991), p. 1.

with individual stockholders actively trading their life savings for shares of stock with little reliable information at hand. Yet this was the state of affairs prior to 1929. The outcome of this unregulated setting was the devastation of personal fortunes and national growth. It is a path no nation needs to tread more than once.

The rationale for regulating the FMIS, then, is an underlying concern that an individual investor has limited access to reliable information, and that other groups, such as management, have better access to the information and can either distort it or trade on it prior to making it public (insider trading). The SEC, in conjunction with the FASB, attempts to ensure the free flow of reliable, consistent information that will enable a "reasonably informed" investor to participate successfully in the financial markets. Meeting these external demands has spawned an *audit mentality* among financial professionals; external informational demands have taken precedence in daily activities.

Unfortunately, what appears to be lost in this focus on meeting external reporting needs is the very real fact that the decisions and activities that take place *internally* determine the results these statements detail. Unrelenting financial reporting demands cannot be avoided, but when they become the focus of the FMIS and the management process, the competitive game is often lost before it has begun. In fact, if the Japanese have taught us anything, it is the importance of understanding *how* outcomes are obtained. To be useful, the FMIS has to shed light on the *how* and *why* of various outcomes; financial *estimates* are needed before action is taken, not after.

The Historical Development of the Financial Function

Contrary to popular belief, the FMIS was initially focused on meeting management's needs for information on costs and efficiency, not external reporting, as noted by Johnson and Kaplan:

> Management accounting developed to support the profit-seeking activities of entrepreneurs. . . . The early management accounting measures were simple, but seemed to serve well the needs of owners and managers. They focused on conversion costs and produced summary measures such as cost per hour or cost per pound produced for each process and for each worker. . . . There could be a separate transactions-based system that recorded receipts and expenditures and produced periodic,

probably annual, financial statements for the owners and creditors of the firm. But the two systems, management and financial, operated independently of each other.[5]

An FMIS focused on management's needs gave way to the demands of external reporting as the Securities Acts of 1933 and 1934 took effect. Faced with regulated levels of external reporting that consumed significant resources, it appears that companies decided to make do with an externally driven FMIS. Given the simple world of manufacturing in the early 1900s, and the fact that the managers of these companies had either founded them or worked their way up from the plant floor, it is quite likely that the externally driven FMIS was adequate; more precise cost information simply wasn't necessary. There was ample information available, both from experience and the engineering records, to meet management's decision needs.

Unfortunately, the downside of this focus on the external financial reporting system was that the management-oriented FMIS went into hibernation. Innovation in this area practically disappeared. This failure to innovate was reinforced by an educational process that placed increasing emphasis on the rigors of auditing and financial reporting. This left financial managers unable to respond in an effective manner to the increasing dissatisfaction of their internal customers—they have not, for the most part, been given the tools needed to create decision-relevant information.

You Can't Drive a Car Looking in the Rear View Mirror

So much of what we call management consists in making it difficult for people to work.

Peter Drucker (3)

The need to bridge the gap between the financial function and the rest of the organization that it serves and supports is one major issue facing the modern company. A second issue, equally important, is often set aside in the search for "better" numbers: The numbers that the financial manager produces on a daily basis affect behavior throughout the organization. They **make** certain outcomes or pro-

---

[5]T. Johnson and B. Kaplan, *Relevance Lost: The Rise and Fall of Management Accounting* (Boston, Mass.: Harvard Business School Press, 1987), pp. 7–9.

cesses visible by reporting on them in detail and serve to *hide* other areas by simply ignoring them.

The most obvious example of this phenomenon is the overhead creep plaguing many major companies today. The financial reporting system has treated overhead as an intractable "glob" that is incrementally increased from year to year, with few questions asked. With minimal disclosure and reporting surrounding expenditures, managers bargain for increased resources using their advocacy skills and political positions. No one really knows where the money went. The cost has always been there, though, and everyone seems to be busy. "Empire building" can easily occur in this semivisible world of overhead reporting, where the key question is not "Why do we do that at all?" but rather "Did you absorb your overhead?"

The "absorption management" game is a direct result of an FMIS that passes out rewards for attaching costs to inventory, whether or not the cost was necessary or the inventory needed. The fact that this game even has a name is a clear signal that numbers can drive behavior. Equally interesting are the games played at budget time, or at period close (such as when goods are shipped out of a warehouse only to return after the closing is complete). In obvious ways, accounting influences ongoing operations, focusing attention on the road behind rather than the challenges ahead.

All Measures Aren't Equal

The impact of the FMIS, though, extends beyond these dysfunctional games. There is increasing proof that the assumptions underlying the calculation and use of the numbers can have a major impact on the organization. Edwin Caplan, writing in 1971, introduced these thoughts into the literature:

> The viewpoint of contemporary management accounting must continue to be expanded from the traditional accounting model to encompass concepts of human behavior in business organizations. . . . In particular accountants should endeavor to develop an increased awareness and understanding of the complex social and psychological forces which motivate organization participants.[6]

---

[6]E. Caplan, *Management Accounting and Behavioral Science* (Reading, MA: Addison-Wesley Publishing Company, 1971), p. 111.

The "traditional" accounting perspective Caplan refers to is based on the principles of Scientific Management developed by F. W. Taylor and others in the 1920s. This perspective underlies most modern management techniques. What is of most concern is the fact that the core assumptions of these traditional approaches are in direct conflict with the assumptions of the Japanese management systems being implemented in many companies today, as suggested in Figure 1–2. The Japanese model, with its focus on the performance of the entire system, rather than its parts, and an underlying respect for and use of the "whole person," directly contradicts the traditional approaches and beliefs that have formed the background of Western business management.

A look through the list of FMIS characteristics under a traditional versus continuous improvement model of management makes it clear that little overlap of objectives or characteristics exists. The basic assumptions of the two settings are radically different; the FMIS that supports decision making in the traditional setting seems out of sync in today's fast-paced global market. What is needed is an FMIS that meets management needs in a flexible and responsive way—an interdependent system that can drive management to focus on the process, rather than the results of prior decisions and activities. Results are the outcome of doing the right job.

FIGURE 1–2
Traditional versus Emerging FMIS Characteristics

Characteristic	Emerging FMIS	Traditional FMIS
Core assumption	Interdependence	Independence
Focus of analysis	Organization/system	Individuals
Key role	Analysis	Cost control
Control emphasis	Activities	Costs
Control point	Process	Outcomes
Variance used to ...	Improve Process	Balance ledger/ assign accountability
Desired standards	Historical/trended	Engineered/static
Goal encouraged	Continous improvement	Meet standard
System features	- n-dimensional - Ambiguous - Strategic - Integrated measures	- One-dimensional - One-to-one mappings - Historical - Financials only

The key difference between the two lists in Figure 1–2 is one of perspective. Whereas a traditional FMIS is concerned with **control**, a system that meets customer requirements emphasizes decision making: The former is after-the-fact record keeping, the latter before-the-fact estimating. In supporting decisions, the emergent FMIS incorporates the objectives of the organization; continuous improvement drives the structure of the estimating process.

Completely understanding the degree of difference between a traditional and continuous improvement–based FMIS is not a prerequisite to putting in motion events that will shake the system loose from its external reporting anchors. In fact, the ultimate design and function of an FMIS dedicated to serving the internal customer is still open to debate, in both business and academic circles. One point is clear, though. Any redesigning needs to start by asking customers what they need, and when; the general ledger and traditional FMIS concerns may need to be deprioritized for a while.

"MISFIT" ACCOUNTINGS

The customer is always right.

Proverb (3)

If the FMIS, with its ability to influence behavior, is based on the traditional school of management, it can be very difficult to implement continuous improvement-based management approaches, such as JIT manufacturing and TQM. The insidious effect of a traditionally defined FMIS is that it continues to highlight behaviors that the new management approaches are attempting to eliminate, often ignoring (i.e., not measuring or reporting) the areas of improvement these approaches target.

A simple example will illustrate the point. The Japanese management approaches focus on continuous improvement through the elimination of waste. Each approach targets a different type of waste for elimination. JIT eliminates unnecessary movement and queuing from the workflow. The improvements are reflected in decreased cycle times and reductions in the level of work-in-process inventory necessary to maintain desired production levels. These improvements occur; there is ample evidence to underscore this fact.

Because JIT approaches the manufacturing process from a **systems perspective,** the effectiveness of the entire area is improved rather than one operation (e.g., man-machine couplet). These improvements are brought about by the active participation of employee teams.

The FMIS, though, has never recorded move, queue, or holding costs for inventory; it focuses on individual efficiency. Therefore, even though physical improvements occur as the company implements JIT, few if any of the areas of improvement are reflected by the ongoing reporting system. This means that they are *invisible.* Operating managers see the improvement, but it's difficult to tie them to the bottom line because the FMIS doesn't support the analysis or identification of linkages.

What the FMIS does detail are labor efficiency and volume variances. These are focused on the *wrong* things: getting more parts out, regardless of quality, in order to meet budgeted output quotas. What is quite likely being built in this case is not finished goods, but rather work-in-process inventories. Manufacturing, given credit for production based on direct labor hours used, runs parts and stores them for future use. This is not the optimal way to produce, but it is the behavior that is rewarded by the traditional FMIS. In a traditional system, the costs of holding excess work-in-process inventories, of moving these components into and out of storage areas, and the idled capital tied up in the inventory itself are buried in overhead. The combined impact of these forces is to promote production at all costs rather than cost reduction through continuous improvement and the elimination of waste. When the fledgling JIT system is evaluated using antipathetic numbers and assumptions, the outcome is often preordained: JIT is abandoned because the numbers show it doesn't deliver on its promised benefits.

A Shopping List of Challenges

The negative impact of traditional accounting systems on the implementation of JIT manufacturing is widely recognized. New forms of accounting have been developed to address the unique needs of this setting. Although this is a positive change, there remain a number of challenges facing the financial function today, as suggested in Figure 1–3.

FIGURE 1–3
Challenges Facing the FMIS

Challenge	Why? Who Cares?	Required Response	Current Progress
Quality costs	Support process improvements	Develop new measures and reports	Cost of quality reporting
Track continous improvement	Baseline for gaining competitive advantage	Revise concept of desired standards to match goals	Trended actual costs/rolling averages
Improved product cost and profit analysis	Need to identify and promote high profit items	Develop new forms of product costing and overhead charging	Activity-based costing
Ongoing cost control	Competitive survival	Proactive cost analysis and reporting	Target costing: Process control costing
Maximize value-added	Competitive advantage	Identify and cost activities throughout organization	Activity-based accounting
Maximize long-term profitability	Survival and growth	Project/product tracking over multiple periods and areas	Life cycle costing
Ongoing decision support	Need to meet or exceed customer requirements each and every day	Flexible, integrated, real-time data base	Integrated performance measurement systems

The first area these challenges engaged was total quality management. Companies, devastated by imports of high-quality products from Japan and Europe, fought back with intensified quality-enhancing efforts of their own. These took the form of process and service improvements under various continuous-improvement plans. In attempting to assess the current state of quality deployment in their firms, managers turned to their financial function for reports of cost and benefits of these efforts. The numbers, unfortunately, weren't available.

This shortfall led to the development of cost-of-quality reporting concepts and techniques. Today, most *Fortune* 500 companies use some type of cost-of-quality reporting, either to focus management's attention on key opportunities for improvement or to ensure that desired performance targets are met. These reports continue to evolve, as concerns with **nonconformance costs** expand to include the entire organization.

The unique demand of the JIT manufacturing environment prompted the second major movement to update the FMIS. Faced with increasing discrepancies between operational and financial per- formance reports, and the heartfelt belief that the JIT philosophy was the basis for regaining a competitive advantage, management turned once again to financial managers. This time, though, the requested changes went beyond a new report: The transaction-intensive, labor- focused reporting systems that had been daily fare for accounting in most organizations were brought into question.

The impact of JIT and its technological counterparts (e.g., computer-integrated manufacturing [CIM] and flexible manufacturing systems [FMS]) on the FMIS was significant. Traditional engineered standard costing was abandoned for a historically oriented cost system based on the rolling averages of actual costs. While textbooks had decried the shortcomings of historical actual costs for costing pur- poses, financial managers in JIT-adopting companies found that these trended actual costs were a better tool for evaluating whether contin- uous improvement was being achieved. Trended actual costs provided a metric of improvement that would coincide with the operational realities in the plant.

In addition to this shift of perspective, the financial function in such progressive companies as Hewlett-Packard began to question their emphasis on direct labor reporting. This led many companies to simplify direct labor reporting and to remove it as the basis for the cost system. As the financial function began to examine itself, it became clear that there was ample justification for criticism and plenty of room for change. Techniques such as backflushing[7] began to appear, as financial managers began to search out ways of doing old tasks more efficiently in order to free up the time to meet the new wave of demand from their true customers: internal management.

---

[7]*Backflushing* is a term that has been coined to represent the simplification of inventory tracking and costing. In contrast to a traditional system that generates an inventory transac- tion each time a part or material moves, in a backflushed system only one transaction takes place—when the product or component is completed. This transaction relieves (backwards, or backflushes) the inventory accounts for all of the materials used at one time. The effect is to eliminate most work-in-process tracking.

The list of items in Figure 1–3 clearly shows that new types of management information are being demanded in companies today. No longer satisfied with outdated financial data that fail to reflect the real story of everyday corporate life, management is pushing the financial function to the edge. Financial managers are being asked to do more with less, and to provide the type of decision support needed to keep the organization on track. To free up the time needed to meet these new demands, financial managers are finding ways to speed up existing tasks or even abandon traditional approaches.

There is increasing recognition that management accounting, or the development of information for internal use, requires a different mindset than that typified by the audit mentality. Relevant internal information is based on reasoned estimates and intuition; financially based external reporting is a collection of historical facts compiled in a tightly defined way. Individuals comfortable with the ambiguous world of estimates are often poorly suited for the highly disciplined world of GAAP-based reporting. The recognition that these two areas of the financial function require different skills, competencies, and orientations is leading many to suggest that management accounting be developed as a separate profession from traditional accounting. Whether this occurs or not, the fact remains that serving the internal customer has to become the first order of business for the financial function.

FINAL NOTES

Go around asking a lot of damfool questions and taking chances. Only through curiosity can we discover opportunities, and only by gambling can we take advantage of them.

Clarence Birdseye (3)

The role played by the financial manager in the modern corporation is a far cry from the green eyeshade days. Chief Financial Officers (CFOs) are being asked to join the decision-making team, to actively participate in the process of (and assume the risks that come with) leading a company through the troubled waters of global competition. The need for financial managers to support efforts for continuous improvement has never been greater. In a value-adding world, even the scorekeeper has to justify his or her existence.

The ultimate issue facing the financial function is how to transform existing, outdated general ledger tasks and "watchdog" roles into decision-support activities and competitive-team ones. The transformation has to be done with an ever-watchful eye to the fact that the financial function must still uphold the organization's ability to pass its external audit, safeguard the assets and interests of the owners (e.g., the stock market), and ensure that appropriate internal control procedures are in place. This may result in several different approaches to the financial function in the modern organization:

1. Splintering of management accounting (e.g., decision-support) tasks, and individuals, from the financial function.

2. Shift in emphasis of existing work being performed, placing heavier emphasis on management information, with reduced time on traditional roles (new computer support packages could be of use in this regard).

3. Reduce the transaction "intensity" of the accounting system by moving to quarterly closings instead of monthlies; simplified accounting approaches, such as backflushing under a just-in-time model; increased reliance on bar coding systems for basic data collection; and other work-reducing approaches.

In other words, to meet the increasing demand for financial estimates and information, financial managers are going to have to find ways to eliminate and streamline existing tasks to free up the time to support other management efforts.

Traditional accounting is not likely to be seen as value-adding in the customer's eyes: It is to be minimized. This does not mean the end of the need for sound fiscal management; instead, it suggests an expanded role for a team-oriented, financially skilled manager who can support ongoing decisions within the organization. It is a brave new world for the financial manager, one which must be entered into in more than words. New demands mean new tasks and new challenges that must be developed, utilized, and applied to ongoing issues.

> We can't be like the little boy with the big dog waiting to see where the big dog wants to go so that he can take him there. We must make decisions and learn to live with them.
>
> Lee Iacocca (3)

SUGGESTED READINGS

Barton, M. Frank, and L. Mason Rockwell. "Who's Responsible for the Content of Financial Statements?" *Management Accounting*, January 1991, pp. 24–27.

Briloff, Abraham. *Unaccountable Accounting*. New York: HarperCollins, 1973.

Brown, Victor H. "The Tension between Management Accounting and Financial Reporting." *Management Accounting*, May 1987, pp. 39–42.

Caplan, Edwin. *Management Accounting and Behavioral Science*. Reading, Mass.: Addison-Wesley, 1971.

Fern, Richard H., and Manuel A. Tipgos. "Controllers and Business Strategists: A Status Report." *Management Accounting*, March 1988, pp. 25–29.

Johnson, H. Thomas, and Robert S. Kaplan. *Relevance Lost: The Rise and Fall of Management Accounting*. Boston, Mass.: Harvard Business School Press, 1987.

Kaplan, Robert S. "One Cost System Isn't Enough." *Harvard Business Review*, January-February 1988, pp. 61–66.

Keating, Patrick, and Stephen F. Jablonsky. *Changing Roles of Financial Management: Getting Close to the Business*. New York: Financial Executives Research Foundation, 1990.

National Center for Manufacturing Sciences. *Competing in World-Class Manufacturing: America's 21st Century Challenge*. Homewood, Ill.: Business One Irwin, 1991.

Pipkin, Al. "The 21st Century Controller." *Management Accounting*, February 1989, pp. 21–26.

Runk, Randall C., and Ralph G. Loretta. "Controllers on the Firing Line." *Management Accounting*, November 1989, pp. 38–42.

Sathe, Vijay. *Controller Involvement in Management*. Englewood Cliffs, N.J.: Prentice Hall, 1982.

Schonberger, Richard J. *Building A Chain of Customers: Linking Business Functions to Create the World Class Company*. New York: The Free Press, 1990.

Shank, John K., and Vijay Govindarajan. *Strategic Cost Analysis: The Evolution from Managerial to Strategic Accounting*. Homewood, Ill.: Richard D. Irwin, 1989.

Shillinglaw, Gordon, and P. Meyer. *Accounting: A Management Approach*. Homewood Ill.: Richard D. Irwin, 1990.

Spiller, E., and P. May. *Financial Accounting: Basic Concepts*. Homewood, Ill: Irwin, 1990.

Welsh, G., 1987. and D. Short. *Fundamentals of Financial Accounting*. Homewood, Ill.: Richard D. Irwin, 1987.

CHAPTER 2

NUMBERS FOR FINANCIAL MANAGEMENT

Every company needs an accountant who thinks of ways to maximize profits.

Joe Griffith, Speaker's Library of Business Stories (7)

The back-room functions surrounding the general ledger and basic asset management still consume a significant amount of the energy and time of the financial function. Building from the basics of the **accrual accounting** model, financial managers attempt to capture the underlying transactions of the company, meet external disclosure rules, and assist their company in constructing and maintaining favorable financial statements. Accrual accounting, and the back-office tasks performed within the financial function, are the source of accounting miracles that turn losses into gains, if that is what is desired, or questionable years into ones that at least meet the minimum expectations of the market. In fact, the definition of a good financial person in some circles is the one that can make the numbers meet management's needs, within the boundaries of generally accepted accounting principles (GAAP).

In this chapter the core tasks that underlie the financial function are discussed, focusing on the mysteries of accrual accounting, which provide the accounting system with the flexibility to support organizational needs. Understanding these approaches is the key to understanding the financial function, its impact on the organization, and the "art" of accounting.

UNDERSTANDING THE FINANCIAL FUNCTION

The safest way to double your money is to fold it over once and put it in your pocket.

Frank McKinney Hubbard (1)

The financial function is concerned with measuring, in monetary terms, the economic effects of exchange transactions undertaken by the organization.[1] These economic transactions are classified according to their effect on the **assets, liabilities,** and **owner's equity** of the organization. Assets are objects, claims, and other rights owned by, and having value to, the organization.[2] Some assets are monetary, or enforceable claims for specified amounts of money. Others are tangible physical holdings, such as inventory, plant and equipment, and office supplies. Finally, assets can be intangible in nature, such as patents and trademarks.

The core task of the financial function is the recording of ongoing transactions as they affect the assets, liabilities, and owner's equity of the firm. It is bookkeeping at its best: Ensuring the ongoing balance between the sources (debt and equity) and uses (assets) of the organization's funds (e.g., assets = liabilities + owner's equity). This balance is maintained through detailed recordkeeping procedures called **double-entry accounting.** The system of checks and balances based on the use of debits and credits is the basis of financial recordkeeping; it is a numbers game that can have a broad range of outcomes, all looking equally precise.

Assets are purchased with funds provided by owners and creditors. Liabilities represent creditor's claims on the company's assets. Liabilities can be incurred for goods or services (accounts payable), short-term operating funds (notes payable), wages and salaries, and long-term funding (bonds payable). Usually, creditors require the payment of interest for the use of their funds. Interest is an ongoing, unavoidable cost of doing business that must be paid out of current cash balances. This can cause major problems for a company that becomes **over-leveraged** (i.e., has an excess amount of its resources funded through debt).

Owner's equity accounts record the funds provided by the company's owners, as well as the retention of portions of income from prior periods (**retained earnings**). These funds are invested for long periods of time. Owners expect a payment for the use of their funds. This payment is made in the form of **dividends.** Dividends are paid

---

[1]G. Welsch and D. Short, *Fundamentals of Financial Accounting,* 5th ed. (Homewood, Ill.: Richard D. Irwin, 1987), p. 5.

[2]The definitions of assets, liabilities, and owner's equity in this section are based on discussions found in G. Shillinglaw and P. Meyer, *Accounting: A Management Approach,* 8th ed. (Homewood, Ill.: Richard D. Irwin, 1986), pp. 4–6.

from the profits of the firm; a company that pays dividends on an ongoing basis when there are no profits to support them will go out of business. Creditors, not owners, have the right to the company's assets in the case of liquidation.

Revenues and **expenses** are the final categories of accounts maintained in the financial records. This series of accounts captures the changes in the owner's equity portion of the basic accounting equation, otherwise known as **net income.** Revenues are the resources received by the business as a result of providing products or services to outsiders during a specified period of time. Expenses are the resources (i.e., assets) consumed by the company to generate the revenues of that period. Net income (or loss) is what is left after all the expenses are subtracted from the revenues they generated. Two basic statements are prepared from this data. The **income statement** captures the effects of changes in the source and use of funds during a period; the **balance sheet** provides a listing of account balances as of a specific date. Financial transactions and the reports that are built from their aggregation create an input–output information cycle.

FINANCIAL REPORTING: INPUTS AND OUTPUTS

Facts are stupid until brought into connection with some general law.

Louis Agassiz (1)

Any information system can be portrayed as a series of inputs and outputs, as suggested in Figure 2–1. Looking at the input side of the diagram, the financial reporting system is made up of data from financial transactions based on historical costs recorded in the general ledger, cost elements for the various inputs used in the productive process, engineering estimates (e.g., standard costs), information on external factors (e.g., the prime rate or cost of capital), policy issues, data on external reporting requirements (e.g., tax law, rates and reporting; SEC and FASB disclosure rulings), and the current financial status of the organization as captured by the financial statements and cash balances. Each of these inputs provides essential details about some aspect of the financial status of the firm.

Outputs from this data base include the published financial statements, tax and public reporting documents, managerial reports (e.g., accounts receivable aging), inventory valuation and standard cost rollups, budgets and financial plans, exception and variance reports,

FIGURE 2–1
Financial Reporting Systems: Inputs and Outputs

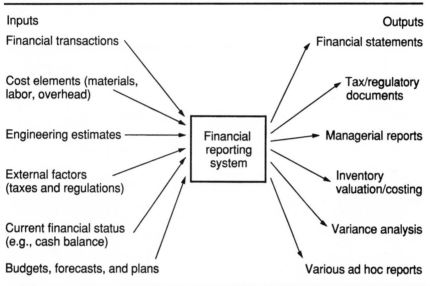

Inputs

Financial transactions

Cost elements (materials, labor, overhead)

Engineering estimates

External factors (taxes and regulations)

Current financial status (e.g., cash balance)

Budgets, forecasts, and plans

Financial reporting system

Outputs

Financial statements

Tax/regulatory documents

Managerial reports

Inventory valuation/costing

Variance analysis

Various ad hoc reports

make versus buy analysis, capital acquisition analysis, product and segment profitability analysis, life cycle cost analysis, and project auditing or monitoring reports. These ongoing and ad hoc reports are based on the input data, managerial estimates, and knowledge about key contending variables in the organization and its environment. Simply listing these inputs and outputs, though, fails to capture the complexity that underlies the financial process.

Inputs: Understanding the Role of Financial Transactions

Financial transactions are the foundation of most of the listed inputs to the financial reporting system in Figure 2–1. An accounting transaction is recorded whenever resources are acquired or used up in production, when cash is obtained or bills paid, when sales are made or returns credited, to list just a few examples. The structure used to record these transactions is the general ledger system, which is built around two basic equations:

$$\text{Assets} = \text{Liabilities} + \text{Owner's equity}$$
$$\text{Debits} = \text{Credits}$$

These equations provide a self-balancing series of accounts because of the following relationships (creating the underlying system of double-entry accounting):

	Increase with a	Decrease with a
Assets	Debit	Credit
Liabilities	Credit	Debit
Owner's Equity	Credit	Debit

Every financial transaction, then, requires a self-balancing entry that exactly matches the debits to the credits, following the rules for the various types of accounts as suggested.

These three account classes are the basis for maintaining the balance sheet, or statement of financial position, which lists the resources the company owns (the uses of funds) and the sources of the underlying capital for their purchase (sources of funds). The financial system is rounded out by adding revenues and expenses to the equation. What are they, and how do they factor into the accounting system? Revenues and expenses increase (or decrease) the owner's equity account. They are reported in the income statement, which provides a summary report of changes in the owner's equity account. This means that the double-entry system will record increases in revenues in the same manner as increases in owner's equity (i.e., as credits), and increases in expenses as *decreases* in owner's equity (i.e., as debits).

Many argue that this basic structure does not need to be understood to understand the financial function. That is equivalent to saying that one can read a novel in French without understanding the language. This self-balancing set of accounts constrains the type of information the financial system can record and forces certain types of reporting and behavior. For the practicing manager, it is important to keep in mind the fact that the financial manager is, at all times, concerned with maintaining the underlying balance of the financial accounts, is required to do so, and is constrained at times (both mentally and physically) from pursuing certain courses of action because of its power. In many respects, it defines the culture of financial reporting.

A financial transaction records changes in the balances of any of these five basic types of accounts. These transactions, although restricted to be self-balancing, can actually be "painted" in many different ways. A financial manager usually has more than one option for recording any specific transaction. The decision made at this point can affect net income radically. That is the mystery of accounting. While the system itself is precise, always balancing the sources and uses of funds, the decision about how to record the transaction provides tremendous latitude for the financial system. When coupled with the fact that the **matching principle**[3] can be used to justify the recording of some expenses or delaying of others, based on the desired "bottom line," the financial system becomes a very fluid version of financial truth. This underscores the common understanding of what makes a good controller: A good controller can provide any set of numbers (any outcome) that the operating manager needs to justify a decision.

Why shouldn't the truth be stranger than fiction? Fiction, after all, has to make sense.

Mark Twain (1)

BASIC FINANCIAL STATEMENTS

In every person, even in such as appear most reckless, there is an inherent desire to attain balance.

Jakob Wasserman, *The Book of Marriage* (4)

The efforts to regulate the disclosures made by companies to investors revolve around the three basic financial statements presented in Figure 2–2: the balance sheet, the income statement, and the statement of cash flows. These three primary financial statements summarize the current financial status of the company (the balance sheet) and how that status has changed over the previous year (income statement and statement of cash flows). They are the culmination of millions of financial transactions, recorded throughout the year, that attempted to capture the key events affecting the financial health of the organization.

---

[3]The matching principle is an accounting "rule" that requires expenses in a period to be matched against the revenues they generated. The objective here is to make sure that the reported profits are not overstated.

FIGURE 2–2
Lawnmasters, Incorporated Financial Statements

LAWNMASTERS, INCORPORATED
Balance Sheets
At December 31, 1990 and 1991

	December 31, 1991		December 31, 1990	
Assets				
Current assets:				
Cash....................	$41,300		$31,000	
Accounts receivable (net of allowance for bad debts)..................	35,000		30,000	
Inventory.................	25,000	$101,300	29,000	$ 90,000
Long-term investments:				
Common stock in Quick-seed Corporation........		10,000		15,000
Long-term assets:				
Property, Plant and Equipment..............	90,500		85,800	
Less: Accumulated depreciation............	31,500	59,000	23,600	62,200
Total assets.................		$170,300		$167,200
Liabilities				
Current liabilities:				
Accounts payable........	$35,000		$32,000	
Income tax payable.......	1,500		2,000	
Short-term notes payable..	15,000	$ 51,500	18,000	$ 52,000
Long-term liabilities:				
Long-term notes payable..		15,000		10,000
Bonds payable...........		35,000		40,000
Stockholders' equity				
Common stock, par $10...	50,000		50,000	
Contributed capital in excess of par..........	5,000		5,000	
Retained earnings (net of $7,000 in dividends paid out each year).............	13,800	68,800	10,200	$ 65,200
Total liabilities and stockholders' equity.........		$170,300		$167,200

FIGURE 2–2 *(continued)*

LAWNMASTER, INCORPORATED
Income Statement
For the Years Ending December 31, 1990 and 1991

		December 31, 1991		*December 31, 1990*
Sales revenue..............		$160,000		$125,000
Cost of goods sold.........		100,000		75,000
Gross margin..............		$ 60,000		$ 50,000
Less expenses:				
Salaries..................	$25,000		$24,100	
Depreciation expense....	7,900		4,300	
Advertising..............	6,500		5,000	
Interest..................	3,000	42,400	2,400	35,800
Net income before taxes...		17,600		14,200
Income taxes............		7,000		5,600
Net income................		$ 10,600		$ 8,600

LAWNMASTERS, INCORPORATED
Statement of Retained Earnings
For the Years Ending December 31, 1990 and 1991

	December 31, 1991	*December 31, 1990*
Retained earnings balance, January 1..................	$10,200	$ 8,600
Plus net income for the year......................	10,600	8,600
Total retained earnings available to stockholders....	$20,800	$17,200
Less dividends paid..........	7,000	7,000
Retained earnings balance, December 31..............	$13,800	$10,200

These three primary statements are linked. In accounting terminology this is called **articulation**, which means that the two "flow" statements (the income statement and statement of cash flows) close into the balance sheet; changes in net income are reflected on the balance sheet, and changes in the definition or composition of resources on the balance sheet affect the bottom line (e.g., net income). The income statement details changes in the **retained earnings**, or owner's equity, section of the balance sheet. As can be see from the income statement, the net income for the year ($10,600) is added to retained

---

FIGURE 2–2 (continued)

LAWNMASTERS, INCORPORATED
Statement of Cash Flows
For the Year Ending December 31, 1991

Cash flows from operating activities:			
Net income, per income statement.......		$10,600	
Add:			
Depreciation...........................	$7,900		
Decrease in inventories................	4,000		
Increase in accounts payable..........	3,000	14,900	
		$25,500	
Deduct:			
Increases in accounts receivable	$5,000		
Decrease in taxes payable.............	500		
Decrease in short-term note payable ..	3,000	8,500	
Net cash flow from operating activities			$17,000
Cash flows from investing activities:			
Cash received from sale of investments..		$ 5,000	
Less cash paid for equipment...........		4,700	
Net cash flow from investing activities....			300
Cash flows from financing activities:			
Cash received from long-term note			
payable		$ 5,000	
Less:			
Retirement of bonds payable..........	$5,000		
Cash paid for dividends...............	7,000	(12,000)	
Net cash flow provided by financing			
activities			(7,000)
Increase in cash..........................			$10,300
Cash at the beginning of the year.........			31,000
Cash at the end of the year...............			$41,300

---

earnings ($10,200) at the beginning of the year (e.g., the residual earnings retained for dividends and operations), dividends paid ($7,000) are removed from the account, and the final reconciled retained earnings amount, $13,800, is reported on the balance sheet for the firm.

The statement of cash flows, a relatively new disclosure (it replaces the statement of changes in financial position, or working capital) performs the same basic type of reconciliation, focusing on the cash account instead. Those transactions generating cash are reported as sources of cash, while those using cash are bracketed, or deducted from existing cash balances. This statement allows the investor to see whether or not the company is financing ongoing operations from profits (a preferred solution) or is borrowing to meet ongoing needs.

Cash is the one resource a company cannot survive without, so this statement serves as a major piece of information on the financial health of the organization. The final number on the statement of cash flows ($41,300) represents the cash balance reported in the current asset section of the balance sheet.

These relationships are reflected in the basic accounting equations,[4] as suggested below:

$$\text{Assets} = \text{Liabilities} + \text{Owner's equity}$$

$$\text{Owner's equity} = \text{Contributed capital} + \text{Retained earnings}$$

$$\text{Retained earnings} = \text{Beginning retained earnings} - \text{Dividends} + \text{Net income}$$

$$\text{Net income} = \text{Revenues} - \text{Cost of goods sold} - \text{Other expenses}$$

This linked series of equations affects the final cash balance, which feeds back to the assets section of the balance sheet. The issues surrounding cash and cash management will be dealt with in more depth in Chapter 4.

ACCRUAL ACCOUNTING: PUTTING DOLLARS WHERE THEY BELONG

The world is governed more by appearances than by realities, so that it is fully as necessary to seem to know something as it is to know it.

Daniel Webster (2)

The basis of accrual accounting is the matching principle, in which the revenues generated within an accounting period are aligned with the costs, or expenses, required to generate those revenues. It is described by A.C. Littleton as follows:

The central problem of accounting is to bring into association, in the present, the revenues identified with the present and their related costs, and to bring into association, in the future, the revenues identified with the future and their related costs. In solving this problem those who use accounting are in effect, matching enterprise efforts and accomplishment . . . The fundamental problem of accounting is therefore to

---

[4]Source for this exact approach is L. Nikolai and J. Bazley, *Intermediate Accounting*, 4th ed. (Boston: PWS-Kent, 1988), p. 44.

cut through a continuing stream of costs and correctly assign portions to the present and to the future.[5]

In performing accrual accounting procedures, the accountant is attempting to sort costs and revenues according to different time periods.

This sorting process has little to do with the actual cash flows for a period of time. In an excellent book on financial reports written for the nonfinancial manager, Tracy notes:

> The main point is this: cash flows are not the correct amounts needed to determine profit for a period of time. Cash flows do not include the complete sales revenue and expense activities for the period. A complete accounting is necessary to measure profit... This "complete accounting" is known as the *accrual basis*. Accrual basis accounting records the receivables from making sales on credit, and also records the liabilities for unpaid expenses, in order to determine the correct profit measure for the period.[6]

Accrual accounting, then, is the booking of receivables for sales on credit, the recording of liabilities for bills not yet paid, and the development of accrual and deferral accounts that capture the differences between when a revenue or expense is paid versus when it is actually expensed in the financial system. The presence of receivables and liabilities is what defines an accrual accounting system; a small company that operates on a **cash basis** will not have these accounts on their records.

Depreciation on plant and equipment is a prime example of an accrual accounting transaction that does not have a cash impact. Cash is paid out when the assets are purchased, but the expense generated by their ongoing usage, which the depreciation charge attempts to capture, does not use cash at all. In depreciating a fixed asset, the company is expensing some part of its value on a regular basis against the revenues that this asset helped provide. This depreciation expense does have an indirect cash effect, as it reduces the taxes that have to

---

[5]A. C. Littleton, *Essays on Accountancy* (Urbana, Ill.: University of Illinois Press, 1961), p. 201.

[6]This is a very good sourcebook for any nonfinancial person concerned with understanding and using financial reports. John A. Tracy, *How to Read a Financial Report: Wringing Cash Flow and Other Vital Signs Out of the Numbers,* 2nd ed. (New York: Wiley, 1983). Later editions are available from Wiley.

FIGURE 2–3
Revenue Recognition Alternatives

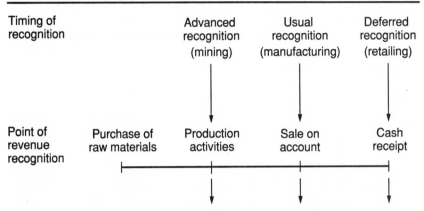

*Transaction recording revenue is booked; expenses
recognized (matched) as appropriate*

be paid by the firm, but the expense itself is an accrual accounting transaction that does not affect cash directly.

The Role of Revenue Recognition

Revenue recognition is the starting point for the accrual accounting process. It is the point at which revenues can be recorded and the related costs matched to them. This may seem to be a simple issue, but in reality, "the emergence of revenue might be recognized at any stage in the investment cycle from initial commitment of capital to its ultimate recovery in the form of cash."[7] As can be seen in Figure 2–3, revenue can be recognized when production activities occur, sales are made on account, or cash is received.

The decision as to when to recognize revenues focuses on three factors:

1. Title to properties has passed hands, or a similar economic transaction has occurred.

2. The receivable so established is reasonably expected to be collected.

[7]W. McFarland, *Concepts for Management Accounting* (New York: National Association of Accountants, 1966), p. 139.

3. The risks and benefits of ownership have been transferred to the buyer.

The most obvious and commonly used revenue recognition point is the point of sale, whether that entails the shipment of the goods to the customer or the direct transference of products to a customer in a retail setting (i.e., face-to-face transaction). Most revenues are booked when goods pass hands.

When this economic transaction occurs, the financial system records an increase to the revenues of the entity, notes the receivable that the customer is now obligated to pay, relieves the **inventory** to record the cost of the goods sold, and expenses these costs into the **cost of goods sold** account. Two balanced transactions take place, one to reflect the sale, the other to match the costs to this revenue.

In each of these cases, the revenue is recorded in accordance with the **realization principle,** which states that revenue is only earned when disposable funds are available. The realization principle, in defining earned revenues, provides the most comparable estimate of revenues and cash flows. It is the most conservative revenue recognition criterion possible. In trying to understand an accounting ruling, always look for the **conservative** solution: the one that will bear the lowest chance of overstating revenues or understating expenses (i.e., show the lowest feasible income number). While there are many different principles or theories used to guide the accounting process, conservatism seems to dominate in many of the rulings made by the various regulatory boards.

Accrual Accounting and the Expense Side of the Equation

The accounting cycle attempts to match revenues with their associated costs within a prespecified **time period.** In making the determination of what costs to include in a specific period, the matching principle is once again called into play:

> In matching, revenue is ordinarily the independent variable and cost the dependent variable. Hence revenues are first assigned to periods, guided by the realization concept. Costs are then matched with those revenues which have been recognized in each period. In general, assigning costs to periods of time is much more difficult than is assigning revenues to periods.[8]

---

[8]McFarland, *Concepts for Management Accounting*, p. 149.

How can it be more difficult to assign costs to a period than revenues? There are many different types of resources used up in a period of time; some continue to have value for several additional periods, and there are others in which outlays have to occur no matter what level of revenue is earned, so it is difficult to tie specific resources to defined outcomes.

Those costs that are deemed to only provide value in the existing time period are called **period costs.** They are reported as either fixed costs in the cost of goods sold account (e.g., overhead), or as free-standing expenses on the income statement. There is also the issue of long-term versus short-term costs; the former includes the costs that are associated with capital equipment, the latter with labor that is utilized in a period-by-period manner. Matching short-term costs with their associated revenues is straightforward. Fixed or long-term costs are much more difficult and have given rise to more analysis, exposition, and confusion than any other aspect of the accounting model. When is a building used up? If an asset continues to provide value after the accounting system has reduced its **book value** (purchase price less accumulated depreciation) to zero, should some form of cost continue to be recognized for its use?

Long-run costs, then, raise the specter of mismatching costs with revenues because of missed estimates of useful life, obsolescence, and a number of other related factors. For example, the most accurate way to match capacity, or fixed asset, costs with output units is the **units of production** depreciation (e.g., multiperiod expensing) methods, yet it is the method employed least often by accounting because of the detailed records it requires. In defining what costs go into the current period, the financial manager is also determining what elements of cost will be **capitalized,** or placed on the balance sheet as an asset. These decisions can have a marked effect on the net income numbers.

Key Concepts Surrounding Accrual Accounting

The key factors to keep in mind surrounding the accrual accounting process are as follows.

1. Focus is on matching revenues to their associated costs in a prespecified period of time (e.g., a month or year).
2. The method used for recognizing revenues, which is set by the realization principle, determines which costs are relevant for current period profit calculations.

3. The preferred method for recognizing revenue is at the point of sale.

4. Some costs can be easily assigned to the period in question due to their short-run nature and nonstorability.

5. Other costs, such as those associated with fixed assets, present a more difficult conceptual problem in determining in what period to recognize specific portions of their use.

Accrual accounting begins with the recognition of revenue, but its key defining characteristic is that it is concerned with **economic transactions,** not cash flows. Sales are recorded when management is reasonably sure that the funds will be collected. If the cash is not received within the accounting period, these uncollected amounts are recorded in an account called **accounts receivable,** to denote the fact that funds are owed to the organization for work that has already been completed. When the cash is received on these credit accounts, revenue isn't recognized. Instead, a simple transaction that reduces the dollar value of accounts receivable and shows an offsetting increase in the cash account is recorded.

On the other side of the equation, a company may obtain and use materials, goods, and services before actually paying for them. These items, if used up in creating revenues in this period, will be recognized as costs, even though the bills to the suppliers haven't been paid. Recorded as **current liabilities,** these unpaid balances are reduced in the future through a cash payment. In other words, in accrual accounting, *expenses do not necessarily equal expenditures* (cash payments) and *revenues do not equal receipts* (cash or funds obtained). Revenues are, instead, recognized when earned, and expenses are recognized when the revenues they create are recorded. The flow of money has little to do with this process.

Money may be paid *before* an expense is recognized, or funds may be received before the income is earned. The former situation sets up a **prepaid expense** account which is slowly written off against the periods in which it provides value. Most insurance companies require prepayments; the unused portion of the insurance coverage is recorded as an asset on the balance sheet. **Unearned revenue,** on the other hand, is the account used to capture those cases where cash has been received prior to the performance of the agreed-upon services or production. The insurance company will use this account to record the payments on insurance made in accordance with its prepayment terms.

The accounting system also employs a series of **accrued revenues, accrued expenses,** and **accrued liabilities** accounts. These accounts are used at the end of an accounting period to adjust the account balances for expenses that have been incurred but not paid (accrued expenses), revenues that have been earned but not recorded or received, and liabilities (e.g., payables or debts) that accumulate in a systematic way, but are not payable in the period in which they are incurred (e.g., accrued liability for compensated or paid sick days and the disclosure of "off-balance sheet" financing or leases).

Offsetting these accounts are all of the situations in which expenditures have been made or receipts taken without a completion of the necessary contractual agreements. These are called **deferrals.** The prepaid insurance example above details a **deferred expense** (prepaid insurance) and a **deferred revenue** (unearned insurance premiums). It can also reflect a catch-all account in which various types of expenditures are accumulated and slowly written off (amortized) over time. The most common deferrals are for income taxes and pension payments. In both cases, **timing differences** between when the expense is booked and when expenditures are made to fund it are the trigger for the development of these accounts.

To understand the accounting process and the tasks performed by the financial manager, the rudimentary differences between accrual accounting and the flows of actual cash within an organization need to be mastered. The flexibility to pull some revenues or expenses forward into the current period, or push them off until the future through the use of accruals, deferrals, and related accrual-based accounts, provides the financial manager with the ability to create the type of financial profile the company needs, or wants, to show to external stakeholders. While GAAP limits this process, there is considerable "play" left in the system.

Finally, the absorption accounting process, in which all overhead is charged to period production, has its roots in the matching principle and accrual accounting practices. In order to fully understand standard costs, variance analysis, absorption costing, and related topics, the nonfinancial manager needs to understand how the pursuit of conservatism in presenting a financial position affects the numbers available from the traditional financial management information system. The need to match revenues and costs within an arbitrarily defined time period, and the separation of cash flows from economic income estimates, all lead the financial manager to focus on reporting past performance. Breaking free of these bonds to the past is the largest challenge facing the financial function today; it has been likened to "cutting the Gordian knot" by some.[9] Whatever terminology is used, the process is the same: Accrual accounting concepts have to play a diminished role in the financial function of the modern organization.

BALANCE AND CIRCULARITY: UNDERSTANDING THE ACCOUNTING CYCLE

Custom will often blind one to the good as well as to the evil effects of any long-established system.

Bishop Richard Whately (1)

Financial statements are the outcome of the financial reporting cycle, which begins with the identification, measurement, and recording of individual transactions, or bookkeeping. Although it serves as the basis for the financial reporting cycle, the classification, reporting, and interpretation of this information transforms the raw accounting data into information for users. The classification process places the raw data into meaningful categories, summarizes individual transactions, and highlights relationships. Interpretation in the financial cycle deals with attempts to understand the information and its implications for the future.

This basic cycle consumes a considerable amount of time for most financial managers. Many of the basic transactions are recorded efficiently, but the trials and tribulations of "closing the books," fondly called "bean counting" by many, are well known. In this process, the accounting department balances the balance sheet after deriving net income and cash flow numbers. Underlying this process is the valuation of inventory, recording of various period-based transactions (e.g., depreciation), adjustments to the various balances, and a fair amount of detective work whenever the "debits = credits" and "net assets = liabilities + owner's equity" rules are violated (i.e., the books don't balance). This closing process usually takes at least one

---

[9]This is a favorite statement of Tom Vollmann. It is reflected in the recent book by J. Robb Dixon, A. Nanni, and T. Vollmann, *The New Performance Challenge: Measuring Operations for World-Class Competition* (Homewood, Ill.: Business One Irwin/APICS Series in Production Management, 1990). See specifically Chapter 4. Note that Vollmann refers to this process as cutting away from the ties of the financial performance measurement system; this breaking away is as critical for the financial manager as for the organization as a whole.

week. Once completed, the financial function generates a series of internal and external reports.

Many companies are beginning to reexamine the need to close the books on a monthly basis. In the financial domain, this may appear sacrilegious, but in reality, there is no external demand for monthly financial statements. Quarterly reports are required by the Securities and Exchange Commission, not monthly ones. Given the amount of resources these activities consume, and the questionable value they add to the organization, it may be preferable to delay the closing process, reduce the number of transactions in the system, and refocus these hours onto tasks that are of more value to management and stockholders. These trends reflect the growing recognition that the role of the financial manager extends beyond safeguarding the assets of the organization to include meeting the needs of management, customers, and other stakeholders.

In meeting changing demands, the financial management function is beginning to reassess its current practices. The objective in redesigning the FMIS is to choose reports that must remain in the accounting "package," streamline the required tasks needed to provide this information, and find creative ways to release the time needed to serve on management committees. In order to successfully participate on design teams in establishing the cost implications of various designs, participate in the continuous improvement efforts of the firm by redesigning the cost management system to more accurately reflect ongoing operations, and develop analytical techniques that will help management choose among competing projects and available solutions, the financial manager will have to rethink and refocus the entire reporting process and the FMIS that supports it. It is a time of challenge and change that starts in the "back room," where external reporting demands are met.

In business, the earning of profit is something more than an incident of success. It is an essential condition of success. It is an essential condition of success because the continued absence of profit itself spells failure.

Justice Louis D. Brandeis (1)

Core Tasks in Financial Management

The critical role played by these concepts in shaping the financial function in an organization cannot be overstated. While a financial manager may perform a broad range of tasks, they all have a common root: They are based on economic transactions that flow from the basic bookkeeping equation. These concepts have served their users well since their development by Luca Pacioli in 1494. Unfortunately, the very dependability and security of the inherent balance in the bookkeeping process is also the source of increasing problems for the financial function.

Because bookkeeping focuses solely on economic transactions *that have already occurred,* the field is often blind to less easily measured costs and benefits of decisions. Estimates are of even greater concern, as they are not based on objective fact. This apparent resistance to less concrete measures of costs and benefits is at the core of the ongoing conflict between managers, who are asked to make decisions in the face of uncertainty, and the financial function, which is most comfortable playing back the score after the game is completed. In the face of increasing competitive pressures, though, the financial function is making the needed changes.

Maintaining the financial records of the organization requires the completion of a core set of tasks by the financial group. In general terms these tasks are

1. **Identification**   Selecting those transactions and events that affect the financial status of the firm.

2. **Measurement**   Measuring the transactions and events in monetary terms.

3. **Recording**   Using a systematic method for keeping track of the transactions.

4. **Classification**   Categorizing the captured data into a logical and useful framework so that they can be reported in a meaningful way to users.

5. **Reporting**   Periodically summarizing the collected and classified financial information into statements and reports.

6. **Interpretation**   Analyzing the statements to explain the meaning and limitations of the financial information.[10]

These tasks reflect the fact that the financial function is concerned with the development, maintenance, and use of one specific database

---

[10]This list of core tasks is adapted from E. Spiller and P. May, *Financial Accounting: Basic Concepts,* 5th ed. (Homewood, Ill.: Richard D. Irwin, 1990), p. 6.

within the organization: the financial reporting system. That is why the term FMIS is preferred for the financial reporting system; it is a data base that sorts, records, aggregates, and produces reports on the monetary transactions of the organization.

Putting the financial function in this context removes much of its mystery. It also underscores the fact that the financial database is only one part of an integrated information system in an organization. Because it selects only a small number of the total transactions undertaken by the company, the FMIS is a biased source of information. If this bias is understood, the numbers and reports created by this database can be properly and effectively used. If, on the other hand, this set of recorded transactions is the only source of management reports, there will be an ongoing bias toward analyzing the past, focusing on short-term profitability, and a related host of problems. The shortcomings of the FMIS are not in its design, but rather the inappropriate (or excessive) use of the information it produces.

MANAGEMENT DECISIONS AND THE BOTTOM LINE

Business without profit is not business any more than a pickle is a candy.

Charles F. Abbott (1)

The FMIS is the corporate scorecard; it reflects the decisions management has made and their impact on the company's ongoing financial prospects. Management is not a passive receiver of financial information; it is the force that shapes it. The types of assets purchased, their use in making a range of potential products, the processes through which those products arise, and the individuals who drive the value-creation process are acquired through management decisions and directed by them.

These decisions can affect the strategy, structure, and process the company employs to meet customer needs. If the value chain put in motion by management provides the customer with the right product or service—at the right time, in the right quantity, and at the right price—the company prospers. If this "mark" is missed, though, the company can flounder. What impact do various types of decisions have on the bottom line? Decisions that affect the way the FMIS is structured, and how GAAP will be applied to the company's financial statements, are addressed in the next chapter under the concept of "accounting policy choice." More important, and less easily identified, are the impact of strategic decisions on the company's financial performance.

Strategic Decisions and the Bottom Line

One of the key decisions made by a company is the type (and manner of distribution) of products or services it is going to offer to the marketplace. At the same time, decisions are made about price and related product characteristics to complete the product's "package." Today, customers buy more than a physical product; they buy a product/ service bundle that fills their needs. The size and composition of this product package, the variety of options available for the customer to choose from, and the cost-to-value ratio of this package all affect the marketability of the company's goods.

The tie between the market potential of a product and the economic performance of the company that provides it appears to be fairly straightforward, but this relationship can be muddied by the very accounting system that was set up to record it. Whenever an allocation of costs serves as the basis for developing a cost estimate for a product or service, or some form of estimating process is employed to charge off the use of resources in the productive process, error enters into the accounting process. Some of these estimates are better than others. If estimated costs are accurately tied to the revenues they generate, management can see the impact of various product-based decisions on overall profitability. Unfortunately, many accounting systems today use imprecise or inadequate methods for assigning costs to revenues; the objective may be clear, but the techniques used to carry them out are poorly suited to their task.

To determine how product-based decisions affect the bottom line, there would need to be a high level of accuracy in the FMIS; matching costs to their revenues would have to take on a new meaning. For instance, the question has been raised as to whether a "fully depreciated" asset should still carry a cost for its use when a product is made using it. The traditional FMIS would never record such a cost; it would generate an "unbalanced" entry (the resources consumed are no longer present on the books). Yet, if old machinery is free and new machinery costly, will not the long-run impact be to discourage reinvestment in fixed assets? Could at least a part of the competitive decline of American business be due to the impact of this accounting "fact" on the decision-making process? As stated earlier, the FMIS cannot be blamed for every wrong decision made in corporations today, but the fact that they affect this process cannot be denied.

If management makes a strategic product-based decision, it may be difficult to isolate its impact on the financial performance of the firm. The more complex a company is—the more products and options it offers to its customers—the more difficult it is to link the outcome of the period's efforts (net income) with any one decision or sale. Today, though, new estimating methods that attempt to more closely associate *all* resources used with their causes are beginning to make the relationship between decisions and their financial implications clearer.

One more point needs to be made. Often management makes a decision to drop a product line, or to outsource components for its products, using direct labor savings (fully burdened with its share of overhead). If these estimates were accurate, *and* if management really eliminated the resources (for instance, direct labor) that they based the analysis on, then these decisions could be made with some level of comfort. Unfortunately, neither of these facts appears to hold in most situations. That makes the decision process much riskier; so much so that it can destroy a company's competitiveness.

Decisions and the Bottom Line

Having established the fact that it may be difficult to trace the impact of one specific decision on the financial performance of the company, does that mean no impact exists? Obviously not. When products are dropped from a company's portfolio, the revenues that the sale of those products generated disappear. This reduction in revenues leads to a reduction in costs, but only those that were *directly caused by* the production, distribution, and support of those products. If these excess resources are eliminated (raw materials not purchased, labor furloughed, etc.), then the total costs of the company go down. These types of cost are called **avoidable costs** in accounting jargon. On the other hand, if resources are not eliminated, costs don't change; there are simply fewer revenues to cover them.

Other types of decisions have a similar effect. For instance, if just-in-time manufacturing is implemented in a company, there are marked improvements in throughput times and a reduced need for inventory. As long as these improvements are followed by a reduction in the resources the company purchases and uses, the impact of the decision will lead to an increase in net income. If these resources are not freed up, or if idle capacity created by the improvements is not redirected to other uses, there may be only a negligible improvement in financial performance.

Management decisions affect the economic performance of the company. If avoidable costs are not eliminated, that decision leads to reduced overall profitability. If the idled resources are redeployed or eliminated, the decision should lead to increased profitability. The tie between the cause (management's decision) and the effect (changes in profitability) may not be immediately clear, but it does exist. Timing differences eventually turn around; decisions that change the composition of the resource package consumed to create the company's products and services will show up in the bottom line. The question is when.

The FMIS builds from a simple set of basic equations to a complex, interconnected set of accounts and statements that provides an estimate of a company's financial position at any one point in time. The process, unfortunately, is only completely correct on the day the company starts operating and the day it closes its doors for good. In between, the FMIS uses a series of estimates, draws imaginary lines in the shifting sands of time that mark the life of the organization, and places these estimated values in front of management and the external market for evaluation and use in decision making. It is an imperfect system, yet it is based on sound principles and proven practice.

Key Points to Remember

The FMIS is built on the accrual accounting model's self-balancing set of equations: (1) assets = liabilities plus owner's equity, and (2) debits = credits. These equations are used to generate entries that record the *completed* financial transactions of the firm, within the boundaries of generally accepted accounting principles. Three basic financial statements are provided by the FMIS: the balance sheet, the income statement, and the statement of cash flows. These statements summarize the financial activities of a company over a designated period of time (usually one year).

Pursuing objectivity and the matching principle, financial managers record, analyze, summarize, and report the outcome of the activities over a year. Their goal is to provide an unbiased report of historical events, not to support internal decision making. The external orientation of traditional financial accounting is one of the overriding problems with this tool. Value is created through the decisions and activities of the FMIS's internal customer, a fact that appears to be overlooked in many financial circles.

The accounting cycle has been described in reasonable detail, providing a basic understanding of what tasks are normally performed within the financial arena. The objective was to detail the accounting mentality (the restrictive nature of external reporting under the auspices of GAAP) and to suggest why many experts argue that these systems are irrelevant in many organizations today.

The traditional FMIS builds from information recorded in various parts of the organization, transformed into financial transactions and placed in the general ledger. The numbers are developed by the financial area using raw data from other parts of the company, and are summarized and reported for external users. Customers, whether inside or outside the company, are not the focal point of the system; GAAP, the SEC, the IRS, and the stock market are. The numbers are targeted to a very different market than the rest of the organization's activities.

To really understand how the FMIS can be used to support management decisions, it is important to know what its core assumptions are, when the system is doing things that coincide with common sense, and when the techniques take on a life of their own that can impair the decision process. The key continues to lie in the matching principle, but the focus has to shift, from matching resources to periods and products after the fact to evaluating the multiple uses that can be made of the resources currently available. The former approach is historical; the latter is strategic. History is useful only if it provides hints about the outcome of future events. If the FMIS is treated as one input to the decision process, and if its strengths and assumptions are fully understood before the numbers it generates are used, then it can be a value-adding tool in the search for competitive excellence.

The marriage of economics and history produces a hybrid which regularly combines the inadequacies of both.

John Kenneth Galbraith, *The Liberal Hour* (3)

SUGGESTED READINGS

Curtis, D. *Management Rediscovered: How Companies Can Escape the Numbers Trap.* Homewood, Ill.: Business One Irwin, 1990.

Delaney, P., J. Adler, B. Epstein, and M. Foran. *GAAP: Interpretation and Application of Generally Accepted Accounting Principles.* New York: Wiley, 1991.

Dixon, J. R., Nanni, A., and Vollmann, T. *The New Performance Challenge: Measuring Operations for World Class Competition.* Homewood, Ill.: Business One Irwin/APICS Series in Production Management, 1990.

Keating, P., and S. Jablonsky. *Changing Roles of Financial Management: Getting Close to the Business.* Morristown, N.J.: Financial Executives Research Foundation, 1990.

McFarland, W. B. *Concepts for Management Accounting.* New York: National Association of Accountants, 1966.

Nikolai, L., and J. Bazley. *Intermediate Accounting.* 4th ed. Boston: PWS-Kent Publishing Company, 1990.

Rappaport, A. *Creating Shareholder Value: The New Standard for Business Performance.* New York: The Free Press, 1986.

Spiller, E., and P. May. *Financial Accounting: Basic Concepts.* 5th ed. Homewood, Ill.: Richard D. Irwin, 1990.

Tracy, John A. *How to Read a Financial Report: Wringing Cash Flow and Other Vital Signs Out of the Numbers.* New York: Wiley, 1983.

Weston, J. F., and Grigham, E. *Managerial Finance.* 7th ed. Hinsdale, Ill.: The Dryden Press, 1981.

CHAPTER 3

NUMBERS BY CHOICE: THE "FLEX" IN THE FMIS[1]

He who chooses the beginning of the road chooses the place it leads to. It is the means that determine the end.

Harry Emerson Fosdick (2)

Managing operations means getting the product to the customer in an effective and efficient manner. Minimizing setup times and keeping the machines "junking and clunking" as scheduled is an internal orientation that has its own set of variables. These variables provide the basis for decision making, planning, and control.

Decision makers outside this internal circle also try to evaluate operations, but without firsthand knowledge. These decision makers include individuals involved in the capital markets in which financial resources are allocated (investors, creditors), government agencies (IRS, SEC), and unions. In fact, operations people may become external users of other companies' data as they try to assess major competitors' operations during benchmarking exercises.

A company's published financial statements are a major source of data used by those outside of a company to assess the effectiveness of internal operations. Financial analyses (such as common-sized income statements, asset turnover ratios, and other financial and operational performance ratios) are used to determine how efficiently a business is operating. These tools provide insight into the management process of the company, its strengths and weaknesses, and potential risk for the investor.

Because these analyses are used by a diverse array of interested parties to place value on a firm, it is important to understand the graded components in management's report card. How the capital markets, governments, competitors, and other interested decision makers view top management is going to affect all employees. For example,

---

[1]This chapter was written by Michael Fetters, Chairperson, Babson College Division of Accounting and Law. His contribution to this book is greatly appreciated.

Digital Equipment Corporation's profit as a percentage of sales dollars has fallen drastically in recent years. It should come as no surprise, then, that there are now major cost-cutting measures in place to combat these trends. In a related vein, Hewlett Packard's material costs have become quite high as a percentage of cost of goods sold. The result? A new program for reducing materials costs has been implemented.

Whether you work for one of these companies or for one of their competitors, understanding the accounting scorecards will help you prepare and plan for likely executive directives. If you know and understand how the capital markets are reviewing and evaluating your company, or how your company compares to benchmark companies, you will know what top management responses will likely be: You can prepare a plan of action. If you occupy one of the top positions in your firm, detailed financial analyses can shed light on areas of opportunity and challenge that lie ahead. Forewarned is to be forearmed; trending financial performance can provide early warning signs of danger ahead.

In order to understand the accounting numbers used by decision makers external to the firm, the impact of accounting choices on the bottom line needs to be understood. These policy choices, based on management discretion, can have marked influence on the financial statements; they effectively define when various revenues and expenses are recognized, and in what amount. This chapter reviews four of the major accounting choices that affect top management's scorecard: revenue recognition, inventory costing, depreciation, and off balance sheet financing (e.g., leases).

REVENUE RECOGNITION: WHEN IS A DOLLAR EARNED?

Better a dish of illusion and a hearty appetite for life, than a feast of reality and indigestion therewith.

Harry A. Overstreet (2)

The impact of accounting policy choice begins at the top of the income statement with the selection of the revenue recognition point (i.e., when is a sale shown on the income statement?). This choice affects many of the income statement items through the matching principle. In terms of location and importance, the policy choice that results in a revenue recognition method is critical. This choice shapes the income statement by what it includes; it affects the balance sheet by what it leaves out (through articulation).

The accounting profession defines **revenues** as the inflow of resources generated through operations. Judging the timing of these inflows is management's choice, within the prescribed boundaries of generally accepted accounting principles. Revenue recognition drives the income statement; reported earnings are based on matching accomplishment and effort for a particular period of time. Accomplishment is revenue. Effort is **expense**, which is defined as an outflow of resources used to generate revenues. Therefore, when management selects the point in time to show a sale, it also affects many of the expenses shown on the financial statements.

Revenue Recognition: An Example

Assume a systems company designs and sells database management systems. The company designs the system, develops the software, assembles the hardware components, and installs the system to the customer's satisfaction. The customer pays 25% when the contract is signed, 25% on delivery of the system, and 50% after the system is successfully installed.

What revenue recognition choices does management have? When can management show a sale?

- *Date the contract is signed.* A contract is signed and the customer has paid a substantial amount of money. The systems company could argue that the contract signing is a critical event in the earnings process; the sale amount is known, the contract is signed, and collection is reasonably assured. A sale could be booked and shown on the income statement.
- *Date the system is delivered.* The company has completed the majority of its work, and the customer has paid 50% of the contract price. The sale could be shown at delivery (close to shipment; many companies use this approach).
- *Successful installation.* At this time, the systems company knows the effort and associated costs of this product. Furthermore, only on customer satisfaction can the systems company be reasonably assured that the entire contract amount will be collected. Revenue recognition could be when the work is completed.
- *Throughout the earnings process.* The systems company may decide to recognize revenue as the various stages are completed:

sale, design, development, delivery, and installation. By matching revenue to these major milestones in the earnings process, accomplishment and effort can be matched in a timely fashion. Therefore a portion of the contract price could be shown on the income statements for the periods in which the stages are completed. (Some of you will recognize this as the percentage of completion method popularly employed in the construction and defense industries.)

Choice Guided by Criteria

Management has many choices and variations within this selection process. From an accounting viewpoint, though, the point of revenue recognition (i.e., "When do we have a sale?") is determined by two key criteria:

1. Completion of the earnings process
2. Reasonable estimation of the revenue can be made.

As long as management can support its selection of the revenue recognition point within the contextual setting established by these criteria, the choice will be generally accepted by the accounting profession.

Figure 3–1 contains two articles about a company named Storage Technology. This hardware/information-systems company combines available hardware and its own software to create and install information systems for a variety of businesses. From these articles, it is clear that Storage Technology has been aggressive in its revenue recognition policies. That is, it has included sales in its income statement early in its business cycle, much to the apparent dismay of the SEC.

Such aggressiveness hastens the revenue recognition process, casting the company's financial statements in a better economic light than a more realistic, conservative approach might indicate. This happens for two reasons. First, sales included in the income statement early in the earnings process may have less definable or reliable links to future cash flows. For instance, quick recognition of sales may make it harder to forecast customer dissatisfaction; this means that estimated product returns may become problematic. Pushing revenue recognition to such an early point in the operating cycle can also make it difficult to estimate potential nonpayments (i.e., bad debts).

Second, when sales are shown aggressively on the income statement, the matching concept requires that all expenses—current and

FIGURE 3–1
Revenue Recognition: Aggressive Policies

Storage Tech Announces Iceberg; Orders For 150 Systems Reported

By Ted Bunker
Investor's Business Daily

NEW YORK—Storage Technology Corp. finally raised the curtain on its long-awaited Iceberg high-performance data storage system yesterday.

The company also reported it has in hand 150 Iceberg orders worth about $1 million each, even though it is still working on the necessary software and doesn't expect to ship production versions of the machine for another five months.

Investors reacted with enthusiasm, bidding up Storage Tech shares by nearly 16% on the New York Stock Exchange. The stock closed at $65\frac{1}{2}$, up 9.

Ryal R. Poppa, Storage Tech's chairman, president and chief executive, said the Iceberg orders are worth more than $150 million. But David E. Weiss, corporate vice president for worldwide market planning, said only $50 million to $75 million of that revenue will be booked this year. Storage Tech only books revenue when a customer has paid for a system or signed a formal letter of acceptance.

Based on a technology called disk array, the Iceberg system harnesses dozens of $5\frac{1}{4}$-inch magnetic disk drives in a single unit, offering a cost-effective means of storing large quantities of data.

Poppa said the company expects to be able to make and sell between 1,000 and 1,200 Iceberg drives next year. He added that as the market becomes less skeptical about the technology used in the Iceberg systems, he expects more customers to buy high-capacity systems carrying higher price tags.

To compete with data stroage systems made by International Business Machines Corp., the Iceberg drives combine disk array and other new techniques to cut overall costs and speed up data access rates.

IBM virtually owns the $10 billion market for high-end data storage systems, and Storage Tech designed Iceberg specifically for use with IBM's largest computer systems. The initial version won't work with computers that are not IBM-compatible.

The Iceberg units use 32 to 128 5.25-inch fixed disk drives supplied by Hewlett-Packard Co. and arranged on racks inside refrigerator-sized cabinets. To boost data storage capacity by up to three times the rated disk space, Iceberg compresses data to be stored and then compacts it on the disk, leaving little or no space unused.

To do that work, Iceberg uses a set of pre-programmed microprocessors contained in a separate cabinet.

FIGURE 3–1 (continued)

SEC Sues Storage Technology

By John Wilke
Globe Staff

The securities and Exchange Commission yesterday filed suit against a Colorado computer-products maker over an accounting practice widely used by Boston-area high technology companies.

Accountants say the SEC's suit against Storage Technology Corp., filed in a Washington federal court, sends a stern warning to computer companies to take a hard look at their own bookkeeping practices.

At issue is the practice of claiming a sale when products are shipped, rather than when the device is installed or formally accepted by the customer. Known as shipping point revenue recognition, it's a common practice among computer and software companies, including Data General Corp., Wang Laboratories Inc. and International Business Machines Corp.

There's nothing wrong with it. And in simpler industries, the practice usually isn't a problem. But in the computer business, when customers often don't pay for a product until it's up and running, or where third-party sales or complicated lease agreements are common, it can cause trouble.

"Every once in a while a company goes overboard, either to help the stock, say, or back up a prediction by the president, and they'll push sales out the door to make the revenue numbers look better," said Edward Noakes, deputy chief accountant at the SEC's enforcement division.

"With this case, what we're saying is, if you do that we're coming after you," Noakes said.

If a sale is put on the books in advance of a firm agreement by a customer to accept it, it overstates current revenue as it borrows from future quarters, accountants say. As long as sales keep growing, and the practice is applied consistently, any problems are masked. But if sales fall off, it can bring a sudden, unexpected crash for firms that looked like high-flyers.

"There's nothing wrong with aggressive sales practices, or with recognizing revenue at the point of shipment," Noakes said. But in the computer industry, especially, "companies need to take care that the numbers accurately reflect final sales."

"The more complex the equipment is, the more steps there are before the sale is final," added Gary Sundick, an enforcement division attorney. "It's not like buying a typewriter."

"The commission is taking a close look at accounting issues and at revenue recognition in particular," Sundick said.

Julian E. Jacoby, a partner at the accounting firm of Lavanthal and Horwath, said that an aggressive revenue recognition policy "means sales can be posted too soon, which has the effect of over-reporting revenue and net income."

For Storage Technology, a $700 million company staging a strong comeback from bankruptcy, the case is ancient history. In a filing yesterday, the company settled the SEC's charges.

The SEC alleged that from 1982 until it went bankrupt in 1984 the company consistently reported revenues before sales were completed. The SEC also charged that the company fraudulently backdated a major transaction in 1983 that made the company appear profitable when it otherwise would have shown a loss.

Storage Technology's chairman, Ryal R. Poppa, said that the company's agreement to settle the SEC's charges "neither admits nor denies any wrongdoing on the part of Storage Technology in the early 1980s" and that it puts the company another step closer to emerging from bankruptcy.

"With this agreement, all material controversies except the Internal Revenue Service claims have been settled." Poppa added that he was "optimistic" that the IRS claim would be resolved.

Sources: *Investor's Business Daily,* 29 January 1992; *Boston Globe,* 28 January 1987.

future—related to these sales must be included on the income statements. Again, many of these expenses must be estimated. These estimates may not be very good proxies for the future cash flows when they are made too early in the earnings process. Fact can become fiction quickly in such a situation. It is this fiction that the SEC tries to guard against when regulating revenue recognition choices.

An example of the problems preemptive revenue recognition can create for investors trying to interpret reported financial results can be found in reviewing the activities of some real estate development corporations. For example, Patton Corporation, a real estate development firm based in New England, realized revenue when the sales contracts were signed and before major portions of the development work were begun. These future development costs had to be estimated and included on the income statement when the sales were shown. Difficulties in making expense estimates made the links between reported income and economic reality hazy at best. Downstream, these hazy estimates proved to be inaccurate, to the dismay of bankers and investors alike.

The point to remember here is that operations managers must be aware of the revenue recognition policies of their company. If these policies are aggressive, future operating costs will need to be estimated, and the pressure to achieve these estimated cost levels will be strong. Furthermore, if there is a business downturn, the company may meet hard times, because top management has already played its revenue "trump cards" before the game got tough. This takes the slack out of the system; sales declines translate almost immediately into profit and cash-flow crises.

Revenue recognition policies of major competitors are also important to know. If they are similar, then comparative financial analysis may yield reasonable data to assess competitors' operations. (See Figure 3–2 for an example of this situation.) However, if revenue recognition policies are different, it is likely that estimated expense levels are also different; the comparison of one's own company with benchmark companies in this situation could be treacherous.

Revenue recognition policies set the boundaries on the profit picture for a firm. Management is given discretion in choosing when to recognize income; how this choice is exercised provides as much information about management's intent as about company performance. For individuals inside the organization, the riskiness of management's choices can create downstream frustration, pressure, and potential job loss. The earlier revenue is pulled into the income statement, the shakier these numbers get; they become farther and farther removed from the cash flows that are the lifeblood of the organization. Profits on paper cannot be spent or reinvested; they may make a good showing, but they won't pay the bills.

INVENTORY COSTING METHODS

Riches do not consist in the possession of treasures, but in the use made of them.

Napoleon Bonaparte, *Maxims* (3)

Inventories flow through a company, providing the potential to make products and provide services. They are purchased for agreed upon prices and paid for with cash. Given this fact, how does the concept of **inventory costing** as an accounting policy choice spring to life? What choice is left in this situation?

FIGURE 3–2
Revenue Recognition and Intercompany Comparisons

Assumptions: Companies A and B both sign $6,000,000 contracts to build a small office building. Both buildings are estimated to take three years to complete at a total estimated cost of $4,000,000. Company A decides to report revenues AS the work is being completed; Company B AFTER the work is completed. The following are the cost flows for the project.

	Year 1	Year 2	Year 3	Total
Costs incurred: year	$1,000,000	$2,500,000	$1,500,000	$5,000,000
cumulative	$1,000,000	$3,500,000	$5,000,000	
Costs estimated to finish	$3,000,000	$1,000,000	0	

Company A

	Year 1	Year 2	Year 3	Total
Revenues:				
($1M/$4M) × $6M	$1,500,000			
(($3.5M/$4.5M) × $6M)				
− $1,500,000		$3,166,667		
($6,000,000 − $4,666,667)			$1,333,333	$6,000,000
Less expenses	$1,000,000	$2,500,000	$1,500,000	$5,000,000
Reported income	$ 500,000	$ 666,667	($ 167,000)	$1,000,000

Company B

	Year 1	Year 2	Year 3	Total
Revenues	0	0	$6,000,000	
Less expenses	0	0	$5,000,000	
Reported income	0	0	$1,000,000	

Company A and B's income streams appear quite different although their operations are the same. Company A is reporting revenues using the percentage of completion method and Company B is using the completed contract method. Both methods are generally acceptable and generally used; as you can see, they make intercompany comparisons difficult.

While the total dollars spent on inventories is a fact, what is open for discussion is what dollar value to place on one specific unit of materials or finished goods. Since these material flows go on continuously, who is to say what "cost" goes with which unit? For large-ticket items, such as computers, buildings, and production equipment, it is easy to attach the actual price paid for the asset to that item. On the other hand, it is difficult to achieve the same level of precision for the large variety of common materials used in creating revenues. Should the average cost for purchased parts be used to cost everything, or should materials used be assigned the latest, market-based cost? Inventory costing, as an accounting policy choice, deals with these questions directly. It is a choice that can have marked influence on reported profits and inventory values.

The inventory costing choice has several accepted procedures, but it has no general criteria to guide it. In other words, management can use any method they desire. While open to any *reasonable* method, the inventory choice made by management will likely be influenced by several factors, such as the projected rate of inflation. Management must weigh income statement and balance sheet concerns, estimate long-term trends, and then make a choice that will optimize its ability to meet stakeholder needs and generate additional capital when needed.

The major inventory costing methods are first in, first out (FIFO), last in, first out (LIFO), and weighted average (WA). As the names suggest, these three approaches choose different valuation points for the units sold in a period; they impact the reported level of cost of goods sold and the value of the inventory remaining on the balance sheet. The definition of these methods is as follows.

> **FIFO:** First in, first out. The cost of the first goods purchased and placed into the inventory are the first ones used to calculate cost of goods sold.
>
> **LIFO:** Last in, first out. Assigns the cost of the last goods purchased and placed into inventory as the first costs in cost of goods sold.
>
> **WA:** Weighted average. Requires calculating an average cost per unit for all goods available for sale during the period and then assigning this average cost between the cost of goods sold and inventory.

These methods deal only with the cost flows for the inventory; obviously, the management of the physical flow of inventories is guided by concerns for obsolescence, spoilage, and related issues. This is important to keep in mind as the discussion unfolds: the methods affect only the matching of dollar values for inventory to the revenues they generate, not the physical flow of inventories.

A Simple Example

Assume a start-up company has manufactured six units of its product, in the order and associated cost noted, and sells three of these units this period:

Manufactured: 3 units @ $10
      1 unit @ $15
      2 units @ $17

Sold: 3 units @ $25

  The upper part of the income statements for the three major inventory costing (IC) methods would be as follows:

	FIFO	LIFO	WA
Sales	$75	$75	$75
−Cost of goods sold	30	49	31
Gross profit	$45	$26	$44

Why do these profits differ? The answer can be found by looking at how the cost of goods sold is calculated under each of the methods:

Cost of goods sold calculation	FIFO	LIFO	WA
3 units @ $10	$30		
2 units @ $17			
+1 unit @ $15		$49	
3 units @ $10			
1 unit @ $15			
2 units @ $17			

Average cost
 per unit: $62/6 = 10.33
  +3 units @ $10.33 . . . . $31

  The above example highlights the fact that if inventory costing methods are not understood, the perceptions of a manufacturing company's operating efficiency will be quite different among FIFO, LIFO, and WA alternatives. Is a company using LIFO less profitable than one using FIFO? The same units have been sold; the only difference is the dollar value assigned to the units. If management's goal is to minimize taxes, LIFO is most effective. On the other hand, should management wish to provide a balanced view of its performance for external use, FIFO and WA (WA is a bit more cumbersome to maintain) are preferred methods. The choice is driven by management's objectives, not a set of defined criteria. Once the choice is made, though, it has to be used consistently; a change in inventory costing policies is closely scrutinized by a company's auditors and the SEC.

Tracing the Impact of Inventory Costing Choice

The impact of inventory costing choices can be seen over time. One way this impact is assessed is through a crude, but commonly used, measure of operating efficiency: the **gross margin percentage** (cost of goods sold/sales). In times of growing inventories and rising prices, the company in Figure 3–2 could show a gross margin of 60% (FIFO), 59% (WA), or 34% (LIFO). (It is important to remember that *operations* for this hypothetical company are the same no matter which accounting method is used.) However, the perceptions of the company held by those external to the firm may be quite different if those perceptions are formed without regard to the inventory costing method.

Figure 3–3 contains two examples of companies that have selected LIFO as an inventory costing method, yet disclose enough information to calculate cost of goods sold under the FIFO method. The first company presented, Dupont, shows a tremendous impact from the FIFO–LIFO decision. Notice this is in 1973, a time of rapid price increases for Dupont.

The second company, Tonka, shows very little variation when the LIFO and FIFO versions of the data are compared. In the early 1980s, the prices experienced by toy manufacturers were relatively stable, and thus very little difference existed between LIFO and FIFO numbers.

Clearly, price trends affect the impact of the FIFO, LIFO, WA selection. If prices are changing rapidly (e.g., Dupont, 1974), then the inventory and cost of goods sold valuation differences created by the LIFO/FIFO/WA selection must be taken into account when companies are being compared and evaluated. If prices are not changing quite as dramatically, then intercompany comparisons can be made without much concern for inventory costing methods. Therefore, knowledge of the industry is critical in helping the reader of financial statements identify those situations where inventory costing differences need to be factored into the analysis.

Factors Influencing Inventory Costing Selection

General economic outlook, industry trends, and various company strategies are factors that affect the inventory costing selection. For

---

FIGURE 3–3
Inventory LIFO Compared to FIFO

1974 E.I. Dupont Neumours & Company

Consolidated
Income Statement

(Dollars in millions, except per share)	1974	1973
Sales	$6,910.1	$5,964.0
Other income	67.1	72.0
Total	6,977.2	6,036.0
Cost of goods sold and other operating charges	5,051.9	3,878.6
Selling, general, and administrative expenses	675.1	595.4
Depreciation and obsolescence	506.4	450.3
Interest on borrowings	62.0	34.7
Total	6,295.4	4,959.0
Earnings before income taxes and minority interests	681.8	1,077.0
Provision for income taxes	267.0	480.5
Earnings before minority interests	414.8	596.5
Minority interests in earnings of consolidated subsidiaries	11.3	10.9
Net income	$ 403.5	$ 585.6

These are the income statements presented in the company's annual report. However, also disclosed in the footnotes was that the company switched from FIFO to LIFO. The impact on pretax income was to lower this amount by $368,600,000. Restated earnings before income taxes would have been $1050.4, only a slight reduction from 1973.

1981 Tonka

Tonka reported cost of goods sold and net income of $66,068,000 and $6,735,000 using LIFO inventory methods. Information included in the footnote disclosed that if FIFO were used, cost of goods sold would have been $64,932,000 and net income approximately $7,300,000.

---

example, in times of rising prices, LIFO yields a high cost of goods sold, making a company look less profitable than if FIFO were used. However, under LIFO, a company will pay fewer taxes and thus will have a better cash flow than if FIFO were used. The opposite holds true if prices are falling.

An interaction also exists between the LIFO inventory costing method and inventory levels. Because LIFO places the most recently purchased items in cost of goods sold, the older, noncurrent prices accumulate in inventory. As long as inventory grows, cost of goods sold contains the costs of the most recent purchases. However, with techniques such as total quality management and just in time manufacturing, inventories are often reduced as process improvements are gained.

In these situations, the older, out of date costs in inventory begin to be assigned to current cost of goods sold. The result? Income — and income taxes — go up, and a cash outflow for the additional taxes occurs. In the short term, the benefits of reduced inventory levels may have an unforeseen and undesirable side effect: higher taxes. Thus, industry price trends, inventory size, income measurement, and cash flow concerns affect management's choice of inventory accounting methods.

In reviewing this area, it is important to keep in mind that the appropriateness of a particular inventory method is not at issue in this discussion. The intent is to help you understand the basic differences in inventory costing methods. When a company experiences rapidly changing prices, if inventory is one of its major assets, or the reported cost of goods sold is a large percentage of total sales, then beware of the impact of the chosen inventory costing method. Failing to take this choice into account will interfere with the assessment of the company's actual performance; it is an analysis that cannot be based on reported financial data alone.

DEPRECIATION POLICIES: FIXED ASSETS AND INCOME

Production is not the application of tools to materials, but logic to work.

Peter Drucker (1)

Companies invest in operating assets with the expectation that future periods will benefit from these purchases. The basis for this expectation is a capital asset analysis, which suggests that the sales generated by these operating assets will be enough to recover the initial investment, as well as yield a level of income (sales − expenses) commensurate with the risk faced in obtaining the business. The very real fact that the asset will wear out (depreciate) over time is a key element of this analysis. Including depreciation as an operating expense helps ensure that the recovery of the original investment will be factored into the income measurement process.

In accounting, then, **depreciation** is the systematic and rational allocation of the original costs of assets as expenses to the operating periods benefited by these assets. And, as with other accounting procedures, management must make choices and estimates in this area that can greatly affect the reported financial data of the company. While depreciation is a *noncash* expense, it has a very real impact on the bottom line. The various depreciation policies, in fact, can be used to markedly decrease reported income by recognizing more depreciation early in the life of the asset. What are the options open to management in choosing depreciation methods?

Depreciation Methods: Underlying Issues

The first issue that must be resolved in deciding on a depreciation policy for a specific asset[2] is whether time or an activity level should be the basis for a systematic and rational allocation of the original cost of an asset to the periods benefited by the asset's use (depreciation, or expensing of the asset's original cost over time). In general, if the asset's period of value to the firm is determined by technical obsolescence, then time will be used as the basis for calculating depreciation. This occurs when the useful life of the asset may be shorter than engineering projections of its productive life because of expected advances in the asset's design or function.

If time is used as the basis for depreciation, then management has a second choice to make: Should the calculation be done using *straight-line* or *accelerated* methods of calculation? The straight line depreciation method assumes that all of the periods in which the asset is used will benefit equally from this use. Thus, the depreciation expense is spread evenly over the expected life of an asset. The annual depreciation charge in this case would simply be the total purchase cost divided by the number of years management believes the asset will be of productive value:

$$\frac{\text{Total purchase cost (basis)}}{\text{Estimated useful life}} = \begin{array}{l}\text{Annual depreciation expense} \\ \text{for the asset}\end{array}$$

---

[2]Each asset can actually be depreciated using a different method. This makes depreciation policy choice a bit more interesting and flexible. Also, policies can be switched during the useful life of an asset, and often are to gain the maximum depreciation expense in any one period (e.g., switching from accelerated depreciation to straight line methods when the latter yields a higher expense). Most companies do, though, have a preferred method, which is reported in the notes to their financial statements.

However, if management expects that the benefits of an asset will decline throughout its useful life, then an accelerated method of depreciation can be used. Under this method, more depreciation expense is recognized early in the asset's useful life and less in the asset's later years, because it is projected to provide declining benefits to the company. There are two accepted methods for calculating depreciation under an accelerated approach: *double declining balance* (DDB) and *sum-of-the-years digits* (SYD).

Double declining balance approaches involve several steps in reaching the annual depreciation expense estimate:

1. Determine the annual percentage depreciation under the straight-line depreciation method for the asset (e.g., assets held for five years would be depreciated by 20 percent each year, or 1/5 of the value).
2. Double this percentage. This is the DDB rate (e.g., for our five-year life asset, the DDB percentage would be 40 percent).
3. Apply this percentage to the *remaining balance* of the asset. In other words, the DDB percentage is multiplied times the *book value* (purchase price less accumulated depreciation expense from previous periods) of the asset to determine this period's depreciation expense (e.g., if our five-year asset was bought for $10,000, the first year's depreciation would be $10,000 × 40 percent, or $4,000. The second year, the book value would be $6,000 ($10,000 − $4,000). That means the second year's depreciation would be $2,400 ($6,000 × 40 percent).

As can be seen, the allowable depreciation expense decreases each year. In the early years of the asset's life, most of its cost would be *written off* against the period's revenues. Usually, in about the middle of the asset's life, the straight-line depreciation for the asset, for its remaining life, becomes larger than the DDB amount. Companies usually switch over to straight line at this point, evening out the depreciation expense for the remaining years of estimated useful life for the asset.

Sum-of-the-years digits methods are a bit more cumbersome to undertake than the simple straight-line method of depreciation. SYD accelerates depreciation by *weighting* the early years of the asset's use more heavily than later years using a fraction derived by summing the years of useful life, based on the following steps:

1. Determine the denominator for the fraction by adding together the years the asset will be used. For our five-year asset, this calculation is $5 + 4 + 3 + 2 + 1$, or a total of 15.[3]
2. Determine how many years of life remain for the asset. This becomes the numerator for the depreciation calculation (e.g., in the first year of use, a five-year asset has a numerator of 5; in the second year the numerator becomes 4, for the years of useful life that were remaining at the beginning of the period).
3. Place the years remaining over the sum-of-the-years figure. This drives the depreciation calculation for the year.
4. Multiply the purchase cost times the SYD fraction for this period. The result is the period's depreciation expense (e.g., returning to our asset costing $10,000, the first year's depreciation would be $(5/15) \times \$10,000$, or $3,333, and in the second year this amount would drop to $(4/15) \times \$10,000$, or $2,667).

Of the available methods for performing depreciation calculations that use time as the basis for matching this expense to its associated revenues, straight-line depreciation is the simplest. But simplicity is seldom the driving factor in making this decision: Tax implications are usually the key issue. That is why most companies prefer the cumbersome accelerated methods. They pull more of the depreciation expense into early periods, reducing the tax expense for that period. Computer programs can be used to do the basic calculations, so there are few reasons not to employ accelerated methods, and many reasons to do so.[4]

---

[3]A formula is available to make this calculation simpler. Calling the number of years of useful life n, the formula is $[n(n + 1)]/2$. For a five-year asset: $(5 \times 6)/2 = 15$ years, the same answer derived here by summing the years.

[4]There is actually quite a bit of controversy around the impact of accelerated depreciation over the long-term, evolving from the fact that a company can actually use one method of depreciation for financial reporting (normally straight line) and another for tax purposes (usually accelerated). If a company is growing and constantly replacing its asset base, in reality the accelerated depreciation never turns around. What this means is that the company is always getting high levels of depreciation expense, and the gap between the tax liability owed based on reported income and that paid to the government (a timing difference) continues to grow. This deferred tax liability has become quite large for many companies, resulting in an elaborate FASB ruling (FAS 96) to try and unravel this complicated issue.

On the other hand, if an asset is likely to wear out before it is replaced, then activity level may be used to calculate depreciation expense. In such a case, total expected output or some measure of input (e.g., total estimated life in terms of machine hours) would be used to calculate depreciation expense. This is an underutilized depreciation approach, so much so that financial managers sometimes fail to consider it. Today, though, as companies are looking for ways to understand the true cost of making one unit of a product, these methods are beginning to regain favor. Called *units of production* depreciation, this approach is well-suited to the units-paced environment of just-in-time manufacturing.

The following decision tree summarizes the basic accounting choices for two of the more common measures under the input and accelerated depreciation categories (see Figure 3–4). A simple example in Figure 3–5 is used to further explain these methods. As illustrated in Figure 3–5, depreciation expense trends follow quite different paths to a total of $30,000. Depreciation is frequently part of inventory costs; product costs can vary drastically among these three depreciation methods. Real operations do not vary, but perceptions based on product costs might.

Note that the units of production method is the only method that explicitly attempts to tie depreciation expense to its logical cost driver: production activity. This is why many companies are beginning to reconsider this method, formerly the poor cousin of depreciation

FIGURE 3–4
Depreciation Choice Methods

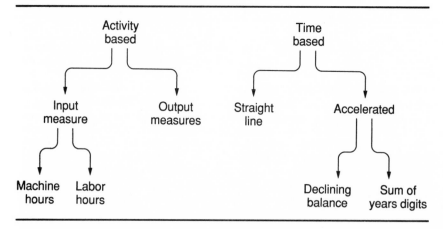

FIGURE 3–5
Depreciation Methods: A Numerical Example

Historical cost $30,000
Estimated life   5 years
Total units expected 30,000

	Years					
	1	2	3	4	5	Total
Straight line						
$30,000 / 5	$ 6,000	$ 6,000	$ 6,000	$ 6,000	$ 6,000	$ 30,000
Accelerated Double Declining Balance	$12,000	$ 7,200	$ 4,320	$ 3,392	$ 5,088	$30,000
Units of production						
Units made	5,000	10,000	3,000	6,000	6,000	
$/* units	$ 5,000	$10,000	$ 3,000	$ 6,000	$ 6,000	$30,000

*Plugged to total 30,000

This example looks at a typical asset over a five year life. The method chosen is assumed to be unchanged once picked, leading to an irregular balance in the DDB method, which is "plugged" in the final year. The calculations follow the same rules as noted in the text: the DDB percentage is twice the straight-line percentage (S/L = 1/5 or 20 percent; DDB is 40 percent) applied against the remaining book value (e.g., year 2 we have $18,000 remaining; 40 percent of $18,000 is $7,200). In the units of production approach, the per unit calculation yielded a depreciation charge of $1.00 for every unit produced ($30,000/30,000 units = $1.00/unit), leading to $5,000 depreciation in year one.

approaches, as a logical replacement for the time-based methods currently used. If the matching principle is used as the basis for the depreciation policy decision, then use, rather than time, seems to be a reasonable approach. Using units-of-production approaches has an added benefit: It brings financial reporting closer to the realities of the business that serve as the basis for internal decision making (e.g., it may better serve the internal customer of the FMIS).

Depreciation and Income

Income can be greatly affected by management depreciation choices. Depreciation is typically included in cost of goods sold, so perceptions of operations can be affected by this selection. Most companies use straight-line depreciation for financial reporting; therefore, this accounting method choice is likely not to affect the comparison of a company against its major competitors. However, this is not always the case. Figure 3–6 highlights changes made in the early 1980s by Wheeling-Pittsburgh Steel.[5] How would this affect Wheeling-Pittsburgh's income statement? If your company remained on time-based depreciation policies, how would this affect intercompany comparisons?

In this case, Wheeling-Pittsburgh's income is positively affected because as production drops, so does depreciation expense. Comparisons with other companies using time-based depreciation could be difficult. Note, however, that what makes for difficult external comparisons likely makes for better internal data. Units of production relates the use of assets directly to products produced. The accounting system helps focus management attention on critical product–cost linkages. If done thoughtfully, units of production serves management's needs much better than time-based methods.

The Impact of Estimates on Depreciation Expense

Perhaps more troublesome than depreciation method variations between companies are variations in depreciation estimates: estimated

---

FIGURE 3–6
Changing Depreciation Methods

Wheeling-Pittsburgh Steel. In the 1982 second quarter, the Corporation changed its method of depreciation for substantially all machinery and equipment from straight-line to a modified units of production method. The modified units of production provides for depreciation charges proportionate to the level of production activity thereby recognizing that depreciation of steelmaking machinery is related to the physical wear of the equipment as well as a time factor. The Corporation believes the modified units of production method is preferable in its circumstances to the method previously used and represents a method common to that used by many major steelmakers.

Excerpted from Wheeling-Pittsburgh Steel's Annual Report.

---

[5]Based on a problem in Spiller and Gosman, *Financial Accounting: Basic Concepts* (Richard D. Irwin, 1984).

useful lives, salvage values, and, to some extent, the historical purchase cost. The straight-line method of depreciation provides a good illustration of this problem. Straight-line depreciation is calculated as follows:

$$\frac{\text{Historical cost } - \text{ Salvage value}}{\text{Useful life}}$$

In this formula, all three numbers are estimates. Historical cost is the cost of acquiring or constructing an asset as well as installing it for normal operating use. While this may seem to be a solid figure, based on quotes and invoices, in reality the installation costs and related expenses to make the asset ready for "normal" use leave room for judgment.

Relatedly, the salvage value (what management believes they will be able to sell the asset for in the open market when it ceases to have sufficient internal value) is an ambiguous estimate. If an asset is seen as having a ten-year life, who can really say what someone else will pay for it downstream? What if the asset develops functional problems that weren't included in the salvage value calculation? The salvage value might be too high, resulting in a failure to fully depreciate the asset over its life (the residual would become a loss in the year the asset is sold). Many companies simply avoid this problem by assuming zero salvage value. When and if the asset is sold, the proceeds become a gain that is added to regular income. If, instead, the asset is traded in, the residual value is simply removed from the basis of the new asset. At this point, it's not an estimate; it's a fact.

Finally, the useful life of an asset is difficult to project, especially as technological advances continue to accelerate obsolescence of existing equipment (e.g., computer systems). The government has taken an active role in setting useful life boundaries for tax purposes through various tax laws and regulations. For external reporting, though, there are few guidelines. Most companies adopt the tax-defined useful life to decrease the complexity of the process.

Depreciation is the most significant noncash expense a company usually faces in any one year. How it is calculated, the basis used for the asset itself, and the estimates that guide the analysis can create significant swings in a company's reported earnings. It is also the area where the maximum advantage can be taken of the tax benefits of owning assets: It's simply good management to minimize current taxes. The more dollars that are kept in the company today, the more potential that remains to take advantage of opportunities that arise.

Because these are management estimates, they can be changed, but GAAP requires consistency in accounting methods between periods. Figure 3–7 is a *Wall Street Journal* article reporting such a change by General Motors. As you can see, this change in depreciation-related estimates had a major effect on the income statement. For GM and most manufacturing companies, depreciation is a significant expense.

The bottom line is that different policies, and different estimates, can make assessment of current operations and intercompany comparisons difficult. Published financial data must be closely scrutinized before conclusions about operations can be made, to ensure that observed differences are not due to accounting policies but to real economic events. At a minimum, one must know the depreciation method and have a rough estimate of the useful lives of the plant and equipment to make comparisons valid. If these are not known, intercompany comparisons can be misleading.

FIGURE 3–7
Changes in Depreciation Estimates

GM 3rd-Quarter Net Jumped as Change In Accounting Erased Operating Loss

By Jacob M. Schlesinger
Staff Reporter of
The Wall Street Journal

DETROIT — General Motors Corp. reported sharply higher third-quarter net income through liberalizing its accounting of equipment depreciation and other items.

Without the changes, however, the No. one auto maker's sales slump would have produced a wider operating loss than the one reported for the year earlier period.

Meanwhile, the auto maker's chief labor negotiator refuted analysts' predictions that GM's new contract with the United Auto Workers will inhibit cost-cutting. He said the pact would enhance GM's competitive position, mainly through closer labor-management cooperation.

Bookkeeping Changes

GM reported net for the quarter more than doubled to $812 million, or $2.23 a share, from $345 million, or 80 cents a share, in the year-ago period.

The increase had more to do with bookkeeping than car making. The most recent earnings were bolstered by GM's decision to lengthen the estimated lives of its plants, equipment and special tools, thus slowing its depreciation and amortization charges. GM said its new practices are more in line with those at other auto makers.

Earnings also were helped by higher profit at GM's three non-consolidated subsidiaries, which reported results earlier this week.

Without the accounting changes, net for the quarter would have dropped 43%, to 46 cents a share. Furthermore, GM's operating loss would have widened to $536.9 million from $251.5 million a year ago.

The accounting change was widely expected, and GM's underlying performance was actually better than some analysts had predicted. Partly as a result of that. GM jumped $3.875, to $59.375 a share, in New York Stock Exchange composite trading yesterday.

"I firmly believe I'm seeing some progress," said Charles Brady, analyst with Oppenheimer & Co. But he added, "I'm not going to be foolish enough to think that within the next quarter or so it's going to be shining brightly through. In 1988, we're going to start seeing the improvements, and in terms of a real increase in the bottom line, it's still a 1989 story."

The main reason for GM's soft performance was the sales slump. Third-quarter revenue of $22.61 billion was about even with that of the year-ago quarter. But sales of vehicles world-wide dropped about 10%. Lower volume and a less-favorable mix of products sold took $1.79 a share out of earnings.

Competitors' Reports

Chrysler Corp. yesterday reported third-quarter net grew 7.7%. Ford Motor Co. earlier this week said net rose 4.4%; the No. 2 maker is on track to pass GM in profit for the second year in a row.

Ford enjoyed the best relative performance of the Big Three. Its net totaled 4.6% of its revenue for the quarter, while Chrysler's was 4.1% and GM's was 3.6%. GM's position was helped because it didn't pay any taxes during the quarter—largely because of unused investment tax credits—while the other auto makers did.

One reason for GM's recent trouble has been its relatively high cost structure. Earlier this year, the auto maker outlined a plan to pare annual costs $10 billion by the end of 1990. Yesterday, the auto maker said it still hoped to meet that goal: It projects reducing costs this year by $3 billion and $4 billion more next year.

And despite the weak earnings performance, executives issued upbeat statements about

GM's future. "We fully expect to improve our market share and competitive position in North America as more of our 1988 models enter the marketplace," Chairman Roger B. Smith said.

Wall Street Worries

Wall Street in general has been concerned about GM in recent weeks because of its new labor contract. The three-year pact includes a job-security program that prevents layoffs except during a sales-drop, prevents plant closings and slows attrition. Many analysts predict the provisions will hamper GM's efforts to restructure operations and shed uncompetitive plants, particularly in parts operations.

But "everyone has missed the spirit of the agreement—analysts aren't willing to put a value on that." Alfred S. Warren, GM's main negotiator, argued yesterday in the company's first public discussion of the pact since it was ratified.

"I feel a willingness in the UAW to sit down and talk as never before about our problems," he added. "Nobody understands how profitable we can become if every man and woman (in the company) is looking to help increase quality."

Specifically, Mr. Warren said he was optimistic about the outcome of committees that will be set up in every plant and that in six months will have to report ways to improve productivity and quality. To ensure that the groups work, GM will educate all plant managers from around the country on what to do with the contract.

Operating Flexibility

Mr. Warren added that the contract preserved GM's operating flexibility. Despite the plant-closing moratorium, he said the company felt it still could cease operations at a non-competitive facility so long as it guaranteed the wages and benefits of the affected workers. The contract even may result in pay cuts at non-competitive plants, although "we don't anticipate that," he said.

Mr. Warren declined to discuss the cost of the contract, but some GM officials are telling analysts and other companies that they expect the pact to increase labor costs a maximum of 7% a year. Although it agreed to a contract largely similar to one that Ford agreed to earlier. GM expects to get more savings than Ford—roughly 20 cents more per worker hour through tougher health-care and absenteeism policies. At Sept. 20, GM's hourly labor cost, was $26.18 per worker.

For the first nine months, GM's net increased 6% to $2.72 billion, or $7.70 a share, from $2.56 billion, or $7.24 a share in the year-earlier period. Revenue eased 2% to $75.4 billion from $77.29 billion.

OFF BALANCE SHEET FINANCING:
THE CASE OF LEASED ASSETS

Facts do not cease to exist because they are ignored.

Aldous Huxley, *Proper Studies* (3)

The final area of accounting procedures is less about management choices and more about the uniqueness of accounting for leases. In accounting for leases, a company faces another set of accounting choices. From management's point of view, leases may be used to purchase a machine on an installment basis, or leases may be used to secure the use of an asset for a period of time. Most individuals believe that in either situation a company has obtained an asset and incurred a related liability. For instance, if the lease is for 10 years and the asset's expected useful life is 10 years, then the lease represents an installment purchase. Even if the lease is a 10-year lease and the asset has a 20-year estimated useful life, then the right to use the asset has a defined value to the company that is commensurate with the liability represented by the lease agreement.

However, lease accounting principles do not recognize the right to control a resource as an asset. Therefore, only if a lease represents an installments purchase will an assets and liability be shown on the balance sheet. Thus, management has an accounting choice: A lease can be structured in order to qualify or not qualify as an asset. The focus of the following discussion is on why the accounting choice is important, and understanding the accounting rules that affect this choice.

Choices in Lease Accounting: Benefits to Management

When leased assets and liabilities are omitted from the balance sheet, it can affect ratio analysis and the subsequent evaluation of a company. For example, two key ratios used to evaluate companies are return on assets (ROA) and debt to equity. ROA is calculated as net income/total assets. This ratio is commonly used as a measure of how well management is using the asset base that it has developed. If leased assets are left out of this calculation, the total asset number is obviously smaller than if the assets were included. This increases the ROA, making the company look financially healthier than it really is.

Relatedly, on the other side of the balance sheet we can compare the existing levels of debt to equity (debt/owners' equity). This number gives a rough idea of how much of a company's long-term financing comes from debt. When the liability for leased assets is left out of this calculation, it understates the total debt faced by the company. This decreases the debt-to-equity ratio, suggesting that the company is on sounder financial footing than it actually is. Most leases have stipulated lease periods, so the lease obligation is just another form of debt.

Another measure, total debt to total assets, helps us assess the company's ability to raise cash if the need arises. If most of the assets are already financed by liabilities, the company may be unable to use debt to finance replacement or growth of assets. This may lead management to turn to leasing. If this is done, the total debt to total asset ratio remains unchanged, even though, in reality, the company may now be in a much riskier financial position. The impact of the lease on future profits is hidden.

If management secures the use of assets through leases, yet does not have to include these resources as assets and liabilities on the balance sheet, then the ROA and debt-to-equity ratios will look more favorable. When such a situation arises, it is called *off balance sheet financing* because management has secured the use of assets to generate income without showing the asset or liability associated with the lease transaction on the balance sheet. It is one of the most controversial areas in financial reporting because it places the investor at risk if it is not properly disclosed.

Lease Accounting: Capital versus Operating Leases

Because management has lease accounting choices, perceptions of operations may be affected by these accounting filters. Lease accounting rules have been written to treat installment purchases made through leasing transactions as assets. If a lease represents an installment purchase, it is termed a **capital lease,** and is recorded as an asset or liability in the accounting system. If a lease is not classified as an installment purchase, it is termed an **operating lease,** and is not shown on the balance sheet: Only footnote disclosure is required.

What characteristics are used to differentiate these two types of lease transactions? First, a lease must be noncancelable to qualify as a capital lease. Once this fact is established, if the lease meets any one of the following four criteria, it is to be considered a capital lease:

1. Title transfers to lessee at end of lease term.
2. Lease contract includes a bargain purchase option (i.e., lessee can purchase the leased asset at significantly less than fair market value).

3. Lease term $\geq$ .75 asset's estimated useful life.
4. Present value of the minimum lease payments $\geq$ .90 of the fair market value of the leased assets at the inception of the lease.

This list highlights the fact that, except for the fourth criterion, these constraints are easily avoidable. In fact, in most cases management can choose to structure a lease contract to create either an operating or a capital lease.

To the extent that ROA, asset turnovers, and debt/equity ratios are used to assess operations, these differences in lease accounting policies between companies can affect operational comparisons. If a major competitor leases most of its equipment and your company owns its machines, comparison of these two companies through ratio analysis will be hard to interpret. There is a remedy for the investor, though. Careful use of the notes that accompany a published financial statement can identify the estimated future obligations faced by a company over the life of its leased assets.

Whether operating or capital, a lease requires the ongoing payment of lease payments that come directly from the cash account. In addition, an asset recorded under an operating lease cannot be depreciated; the firm sacrifices this tax benefit to avoid listing the lease liability on their books. When such approaches are detected, it is important to factor in their impact on the financial position of the firm, its solvency, and future profitability. Legal technicalities and accounting policy choices do not change the economic facts: A debt has to be paid, whether recorded in the balance sheet or not.

FINAL COMMENTS

In everything we ought to look to the end.

Jean de la Fontaine (2)

Capital markets assess a company's operating performance, in part by evaluating published accounting data. A company's chief executive assesses competition, in part by evaluating published accounting data. Based on these assessments, strategies are modified and developed, objectives are established, and operations planned. Operations-managers must understand the data used in these assessments in order to be proactive rather than reactive in their activities. Operations managers must be able to think like the capital markets and assess benchmark companies in order to understand likely management directions and their implications for operating activities.

This chapter focused on accounting choices that can have a tremendous impact on published accounting data. Revenue recognition, inventory costing methods, depreciation policies, and lease accounting procedures include estimates and choices that can make it difficult to separate the results of accounting procedural manipulations from real economic changes to a business. The discussion of these accounting choices should enable the internally oriented manager to better understand, and therefore use, accounting data, as well as to be more alert to other accounting choices at the discretion of management.

Accounting choices can make a major difference to a company, saving countless dollars in tax payments. It is good management to choose policies that improve cash flows. But, when these choices impair the ability of other managers to make sound decisions, or drive undesirable behaviors, they have to be looked at more harshly. There is, it seems, a lot of room for management to maneuver in defining current income and financial position. Being aware of how these decisions can impact internal and external decision making is one way to ensure that these choices, and the numbers they create, do not divert attention away from the facts: Internal decisions and effective management of daily activities form the cornerstone to *sustainable* competitive advantage.

SUGGESTED READINGS

Berton, Lee, and J. Schiff. *The Wall Street Journal on Accounting*. Homewood, Ill.: Business One Irwin, 1990.

Briloff, A. *Unaccountable Accounting: Games Accountants Play*. New York: Harper and Row, 1973.

Brown, L. *The Modern Theory of Financial Reporting*. Plano, Tex.: Business Publications, 1987.

Delaney, P., J. Adler, B. Epstein, and M. Foran. *GAAP: Interpretation and Application of Generally Accepted Accounting Principles*. New York: Wiley, 1991.

Nikolai, L., and J. Bazley. *Intermediate Accounting*. 4th ed. Boston: PWS Kent, 1988.

Tracy, John. *How to Read a Financial Report*. 2nd ed. New York: Wiley, 1983.

CHAPTER 4

NUMBERS IN THE BANK

Money is a terrible master but an excellent servant.

P. T. Barnum (1)

The accounting system focuses on economic transactions, attempting to match revenues with the resources they consume on a period-by-period basis. This is an important objective, but the true bottom line in any organization is its bank balance. Cash is the great equalizer; its lack can fell the large and the small. Retailing giant W. T. Grant met its demise when it could no longer pay its bills; in the end the rules were the same for this organization as it is for the individuals who populated it. Having enough funds to pay the bills in a timely manner isn't an option; it is the core principle of economic survival.

The role of a company's cash position in determining its overall economic health is so important that the Financial Accounting Standards Board mandates the detailed disclosure of changes in the cash position of a firm on an annual basis via the **statement of cash flows.** This mandated statement, first required in 1987, replaced a more general statement of changes in financial position. In moving to the statement of cash flows, FASB was reflecting the market's concern with the liquidity of a company and its impact on the long-term survival of the firm, as suggested by the following statement:

> Financial reporting should provide information to help present and potential investors and creditors and other users in assessing the amounts, timing, and uncertainty of prospective cash receipts from dividends or interest and the proceeds from the sale, redemption, or maturity of securities or loans. The prospects for those cash receipts are affected by an enterprise's ability to generate enough cash to meet its obligations when due and its other cash operating needs, to reinvest in operations, and to pay cash dividends.[1]

---

[1]*Statement of Financial Accounting Concepts,* No. 1, "Objectives of Financial Reporting by Business Enterprises," Stanford, Conn.: The Financial Accounting Standards Board, 1978, paragraph 37. This quotation appears in P. Fess and C. Warren, *Accounting Principles.* 16th ed. (Cincinnati, Ohio: South-Western, 1990), pp. 691–92.

The statement of cash flows details the inflows and outflows of money into the organization. It provides a clear, objective measure of the financial health of the organization, devoid of the machinations of accrual accounting. How does cash-based reporting differ from accrual accounting?

ONLY THE FACTS, PLEASE

It is always a relief to believe what is pleasant, but it is more important to believe what is true.

Hilaire Belloc, *The Silence of the Sea* (4)

Cash-based reporting provides an accurate and undistorted view of **liquidity,** or the company's ability to generate enough cash from its daily operations to pay the bills those activities create. It doesn't focus on the illusive concept of matching the use of a resource with the revenues it generates, but merely records, instead, when the bills are paid and when cash is received from customers on account.

Cash-based reporting is the same for a business as it is for an individual. When checks are received, deposited, and clear the financial markets, money is available to pay for past purchases, to buy new goods, or to put in the bank for later use. In examining the source and use of cash in a business, three major categories of transactions appear: (1) cash flows from operations; (2) cash flows from investing activities; and (3) cash flows from financing activities (see Figure 4–1). In other words, cash is generated and used to fund ongoing operations, through the buying and selling of investments in physical plant or nonphysical assets, and from the debt and/or equity markets.

When the focus is on cash flows, the objective of the accounting process is quite clear. As with a checkbook, the only point of concern is determining when and how much cash is required, and then making sure those dollars are in place. Not every dollar needed over the next month has to be in the checking account of a company on the first of the month; in fact, it is wiser to keep those dollars earning interest as long as possible. The objective, then, is to make sure that there is enough cash to cover, and only cover, daily expenditures. A well-functioning cash-based accounting system keeps the actual cash balance at the minimum level needed to cover those bills that must be paid on any given day; any residual cash should be invested in some easily accessible, "near-cash" instrument, such as a money market account.

FIGURE 4–1
Sources and Uses of Cash

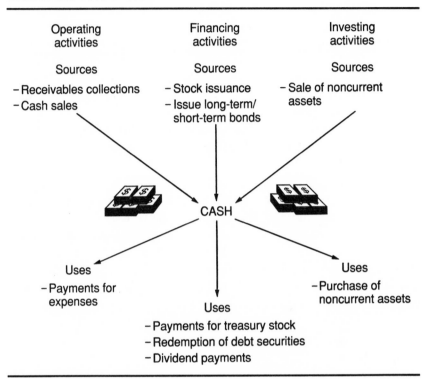

| Operating activities | Financing activities | Investing activities |

Sources
- Receivables collections
- Cash sales

Sources
- Stock issuance
- Issue long-term/ short-term bonds

Sources
- Sale of noncurrent assets

CASH

Uses
- Payments for expenses

Uses
- Payments for treasury stock
- Redemption of debt securities
- Dividend payments

Uses
- Purchase of noncurrent assets

In summary, accrual accounting differs from cash accounting in one key way: accrual accounting attempts to match, from an economic perspective, all revenues earned in a period with all the resources consumed to generate them. Cash accounting, on the other hand, concerns itself only with the flow of funds through the cash account; it attempts to correctly record the receipt and expenditure of cash on an ongoing basis. The differences between these two approaches comes down to one of *timing*—cash accounting records the event when dollars change hands; accrual accounting records it when the economic transaction is completed or assured.

Selling Goods on Credit: Separating Revenues from Receipts

One of the most common examples of the timing differences between cash and accrual accounting occurs when a company sells its goods to customers on credit. When the sale takes place, the accrual accounting system records an increase to the period's revenues and a corresponding increase in the accounts receivable account. In other words, the customer's obligation to pay the company for the goods is recorded at the time of sale. Should the period close immediately after this sale, the cash account would be unchanged, while revenues and the asset accounts receivable would show the impact of the sale. When the customer pays for the goods, the cash receipt is recorded and the account receivables account is reduced for the amount. That's the accrual accounting approach; it separates the recognition of the revenue from the receipt of payment for the goods.

If the company were operating on a cash basis, revenues would not be recorded until the cash for the goods was actually received from the customer. While a "memo" entry might be used to keep track of the debt, the revenue from the sale would not be recognized until collection on this debt was made. In accounting terms, the cash basis of revenue recognition focuses on the actual transference of cash as its starting point. The same rule applies to the payment of bills; until the check is written, the expense is nonexistent, or transparent to, a cash-based FMIS. Cash accounting is based on the concrete flows of funds between a company and the external marketplace.

Capturing Cash Flows

The statement of cash flows attempts to proxy the flow of cash through the business, detailing when and why cash was received, and how it was used by the company (see Figure 4–2). Looking at Lawnmasters' financial statements once again, we can see that the cash statement begins with a detailing of "cash from operations." This number does not correspond, though, to the net income number that is derived from the accrual accounting system. Instead, as suggested in Figure 4–3, it is based on the actual flow of funds.

Under the **direct** cost method of determining cash flows from operations, all the transactions involving cash are summarized following an analysis of the cash account. This is the most straightforward way to derive the cash from operations figure, but it is impossible for someone outside the company to develop it. The second part of Figure 4–3 illustrates the differences between the **direct** and **indirect** **cost** methods for determining the cash from operations figure. Looking closely, it is clear that in deriving this number indirectly, we *undo*

FIGURE 4–2
Lawnmasters, Incorporated Financial Statements

LAWNMASTERS INCORPORATED
Balance Sheets
At December 31, 1990 and 1991

Assets	December 31, 1991		December 31, 1990	
Current assets:				
Cash....................	$ 41,300		$ 31,000	
Accounts receivable (net of allowance for bad debts)...........	35,000		30,000	
Inventory...............	25,000	$101,300	29,000	$ 90,000
Long-term investments:				
Common stock in Quick seed Corporation.....		10,000		15,000
Long-term assets:				
Property, plant, and equipment...........	90,500		85,800	
Less accumulated depreciation..........	31,500	59,000	23,600	62,200
Total assets...............		$170,300		$167,200

Liabilities				
Current liabilities:				
Accounts payable......	$ 35,000		$ 32,000	
Income tax payable.....	1,500		2,000	
Short-term notes payable..............	15,000	$ 51,500	18,000	$ 52,000
Long-term liabilities:				
Long-term note payable		15,000		10,000
Bonds payable.........		35,000		40,000

Stockholders' equity				
Stockholders' equity:				
Common stock, par $10..............	50,000		50,000	
Contributed capital in excess of par........	5,000		5,000	
Retained earnings (net of $7,000 in dividends paid out each year)..........	13,800	68,800	10,200	$ 65,200
Total liabilities and stockholder's equity........		$170,300		$167,200

FIGURE 4–2 (*continued***)**

LAWNMASTERS, INCORPORATED
Income Statement
For the Years Ending December 31, 1990 and 1991

	As of December 31,1991	As of December 31, 1990
Sales revenue..................	$160,000	$125,000
Cost of goods sold.............	100,000	75,000
Gross margin...................	$ 60,000	$ 50,000

Less expenses:

Salaries.....................	$25,000		$24,100	
Depreciation expense...................	7,900		4,300	
Advertising..................	6,500		5,000	
Interest......................	3,000	42,400	2,400	35,800
Net income before taxes......................		17,600		14,200
Income taxes...............		7,000		5,600
Net income....................		$ 10,600		$ 8,600

LAWNMASTERS, INCORPORATED
Statement of Retained Earnings
For the Years Ending December 31, 1990 and 1991

	As of December 31, 1991	As of December 31, 1990
Retained earnings balance, January 1	$10,200	$ 8,600
Plus net income for the year.......................	10,600	8,600
Total retained earnings available to stockholders.......	$20,800	$17,200
Less dividends paid.............	7,000	7,000
Retained earnings balance, December 31.........	$13,800	$10,200

---

the timing differences that exist between the accrual and cash-based accounting systems. Specifically, those transactions that affect net income but do not require a direct cash outlay (such as depreciation) are added to the net income number.

FIGURE 4–2 *(continued)*

LAWNMASTERS, INCORPORATED
Statement of Cash Flows
For the Year Ending December 31, 1991

As of
December 31, 1991

Cash flows for operating activities:			
Net income, per income statement........		$10,600	
Add: Depreciation.........................	$7,900		
Decrease in inventories..............	4,000		
Increase in accounts payable........	3,000	14,900	
		$25,500	
Deduct: Increases in accounts receivable .	$5,000		
Decrease in taxes payable	500		
Decrease in short-term note			
payable........................	3,000	8,500	
Net cash flow from operating ac-			
tivities.........................			$17,000
Cash flows from investing activities:			
Cash received from sale of investments ...		$ 5,000	
Less cash paid for equipment............		4,700	
Net cash flow from investing activities.....			300
Cash flows from financing activities:			
Cash received from long-term note			
payable................................		$ 5,000	
Less: Retirement of bonds payable........	$5,000		
Cash paid for dividends............	7,000	(12,000)	
Net cash flow provided by financing activi-			
ties......................................			(7,000)
Increase in cash			$10,300
Cash at the beginning of the year...........			31,000
Cash at the end of the year.................			$41,300

The indirect method of reconciling the accrual and cash-based systems drives home the fact that some of the differences between these two methods are permanent, while others are simply timing differences. Yet an operating manager needs to know how to control these cash flows, not simply how get them in the right bucket. How do management policies affect the flow of cash through a business?

FIGURE 4–3
Lawnmaster, Incorporated Statements of Cash Flows

LAWNMASTERS, INCORPORATED
Cash Flows vs. Net Income
For the Year Ending December 31, 1991
Cashflows

Sales..................	$ 155,000	−$5,000
Cost of goods sold.....	(93,000)	−$4,000
		−$3,000
Operating expenses...	(37,500)	+$3,000
Depreciation...........	-0-	−$7,900
Cash increase from operations......	$ 17,000	

Accounts receivable (sales were made this period even
  though cash will not be collected until next period)....... $160,000

Inventory reduced during period (more sold than bought)
Accounts payable (goods were purchased this period but
  won't be paid for until next period)...................... ($100,000)

Accounts payable (goods were purchased this period but
  won't be paid for until next period)...................... ($100,000)
Accumulated depreciation (this contra account is increased
  when depreciation is recognized; the cash impact was
  noted when the asset was originally purchased)......... ($ 7,000)
                                         Net income............ 10,600

As can be seen from the above table, it is possible to reconcile the cash from operations figure, noted in Lawnmasters Statement of Cash Flows as $17,000 for fiscal year 1991, with its stated accrual accounting income from operations, reported in the income statement as $10,600 for the same period. Each noted difference reflects a timing difference between the point at which an obligation was incurred or payment on account earned and the actual payment or receipt of cash.

MANAGEMENT POLICIES AND THEIR IMPACT ON CASH

A fool and his money are soon parted. What I want to know is how they got together in the first place.

Cyril Fletcher, BBC radio program, May 8, 1969 (3)

Management affects the flow of cash through a business by the policies it creates and enforces. If customers are allowed to "slide"

FIGURE 4–3 *(continued)*
Direct vs. Indirect Method for Determining Changes in Cash

LAWNMASTERS, INCORPORATED
For the Year Ending December 31, 1991

Direct reporting of cash from operations:

Cash inflows:

Collections from customers.....................	$155,000	
Sale of investments............................	5,000	
Issuance of long-term note payable............	5,000	$165,000

Cash outflows:

For inventory purchases.......................	$ 93,000	
For employee salaries.........................	25,000	
For advertising................................	6,500	
For interest payments.........................	(500)	
For income taxes..............................	7,500	
For payment on short-term note payable.......	3,000	
For capital equipment.........................	4,700	
For retirement of bonds payable	5,000	
For dividends.................................	7,000	154,700
Net cash inflow...................................		$ 10,300

Indirect reporting of cash flows:

Net income......................................		$10,600
Adjustment for noncash expenses:		
Depreciation expense.........................		7,900

Adjustments to reconcile to cash basis:

Decrease in inventories.......................	$ 4,000	
Increase in accounts payable..................	3,000	
Increase in accounts receivable...............	(5,000)	
Decrease in taxes payable....................	500	
Decrease in note payable.....................	(3,000)	
Decrease in investments......................	5,000	
Increase in plant and equipment..............	(4,700)	
Increase in long-term note payable............	5,000	
Decrease in bonds payable...................	(5,000)	
Decrease in dividends payable................	(7,000)	(8,200)
Net cash inflow...................................		$10,300

---

on paying their invoices, cash will not be available for the company to pay its bills. Conversely, if a company delays paying its bills until the last possible moment (or perhaps even later than that), cash is retained for other uses. Only if penalties are brought to bear can these payment patterns be influenced. How does management influence the cash balance?

Cash and Accounts Receivable

There is a clear, direct tie between a company's collection policies and its cash balance. When customers are allowed excessive time to pay for goods they have already received, they are implicitly being granted interest payments as a reward. How? When customers fail to pay their invoices in a timely manner, they are able to keep their cash on hand longer, earning interest for them in their own bank accounts. The company that sold them the goods, though, is simply out of pocket all the way around; they have neither the goods nor the cash.

One solution for a company faced with slow-paying customers is to release goods only when cash is received. Credit policies, however, are part of the competitive arsenal for most companies; granting a customer credit can spell the difference between making a sale and walking away empty-handed. In most situations, then, the credit policies of a company are based on established industry practice; this practice doesn't have to be followed, but it is what customers have come to expect.

How can company policies affect these practices? First, before credit is granted, a company can establish procedures that limit who they will grant credit to. Not every customer is equally worthy of credit. If everyone who asks for credit is granted it, the company places itself at risk. When goods are delivered but not paid for, the customer comes out ahead (at least in the short run), but the company that furnished them loses on all counts. This makes it imperative that a company screen its customers for their ability, and tendency, to pay their bills on time.

Excessively tight credit policies, though, can squeeze out some good customers with the bad. The objective is to aim for the optimal level of sales within an acceptable level of risk of nonpayment. A company may be willing to live with 5 percent bad debts in order to maximize its overall sales. But if it grants credit too liberally, the company is passing along the bad debt costs from nonpaying customers to those who pay on time. The banking crisis reflects what happens when the default level on loans rises above the preset limits; each additional dollar of bad debt comes directly out of the profits of the company. It has a bottom-line effect that can rapidly consume available cash resources and place the firm in financial jeopardy.

These credit policies are policed by the financial manager, who screens all applications for credit from new customers, and unusually large requests from existing ones. Once approval has been granted, the focus shifts to collecting the funds. Obviously, the company would like its customers to pay on receipt of the invoice, but achieving this can be difficult. The customer knows it is in his or her best interest to delay payment as long as possible.

To combat the tendency to put the new invoice at the bottom of the payment pile, companies often use **sales discounts** to entice customers to pay more rapidly. A sales, or trade, discount is reflected in the credit terms as "2/10, net 30." This means that if the invoice is paid within ten days of its receipt, the customer can deduct 2 percent of the total from the amount due. If the discount is not taken, the customer is expected to send the entire invoice amount to the company within thirty days of the sale.

It is good practice to take the discount. Why? How can 2 percent of an invoice offset the 5- to 10-percent interest the customer's money can earn in the market? The answer is simple. The 2-percent discount translates to 36 percent effective interest within a year. The company that takes the discount gets to keep 2 percent of the invoiced amount and put it in a bank account for the 20 days remaining on the invoice. There are 18 (360 days in a year divided by the 20 days of interest) such **compounding periods** in a year. So the company earns the 2 percent compounded 18 times, or an equivalent of 36 percent interest on the discount.

Offering a trade discount can markedly speed up the collection of cash on accounts receivable. It also helps identify those customers who are in the best financial position for future reference. A customer who never exercises the trade discount option may be having difficulty generating enough cash to pay its bills. If few customers are taking the discount, it may be too low to be of any use. Finally, customers who don't take the discount may be having trouble collecting their own accounts receivable. Collection and payment policies are intimately connected within a company and an industry.

Before leaving the accounts receivable area, it's interesting to note that the accrual accounting system actually records bad debts *before* they happen. Based on a traditional collection pattern, the financial manager will automatically expense a certain percentage of the existing accounts receivable balance as bad debts. This amount is established during negotiations with the auditor; it is a required calculation and disclosure. In this setting, the accrual accounting system is preempting the actual cash flows that may arise from any one sale, setting aside a fund, or provision, for nonpayment. In doing so, the FMIS more accurately details the value of the accounts receivable balance; if certain customers are not expected to pay their bills, recording the potential payment in the receivables account is nonproductive game that can mislead investors, banks, or other interested parties.

In looking at a financial statement for a company, the accounts receivable figure will reflect the **net** amount, or the number of dollars the company expects to be able to collect. If all goes well, the company may actually collect all of these receivables plus those expensed as bad debts.[2] The accounts receivable balance is an estimate of what the receivables are worth in terms of cash at some time in the near future.

The Impact of Inventories on Cash

Inventory policies and levels have an immediate effect on the cash position of a firm. Why? Each dollar of inventory has to be paid for, recorded, stored, moved, and perhaps even thrown away in the course of doing business. As inventories grow, more and more cash is tied up. The slower inventory "turns over" or is sold, the longer it takes to convert raw materials or purchased goods into cash receipts. Inventory is profit waiting to be made, goods waiting to be sold, and cash waiting to be freed for other uses.

The cash impact of inventories is often overlooked by management; when it is taken into account, it is often seen as a **cost of capital** issue. This means that management focuses solely on the opportunity cost, in terms of foregone interest from investing the cash in other goods or financial instruments, in determining the impact of

---

[2]As a point of clarification it is important to remember that the company expects all of its customers to pay; that is why they were granted credit in the first place. The allowance for bad debts is not tied to any one account or customer; it reflects an overall estimate of what percent will remain unpaid (not *who* won't pay).

the inventory on cash balances. This approach ignored the concept of *velocity*, or turnover, in the cash generation cycle.

Just as a 2 percent trade discount can be misinterpreted or ignored if not fully understood, inventory costs are often understated. The costs of holding inventory are greater than the direct costs for interest and storage contained in the carrying cost estimate. Large inventories bring with them a host of problems, indirect costs, and complexity, all of which increase the number and cost of transactions conducted inside the company, and the cost of the products and services it provides.

Inventories remove cash from bank accounts or other investments, eliminating any potential for interest, but the costs don't end there. For instance, in companies adopting just-in-time inventory and manufacturing methods, there is a marked decrease in the level of inventory required to maintain ongoing production (due to process improvements, not management directive). It is not unusual for a company that had been experiencing two "turns" in the inventory value per year to be able to achieve 12 turns per year before the implementation is complete.[3] Looking at the cash impact of this improvement provides some interesting insights:

Average annual sales:	$480,000	
Average inventory, before JIT:	$240,000	
Average inventory, after JIT:	40,000	
Direct increase in available cash	$200,000	per year
Interest earned on funds at 10%	$ 20,000	per year
Reduction in other carrying costs (10%)	$ 20,000	per year

Right away, $200,000 of cash is available for other uses. If this money is simply put in a bank account, $20,000 of additional income falls directly through to the bottom line of the income statement from this inventory reduction. In addition, as inventory shrinks, related carrying costs (e.g., insurance and warehousing) drop. Assuming

---

[3]Sales divided by average inventory is used to develop this figure. For Lawnmaster, $160,000 in sales is generated with $25,000 in average inventory. This translates to 6.4 turns per year.

that total cost of holding inventory is 20 percent (10 percent interest, 10 percent other direct costs), another $20,000 of profit is generated through reduced expenses; this savings also drops directly to the bottom line. $40,000 of additional profit on sales of $480,000 is an 8.3 percent improvement before taxes. It would take a tremendous amount of effort to generate this type of profitability through other means.

What are the direct costs of holding inventory? These include the opportunity cost of holding the inventory, storage costs of the inventory, taxes on the inventory investment, the cost of creating and maintaining inventory records, and the cost of recording, tagging, moving, and disposing of it. Increases in inventory bring direct and measurable increases in the costs of maintaining it.

JIT manufacturing and inventory policies can have a direct impact on the bottom line through the reduction of required inventory levels. As companies attempt to eliminate their raw materials inventories by creating fluid, responsive supply channels that deliver these materials on demand, when needed and no sooner, they reduce the complexity and cost of doing business. In implementing just-in-time supply channels, a company is actively managing the velocity of materials through its plant by recognizing that any idle asset is money lost.

If a company can, through the development of effective manufacturing processes such as JIT manufacturing, start and finish a product in less than a day, it doesn't need finished goods inventories either. One company, Allen Bradley in Milwaukee, Wisconsin, is using a computer integrated manufacturing system (CIM) to accomplish just this goal. Customer orders received by a prespecified cutoff time are shipped the day they are received. The promise of "same day delivery" may not seem spectacular; the fact that it is attained with zero finished goods inventory, zero work-in-process inventory, and only a minimal level of raw materials inventory, though, establishes its importance. Minimal dollars are needed to support the inventory levels, freeing up the cash for other uses.

The Hidden Costs of Holding Inventory

Unfortunately, these direct costs barely begin to scratch the surface of the total costs caused by carrying excessive inventories. The nightmares of excessive inventory write-offs at the end of the year because of shrinkage and obsolescence are all too familiar to most companies. Some of these costs are increasing exponentially, as the impact of shorter product life cycles is beginning to be felt. A company cannot afford to keep a year's worth of inventory for a product that has a six-month life cycle; this applies both to the materials used to make the product and to the finished goods. Obsolescence is not a problem for a small number of volatile industries (e.g., food and drug companies); it is harsh reality across diverse industries with diverse product offerings. It is a cost and risk that cannot be ignored: Each dollar of inventory written off is a direct expense, or reduction, of period profits. These are dollars that can't be regained as well as future opportunities that can't be reaped.

In addition, there are ongoing inventory costs that are often overlooked by management. Every time inventory is counted, tagged, stored, moved, or in any way "touched" (physically or on paper), costs are generated. These costs show up in the company's manufacturing and administrative overhead accounts and are seldom attached to the inventory in any calculations or analysis performed by management. Yet these activities consume resources, use cash, and limit profits the same as interest payments and insurance premiums.

When inventories grow, a large number of observable and unobservable costs grow with them. There are a million stories of companies who have had to rent outside warehouse space to store inventory. Each time a new product, or a new option, part or process is added to the company's mix of activities, more inventory is required. This inventory takes on a life of its own, filling warehouses, requiring more and more people to record it, move it, record it, rotate it, record it, count it, move it, and so on. Inventories can create an excessive amount of non-value-added costs, eating up cash balances as the invoices come due.

A good manager knows that more inventory is not a viable solution to ongoing problems in meeting customer requirements. Yet as long as the FMIS hides the full financial impact of creeping inventories, it is difficult to justify technologies and processes that would make these inventories unnecessary. Inventories are recorded on the balance sheet as an asset; they are a visible store of value. Most of the costs associated with maintaining these inventory levels are hidden in various overhead accounts sprinkled throughout the company. It is very hard in a traditional FMIS to isolate the costs of excessive inventories or the benefits that will arise from better management of them.

Whenever resources are consumed, profits are affected. Each turn of the inventory generates profits, as cash invested in goods is released to buy more goods. Business enterprises are based on the recognition that profits are made when goods are sold, not when they're sitting idle in a warehouse. Cash, and profits, are generated from the *velocity* of material, or goods, through a company; the faster inventory investments can be turned over, the better.

The Operating Cycle and Cash

Inventory policies tie up cash, create a number of current and potential costs that will further reduce the cash available for other uses, and increase the time between the purchase of and payment for raw materials and the receipt of cash from customers. The period that elapses from the time payment is made on raw materials purchases to the time a customer pays the company for completed goods is called the firm's **operating cycle** (see Figure 4–4). The longer the operating cycle, the more cash a company has to retain to cover the timing differences.

Focusing on cash helps simplify the problems facing management. The longer it takes to generate a profit from the purchase of raw materials, the less flexibility the company has. The longer the operating cycle, the more resources are tied up in financing day-to-day activities. That leaves fewer dollars for long-term projects and investments. Every dollar tied up in inventory means one less dollar for developing a new product or process. The shorter the operating cycle, the fewer total dollars that are tied up at any one time for these basic activities, and the more cash that is available for other uses.

The impact of the operating cycle on the cash position of a firm is most obvious when a company is undergoing a period of rapid growth. When sales are growing at a rapid pace, both inventories and accounts receivable usually grow at the same speed as sales, or faster. The inventory and accounts receivables consume cash, placing it temporarily out of reach. The related inflows from collections on accounts receivables, though, usually lag behind the growth in sales and inventories, based on the established credit and inventory policies. The longer the operating cycle, the more rapidly the cash account is depleted. Once this point is reached, a company has few options left; it has to cease operations or borrow cash to meet its obligations.

The list of companies that have been felled by success is long. People's Express expanded so fast that it disappeared from the skies

FIGURE 4-4
Operating Cycles

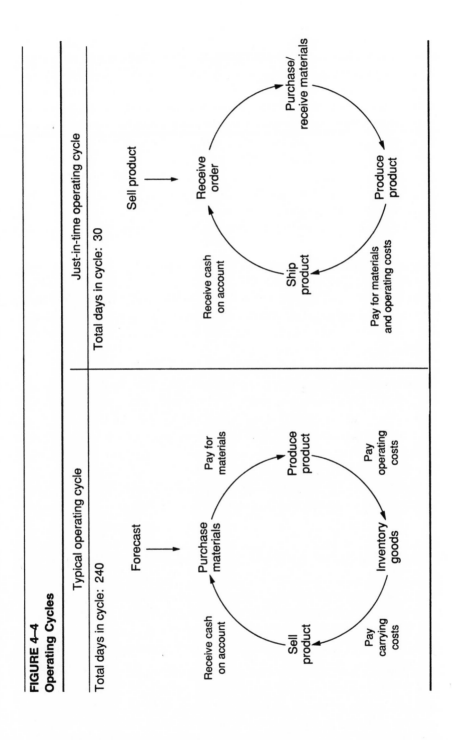

Typical operating cycle

Total days in cycle: 240

Just-in-time operating cycle

Total days in cycle: 30

almost as suddenly as it had appeared. Department stores are infamous for overexpanding and driving themselves into bankruptcy in the process. The cash strain of absorbing more and more business with extended operating cycles, as well as the demands for payment on physical assets and employee wages to generate the business, lead the over-aggressive into an early grave. In fact, a failure to have enough available cash and near-cash resources to cover the operating cycle and overall sales shortfalls is the number-one culprit behind the failure of most small businesses. Cash is not an optional asset; it is the lifeblood of the organization.

As can be seen in Figure 4–4, the impact of World-Class manufacturing techniques (such as JIT manufacturing) on the length of the operating cycle is significant. By reducing total cycle times, from the ordering of raw materials unit finished product is shipped to customers, to less than the customer's *expected* delivery window, a company is able to effectively become a make-to-order supplier, holding minimal inventories and providing maximum flexibility to respond to changes in product demand.

This is, perhaps, one of the least-touted benefits of JIT and related, advanced manufacturing technologies. Because they nibble away at the time needed to meet customer demands, they eliminate many of the hidden costs that come from holding inventories. In fact, for the company suggested in Figure 4–4, cash inflows are almost perfectly matched to outflows; cash may be received for an order before the material invoices have to be paid. The additional cash this makes available for other uses provides productive capability that can be turned into a strategic advantage.

UNDERSTANDING AND MANAGING CASH FLOWS

In short, business managers have a double duty: to earn profit, and to convert the profit into cash reasonably soon. Waiting too long to turn profit into cash reduces the value of the profit.

John A. Tracy, *How to Read a Financial Report*

Returning to the cash-flow reconciliation in Figure 4–3, it is clear now that any increase in a current asset account translates to a use of cash, while reducing these asset accounts frees up cash. Conversely, increases in short-term liabilities increase the amount of cash available, and decreases in these items use cash. In the former case, cash is redirected out of its natural form into some other type of resource. Assets are purchased with cash and with promises to pay in the future (liabilities). When these promises are fulfilled, cash is paid out. In essence, every resource that is used and every transaction that occurs within a company affects the cash position of the firm. Poor asset management can rapidly lead to bankruptcy, as more and more cash becomes tied up in nonperforming assets.

The accrual accounting process hides this fact from view, detaching the cash generation process from reported net incomes. As can be seen in the analysis of Lawnmasters' 1991 performance, the net income figure of $10,600 understates the healthy cash flow this firm is generating ($17,000 increase in available cash). This created additional funds that Lawnmasters' management then redeployed to buy additional equipment ($4,700), reduce debt, and pay dividends.

Short-Term versus Long-Term Cash Concerns

A celebration on Lawnmasters' behalf, though, may be premature, as can be seen in Figure 4–5. When the current rate of growth in revenues is extended over the period 1992 to 1996, cash problems become apparent. Growth brings with it excessive demands on a firm's cash flows that if understood and managed, can provide little or no constraint on its sustainable profits. The key is understanding the cash implications of existing policies and structures.

A cash budget is the best way to get a thorough understanding of how current plans may affect the company's long-term health. In fact, the cash budget is the "stop light" that serves as the ultimate screen on any budget or plan. Unfortunately, if the numbers used to create the cash budget don't hold when reality takes over, problems can arise. In addition to the general issues surrounding operating and collection policies, there are other ways that management affects the cash position of the firm.

Looking at Lawnmasters' projections, it is clear that its expected growth cannot be financed from operating revenues. In fact, there are additional financing requirements in each of the years analyzed, beginning with a shortfall of $19,300 in 1992, which grows to a capital requirement of $81,175 by 1996. These are not total amounts, but the actual dollars of additional financing required *each year* to keep the firm afloat.

FIGURE 4-5
Forecasting Cash Requirements

LAWNMASTERS, INCORPORATED
Fiscal Years 1992–1996

Sales forecast in 1992	$200,000	To meet ongoing needs, current assets are expected to be 50 percent of sales budgeted for the following year.
in 1993	$250,000	
in 1994	$300,000	Net fixed asset expected to be required to meet the budgeted sales are 30 percent of the sales budgeted for the next year.
in 1995	$375,000	
in 1996	$450,000	
in 1997	$550,000	
		The desired current ratio is 2:1, which means that current assets have to be kept at twice the level of current liabilities for each period.
Stockholders' equity as of 12/31/1991	$ 68,800	
		The desired long-term debt-to-equity ratio should be no more than 50 percent (only 50 cents of long-term debt is desired for each dollar of equity).
Net income is expected to be 10 percent of sales over the period of the forecast.		
Dividends of 50 percent of net income will be paid each year.		

FIGURE 4–5 (continued)

Projected Financing Requirements for Lawnmaster, Incorporated

	1992	1993	1994	1995	1996
(1) Sales	$200,000	$250,000	$300,000	$375,000	$450,000
(2) Net income [(1) × 10%]	20,000	25,000	30,000	37,500	45,000
(3) Dividends [(2) × 50%]	10,000	12,500	15,000	18,750	22,500
(4) Increase in stockholder's equity [(2) − (3)]	$ 10,000	$ 12,500	$ 15,000	$ 18,750	$ 22,500
(5) Estimated current assets needed [(1) for next year × 50%]	$125,000	$150,000	$187,500	$225,000	$275,000
(6) Current liabilities allowed [(5) × 50%]	62,500	75,000	93,750	112,500	137,500
(7) Working capital that needs to be financed using long-term sources [(5) − (6)]	$ 62,500	$ 75,000	$ 93,570	$112,500	$137,500
(8) Estimated fixed assets needed [(1) for next year × 30%]	75,000	90,000	112,500	135,000	165,000
(9) Required long-term financing [(7) + (8)]	$137,500	$165,000	$206,070	$247,500	$302,500
(10) Stockholder's equity [prior year + (4)]	$ 78,800	$ 91,300	$106,300	$125,050	$147,550
(11) Long-term debt allowed [(10) × 50%]	39,400	45,650	53,150	62,525	73,775
(12) Estimated total long-term financing available [(10) + (11)]	$118,200	$136,950	$159,450	$187,575	$221,325
(13) Additional requirements [(9) − (12)]	$ 19,300	$ 28,050	$ 46,620	$ 59,925	$ 81,175

Where do the problems appear to lie? To start with, it is questionable whether Lawnmasters can continue to pay out 50% of its earnings in dividends. While dividend growth is expected by investors, the marked increase indicated under existing policies may be excessive. On the positive side, though, its dividend payout policy (dividends paid/net income) should help Lawnmaster attract the additional equity funds it needs to meet its projected demands.

Other areas of concern begin with the assumption that net income cannot be increased above 10 percent of sales. Many of the costs of doing business do not go up, dollar per dollar, with an increase in sales. Even more importantly, Lawnmasters' management needs to be looking for ways to control costs and to eliminate non-value-added activities that are consuming excess resources. Rather than budgeting for a flat 10 percent growth, management might want to build *continuous improvement* goals into this budget. A realistic target might be to increase net income to 15 percent of sales by 1994 and 18 percent of sales by 1996. This would create the potential for an additional $91,250 in internally generated funds for growth.[4] There would still be a shortfall, but the gap would be reduced.

Where else can management turn? Item number seven details the working capital (current assets minus current liabilities) that management feels will be needed to meet sales projections. Once again, there is no questioning of existing practices in the cash forecast. Working capital, though, encompasses items like cash, receivables, and inventory. As this chapter has shown, process improvements, such as JIT, can reduce the level of working capital needed by a firm. If Lawnmasters could find a way to improve the management of its current assets, it might be able to reduce these to 40 percent of next year's projected sales. That would free up a significant amount of capital (e.g., $25,000 in 1992 alone: $250,000 × (.5 − .4)). Reducing current assets also reduces the level of current liabilities the firm can comfortably manage (50 percent of the savings is $12,500), but that

---

[4]Assume that in 1992 net income becomes 12% of sales; in 1993, 14%; 1994 grows to 15%; and on to 17% in 1995 and the desired 18% in 1996. The incremental increase in net income for each year would be: $4,000 in 1992 ($200,000 × 2%), $10,000 in 1993 ($250,000 × 4%), $15,000 in 1994 ($300,000 × 5%), $26,250 in 1995 ($375,000 × 7%), and $36,000 in 1996. The cumulative total provided would be $91,250.

still reduces the total required working capital by $12,500 for 1992.

Adding the changes suggested above, Lawnmasters could use more effective management policies to increase net income as a percentage of sales ($10,000 gain in 1992) and reduce the level of working capital required ($12,500 in 1992). The combined impact of these complementary goals (continuous improvement applied to the entire organization) is that Lawnmasters could become self-funding. For each shortfall noted in Figure 4–5, the suggested improvements would eliminate the need for additional financing. This opens up tremendous opportunities for management to develop new products, implement new technologies, and create a sustainable competitive advantage.

Cash forecasting provides management with the tools necessary to make changes to the way business is currently done *before* a crisis occurs. Proactive management of the existing processes and products, or **cost control,** creates a long-term perspective and awareness among the management team, prevents excessive expansion without recognition of downstream consequences, and helps a company identify areas of opportunity where cost reduction can be used to generate growth in other areas. Departing from historical cost and ledger-based accounting, the financial manager is able to support internal customers, add value to the firm, and identify long-term opportunities for growth.

Long-Term Projects and Cash

New capital assets are usually evaluated through an elaborate cash and return on investment analysis before they are purchased. In fact, most companies set their capital budget spending limits based on the FMIS's projections of cash availability and timing of various cash inflows and outflows. The secondary role played by long-term investments in cash-constrained periods is one reason why these expenses are called "discretionary."

Are these outlays necessary, though? Few would argue that the long-term survival of any organization is based on its ability to generate new products and processes, or to find ways to boost the productivity of its existing asset base. These dollars can be redeployed to meet current operating needs, but continuing to ignore these long-term growth items can ultimately destroy the competitiveness of the organization.

Management is faced with a constant, demanding task. If it is to ensure the long-term success of the company, it has to find innovative ways to decrease the impact of daily activities on the cash available to the firm. The more resources that are tied up just meeting day-to-day needs, the less are available for growth and investment in the future. Each dollar of inventory or accounts receivable limits the dollars available to develop new products or processes. It is a zero-sum game that can't be avoided, and consistent errors will lead to defeat.

Aggressive management of a company's resources is reflected in high turnover rates, short operating cycles, and the ever-present drive to eliminate waste from the products and processes used to meet customer needs. The more time it takes to turn a pound of raw material into profits, the less those profits are worth, and the fewer dollars there are for other uses. Individuals know that saving is the precursor to getting a house or a new car; in business the same rules apply. The equity market can provide some respite from the harsh realities embedded in cash flow dynamics, but investors are interested in companies that can generate cash for them in the form of dividends. The money received from investors is not a gift; there is an expectation that the firm can generate a high rate of return (profitability) with these funds. If not, the investor will put his or her money to work elsewhere.

If a company aggressively manages its assets, but then pays out all of the profits it generates in dividends, interest, and top management salaries, once again the long-run is shortchanged. Dividends compete with research and development for the available funds; a dollar that leaves the company can no longer be used to fund new projects. It is this basic fact that can lead a company to reduce its dividends for a period of time, or to substitute a stock dividend for a cash dividend. Often the equity market sees this as a sign of poor management or of weakness in the company. Yet, if a company is being managed for the long-run, this is the very type of policy it needs to pursue. There are times, it seems, when the demands of the financial market may push management in exactly the wrong direction. It is an ever-present danger that isn't solely rooted in the accrual accounting system; it is reflected in the dynamics surrounding the cash account.

Generating Dollars for Growth

All that is human must retrograde if it does not advance.

Edward Gibbon, *Decline and Fall of the Roman Empire* (3)

Growth is one of the primary objectives of management. It is the source of vitality and long-term improvement in the organization's profits and value. In fact, growth is intimately tied to the survival of a company; if a company stands still it will soon find itself out of the race. Yet growth places a major strain on the available cash flows of the company. Much of this strain comes from the built-in lag between the purchase of materials to the collection of funds owed by customers on account (the operating cycle). The longer the operating cycle and faster the rate of growth, the more difficult sustaining growth can be.

Given that growth is desired, but brings with it excessive demands for cash, what options can management exercise? There are a number of ways management can shortchange the operating cycle and its impact on available cash balances. One of the most common is called **factoring**—some or all of the accounts receivable are "sold" to a bank in return for immediate access to cash. Some companies make a policy of factoring their accounts receivable, leaving the collection concerns with the bank or broker.

Unfortunately, though, factoring is not a riskless or costless option. First, the factoring agent charges a fee, often quite large, to handle the accounts receivable function for the company. Second, if a customer should default on their account, the company has to reassume the bad debt, paying the factoring agent the defaulted amount. In other words, in factoring, ownership of the accounts stays with the company; the agent simply advances cash to the company, which it expects to recoup by collecting on the factored accounts.

Another way a company can generate cash for growth is to shorten its operating cycle. Each day taken off the cycle frees up cash for other uses. This is often an overlooked option, but is actually the most logical approach, especially if the days that are removed from the cycle actually improve the service level for customers. Whenever materials or finished goods sit idle in a company, they consume resources. Minimizing the cost of idle inventory is one way to generate more cash. Relatedly, if the throughput or velocity of materials through the plant can be increased, fewer dollars will be needed to fund ongoing operations. Careful management of noncash assets frees up cash for other uses.

Looking toward the Financial Markets

Management can always turn to the financial markets for cash. Here the options include creating a **line of credit** that provides the company with readily available credit whenever a temporary cash shortfall occurs. Most companies have this type of arrangement with one or more banks. Unfortunately, when a company has to access these emergency funds on an ongoing basis, it is a signal to the financial markets that the firm is in financial trouble. That can cut off, or make excessively expensive, other funds. When a company is drawing down on its line of credit the message is clear: It is not generating enough cash from its daily operations to cover its normal expenses. A negative cash flow is not a long-term option for a company or an individual.

It is often possible for the company to turn to the financial markets directly for an inflow of cash, by either selling additional stock or issuing long-term bonds. This is a good way to generate funds for growth, but it can be a time-consuming process unless the company has already **registered** the financial instruments with the Securities and Exchange Commission. Before a company can trade stocks and bonds in the market, it has to get these instruments registered and approved. This process is expensive and can take six months or more to complete, as the SEC examines the company's financial status, its annual reports, and all related financial documents. If a company is planning for growth, it can preapprove a block of stocks or bonds and "put them on the shelf." These authorized but unissued financial instruments can then be released to the market whenever prices are favorable or the need is great.

Stocks and bonds are not equal in terms of their long-term impact on the financial position of the firm. When bonds are issued, the firm is agreeing to pay interest on a semiannual basis at the defined rate based on the face amount of the bond (regardless of the amount of cash actually received when the bond was issued). That places a new type of cash strain on the company, which can hurt future growth. Issuing stock brings with it an expectation of dividends, though. These dividends are also paid out of the cash account, but the expenditure can be delayed or canceled if the funds are not available.

That may not make it easy to issue more stock in the future, but the flexibility for setting the amount and timing of dividend payments can be a benefit for the firm. Finally, interest paid on bonds is tax deductible, but dividend payments are not. That makes the effective cost (cost net of tax) much lower, on a dollar-per-dollar basis, for debt instruments. The decision to issue stocks versus bonds is complex. Before a decision is made, a careful analysis of the process has to be undertaken.

NO MATTER WHAT THE P&L SAYS, WE'RE BROKE

Credit is like a looking-glass, which when once sullied by a breath, may be wiped clear again; but if once cracked can never be repaired.

Walter Scott (2)

The objective of this chapter has been to drive home the fact that cash is the most important asset a company can have. Major corporations often acquire another company in order to access their cash account. If all available sources of credit are used but bills are still unpaid, the company enters bankruptcy. Restructuring can take place, but often only the barest skeleton of the company remains after the courts complete their task.

Cash-based reporting is the baseline FMIS performance measure; it provides an accurate, undistorted view of liquidity. Cash is provided and used by operating activities, financing activities, and investing activities. Operating activities are the daily business of the firm, from the purchase of raw materials to the receipt of payment for goods and services. Financing activities cover the use of lines of credit, bonds, stocks, and related tools to generate additional cash for the firm; they can also reflect the use of cash for dividends and interest payments. Investing activities reflect the purchase and sale of fixed assets and other large assets used to support a broad range of activity. Only operating activities are ongoing sources and uses of cash; if a company doesn't generate enough cash to pay its bills, it will show up in this number.

Cash accounting differs from accrual accounting because of *timing differences*. Accrual accounting records revenues when legally earned and expenses when legally owed; cash accounting waits until checks are mailed and received. A lot of flexibility is available within the accrual accounting model, but cash balances represent the hard facts. There is very little space for arguing whether or not the firm has money in the bank. A simple phone call will settle the matter.

In looking at issues surrounding cash accounting, this chapter has attempted to look at the way cash is used, and misused, in organizations by detailing examples, such as inventory management, where ongoing cash balances can be radically affected by management practices. Inventory ties up a tremendous amount of cash, removing the potential to take advantage of other opportunities as they arise. Effective cash management is the key to long-term profitability.

The FMIS can make it difficult to see the important role played by cash in the survival of a firm. Yet all the accrual accounting system is really doing is recording the economic event and the financial transaction at separate times, based on when they actually occur. If it is clearly understood that net income is not the same as money in the bank, the problem is a minor one. With the help of a statement of cash flows or a projected forecast of cash demands, management can easily maneuver the company through the most difficult financial waters. It is only when the cash balance is ignored and the impact of various policies on the available cash is overlooked that problems occur.

Advances being made in other areas of management (such as JIT and TQM) are providing companies with the tools needed to reduce their ongoing need for cash by eliminating the cost of defects from ongoing production expenses, driving down the operating cycle through more effective management of existing processes and products, and paring inventory requirements, often quite drastically. As was shown with the Lawnmasters analysis in Figure 4–5, a cash forecast helps management focus on its assumptions and what impact they may have on the firm's ability to survive, let alone prosper. It can generate the right kinds of questions, but only when management is willing to say, "Things have to change."

With the multitude of new operating and management tools becoming available, the potential for more effective asset management and a healthier financial position are at hand. Simple changes, such as instituting total preventive maintenance (TPM), can reduce unnecessary expenses for breakdowns, idle time, scrap, and inventory buffers. Reducing these ongoing costs frees up funds to support research and development, helping a company get more new products to market faster (which can generate improved cash flows in and of itself).

Continuous improvement and the use of World-Class management techniques can generate the funds needed to grow, providing a buffer between the short-term focus and demands of the equity markets and the firm. (If a company never needed new capital, the games played in the stock market would be of little concern.) The goal is to regain control over the management of the organization by making more with less.

The rule is simple. No matter what net income number the FMIS may provide, if the cash balance hits zero the company is broke. If this fact is kept in management's mind, and the cash balance is carefully managed (through the use of innovative cash collection procedures or improvements in operating conditions that shrink the daily demand on the cash account) the company can ride out periods of growth and decline safely. Conservative cash management is one of the keys to long-term survival. The bottom line, it seems, is not the one on the bottom of the income statement, but the one in the checkbook.

Money won't buy happiness, but it will pay the salaries of a large research staff to study the problem.

Bill Vaughan (1)

Money is always there but the pockets change; it is not in the same pockets after a change, and that is all there is to say about money.

Gertrude Stein (1)

SUGGESTED READINGS

Besley, S., and J. Osteryoung. "Survey of Credit Practices in Establishing Trade-Credit Limits." *Financial Review,* February 1985, pp. 70–81.

Carpenter, M. D., and J. E. Miller. "A Reliable Framework for Monitoring Accounts Receivable." *Financial Management,* Winter 1979, pp. 37–40.

Hill, N. R. Wood, and D. Sorensen. "Factors Influencing Corporate Credit Policy: A Survey." *Journal of Cash Management,* Fall 1980.

Kallberg, J., and K. Parkinson. *Current Asset Management.* Chap. 6. New York: Wiley, 1984.

Kamath, R., S. Khaksari, H. Meier, and J. Winklepleck. "Management of Excess Cash: Practices and Development." *Financial Management,* Autumn 1985, pp. 70–77.

Richards, V. D., and E. J. Laughlin. "A Cash Conversion Cycle Approach to Liquidity Analysis." *Financial Management,* Winter 1984, pp. 39–43.

Scherr, Frederick C. *Modern Working Capital Management: Text and Cases.* Englewood Cliffs, N.J.: Prentice Hall, 1989.

Shulman, J., and R. Cox. "An Integrative Approach to Working Capital Management." *Journal of Cash Management,* November/December 1985, pp. 64–67.

Snyder, A. "Principles of Inventory Management." *Financial Executive,* April 1964, pp. 13–21.

Tracy, John A. *How to Read a Financial Report.* 2nd ed. New York: Wiley, 1983.

PART TWO

NUMBERS TO SUPPORT WORLD-CLASS OPERATIONS

CHAPTER 5

NUMBERS FOR UNDERSTANDING OPERATIONS

No gain is so certain as that which proceeds from the economical use of what you already have.

Latin Proverb (2)

The financial manager performs a myriad assortment of activities for stakeholders both internal and external to the corporation. These tasks can require the manipulation of various cost estimates, the recording of economic transactions and tallying of the books of account at period end, or the development of management control procedures (e.g., budgeting and variance analysis). External users of financial information are concerned with *disclosure* issues: Are the financial statements provided by the firm reliable and unbiased summaries of financial performance? The various rules and regulations incorporated in generally accepted accounting principles help ensure the needs of these external users are met.

Where do the demands of the financial function's internal customers begin to be addressed? Most experts would point to product costing as the primary area where the needs of both internal and external FMIS customers are met. To a limited extent this is true, but as the following discussion will reveal, the FMIS's ability to serve these two diverse groups of stakeholders with a common set of data is more a myth than a reality.

In getting to the heart of the impact of the FMIS on internal decision making, an understanding of the basic issues in cost accounting is required. Specifically, it is important to grasp how the traditional FMIS constructs a **product cost,** assigns **overhead** to these output units, and deals with the very real fact that resources often cannot be purchased on an as needed basis in an amount perfectly matched to the number of units of output (e.g., product or service) produced in a period. That means that the financial manager has to make a series of estimates and approximations to get all the costs incurred in one period into buckets that roughly correspond to the outputs that were produced.

KEY ISSUES IN COST ACCOUNTING

The fact is, that in everything we do we give up something and attain something. In every act, therefore, there is really a double character present. In very many cases one side of it or the other may not be noticeable, but both are always present.

Bernard Bosanquet, *Some Suggestions in Ethics* (4)

Cost accounting is the segment of the FMIS that is concerned with assigning the expenses incurred in a period to the products and services that benefit from them. In other words, cost accounting is a direct outgrowth of the *matching principle,* applied to individual units of output rather than period revenues. A **cost** is defined as "an outflow of service potential or the creation of an obligation to relinquish serviceable items owned by the organization."[1] In layman's terms, costs are *the resources used up in making a product, performing a service, or supporting operations over a defined period of time.* A cost is the attachment of the expenses noted in the financial statements to specific time periods, activities, or outputs.

Cost accounting is the branch of the FMIS concerned with attaching costs to the **cost object,** or reason for, the use of the resource. The choice of a cost object defines the costing process. It sets a boundary on the types of resources that need to be considered in developing the cost of the object (e.g., product), and defines how the analysis and use of that information will proceed. The basic structure of cost accounting is built around the need to match costs to their benefits (e.g., cost object or output).

If these definitions of cost accounting and the costing process sound a bit ambiguous, it is because they are. Cost accounting deals with assigning estimates of resource consumption to the question of the day. This is captured in accounting circles by noting that there are *different costs for different purposes.* The purposes, or cost objects, define what numbers (costs) and issues are included in the cost analysis.

Flexibility is the underlying basis for cost accounting, but these systems are seldom as pliable when used on a daily basis in companies. This is because there is a tacitly assumed cost object that appears

---

[1]George Staubus, *Activity Costing for Decisions* (New York: Garland, 1988), p. 2.

to drive almost everything done under the umbrella of cost accounting today: **output units.** Cost accounting, as it is practiced in most companies, has one underlying goal: assign the costs of production to the units produced in a specific period. This myopic focus on units of output as the basis for the internal FMIS places artificial constraints on the system and its ability to meet the needs of its internal customers. These constraints are unnecessary and unnatural; the cost accounting system was never meant to be a servant to the external financial statements.

In reality, the ongoing structure of the internal FMIS in most companies is built around the demands of GAAP for **full cost** inventory valuation. The majority of the work performed by cost accountants revolves around determining what costs to apply to each specific unit of output, whether it is a product or a service. This costing process has very little to do with the market's perceived value for the item; value is not of concern. In fact, the basis of cost accounting under the *traditional* FMIS is, stated simply:

> *To get all of the dollars incurred to support production attached to a specific product or service.*

This goal drives internal FMIS functions. Its presence is signaled by comments such as, "We've got to cover all our costs." In fact, most of the internal calculations done in the financial area are driven by the same concerns as external reporting: keeping the books in balance.

Understanding the basis for traditional approaches to cost accounting is critical to coming to terms with the weaknesses of this system and how these problems can be addressed. These assumptions underlie the material presented in the rest of this chapter, as well as many of the issues and concerns detailed in Chapter 6. Getting comfortable with the implications of these assumptions is the key to understanding the root cause of the current crisis surrounding the FMIS. How do these assumptions play out through the basic costing process?

The Full Cost Model

The basic equation used to drive the costing process in most companies is based on the assignment of **direct** cost, or those that can be cleanly attached to a unit of output, to those units and the **allocation** of the remaining unassigned, or **indirect** costs (commonly called **overhead**) using a preset method. The direct costs and allocated indirect costs are combined to create a product's full cost estimate, as suggested in the following equation:

$$\text{DL} + \text{DM} + \frac{O}{N} = \textit{Estimated full cost}$$

where DL is direct labor costs, DM direct material costs, and O/N the "fair share" of overhead. The basic "cost" of a product is developed from understanding the amount of labor and materials used to make it, and then assigning it some share of the common overhead. The share of overhead assigned is driven by some aspect of the production process, some definable activity level that can be used to trigger the overhead assignment in a reliable way.

Allocation schemes and issues are complex. There are very few rules guiding internal decision making outside of full cost requirements, so the choice of an allocation basis is open for discussion. Realistically, though, with the defined cost object being "units produced," the number of allocation bases available is limited to those facts known about each product: its direct costs or resource usage. The list of allocation bases available within this tightly defined and unnecessarily constrained approach include:

- Direct labor hours.
- Direct labor dollars.
- Direct material dollars.
- Machine hours.
- Units produced.

Once an activity basis (one of the items in the above list) is chosen, an overhead rate is developed. For simplicity, direct labor hours will be used in the following example. (This is not a random choice; it has traditionally been the method of choice in cost accounting.)

A Basic Example

Lawnmasters, Incorporated sells a full line of products for lawn care. It buys some of the items on its product list from outside suppliers, but its most successful product, TurfMaster, is made internally. Its patented formula is one of the company's prize possessions. Applied on a monthly basis, TurfMaster transforms patchy, weed-filled yards into showcase lawns. How it does so is hidden in its complex

---

FIGURE 5–1
Lawnmasters, Incorporated Cost Analysis

Direct materials:		*Cost per bag*
Nutrients/fertilizers (12#/bag).........	$0.30 per pound	$3.60
Grass seed (1/2 #/bag)	$1.50 per pound	.75
Weed killers (7 1/2 #/bag)............	$0.20 per pound	1.50
"Secret" ingredients (5 #/bag)	$0.25 per pound	1.25
TurfMaster bag	$5.00 per hundred	.05
		$7.15

Direct labor ($15.00/hour with all benefits & payroll taxes):

Assemble and weigh materials........	4 hours per batch	.60
Mix TurfMaster.......................	10 hours per batch	1.50
Measure and package individual bags	2 hours for 100 bags	.30
		$2.40

Average batch size: 2500 pounds, or 100 bags

Plant overhead costs for 1991:	*Monthly*	*Annual cost*
Rent on building...................	$1,000	$12,000
Supervisor's salaries...............	800	9,600
Indirect materials	300	3,600
Indirect labor (shipping, etc.).......	400	4,800
Utilities	450	5,400
Insurance..........................	293	3,512
Total overhead..................	$2,838	$38,912

Total production in 1991: 6,400 bags
Total labor hours in 1991: 1,024 [64 batches @ 16 hrs/batch]

---

mix of nutrients, grass seeds, and weed-killers, and a few key "secret" ingredients. In addition to these direct costs of making a batch of TurfMaster, the company has overhead for renting the building, storing products, and paying for supervisory labor (see Figure 5–1).

Using Figure 5–1, it is possible to derive the direct costs and overhead per bag of TurfMaster sold in 1991, as shown in the table at the top of the next page. In looking at the cost accounting process, it is easy to see how the various elements of production enter into the equation. By its very construction, the costing model ensures that every dollar spent in production is assigned to good units produced. The obvious conclusion would be that projecting future period costs could be done by simply multiplying the units expected to be made

---

Overhead cost per direct labor hour:

$$\frac{\text{Total overhead cost}}{\text{Total direct labor hours}} = \frac{\$38,912}{1,024} = \$38.00 \text{ per direct labor hour}$$

Overhead cost per bag:

Batch overhead cost (100 bags): $38.00/hour × 16 hours/batch = $608.00
Overhead cost per bag: $608.00/100 or $6.08 per bag

1991 cost per 25# of TurfMaster:

Materials........	$ 7.15
Labor............	2.40
Overhead........	6.08
Total cost/bag....	$15.63

---

by the $15.63 per bag cost calculated here. Unfortunately, the process is not quite so simple.

The Impact of Volume Changes on Cost

Costs do not occur in the same types of patterns for every resource. Some resources can be bought in the same quantity that they are used in, but others have to be bought in larger amounts than may be currently needed. This fact underscores a key concept in cost accounting: the **behavior of costs.** As volumes change, the cost per unit of good produced may or may not stay the same, depending on how closely the input and output flows can be matched on a unit by unit bases; different costs *behave*, or change, in different ways when volumes change.

Variability describes the relationship between a unit of output to the amount of a specific input it consumes. **Variable cost** refers to a resource that is consumed each and every time a unit of output is produced (e.g., an activity occurs), in roughly the same proportion. For instance, the materials used to make a chair are used up in direct proportion to the number of chairs made. The term *variable* captures the fact that, in total, the resources consumed vary with the number of units produced.

Of course, costs can vary with something other than physical units of output. In the FMIS, this is noted by saying that other *drivers,* or outputs of the organization, can cause cost (e.g., resource consumption). The key factor that defines the term *variable cost,* though, is the relationship between changes in the **volume** of the identified driver and the total resources consumed. If a unit of resource is used up each time an activity occurs, that cost is variable with respect to that activity.

At the opposite end of the costing spectrum are **fixed costs.** They *do not* change, in total, no matter what volume of product or activity is undertaken. These are the costs that do not immediately "go away" when a decision is made to shift volumes overseas or to close a plant for a short period of time. The resources these fixed costs represent can only be purchased in fairly large chunks of available capacity and are not easily disposed of should the level of activity diminish.

Fixed costs are the nemesis of accountants and operating managers; they are radically affected on a *per unit* basis by changes in the total volume of work performed with a set of resources. The more work that can be performed with the same set of fixed resources, the less each unit of output or activity costs *on the average.* This core concept—average fixed cost per unit produced decreases as the number of units produced increases—is the basis for the economic concept of **economies of scale.** It is also at the root of many ongoing problems in the FMIS; it is easy to get caught up in generating volume to absorb these fixed costs. This can lead to excessive inventories, obsolescence, waste, and all the other ills of modern Western manufacturing.

Adding some substance to the concept of the behavior of costs, Figure 5–2 indicates the cost patterns for some common resources used in a manufacturing company. As can be seen, there are a series of costs that do not change *in total* as the volume of production changes; they are fixed with respect to these changes. Yet on a per unit basis, they are influenced by volume changes. Variable costs respond in exactly the opposite way; they are the same for each unit produced, but vary in total as volume changes.

In between these two extremes there are a series of costs that change in "steps." These types of costs support a range of volume. The underlying resources, though, can only be purchased in **indivisible** chunks, or units. So, if the volume produced moves one unit beyond that supportable by the existing resources, another complete unit of the resource has to be purchased.

FIGURE 5–2
Common Cost Patterns

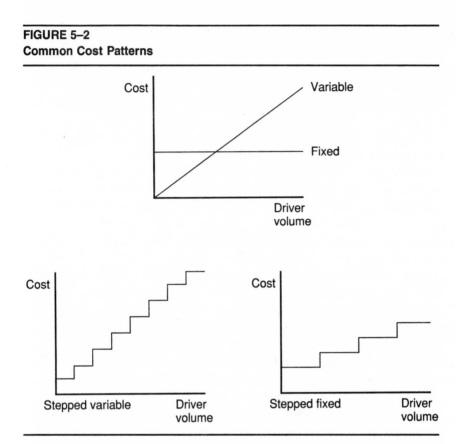

The easiest way to think of these types of costs are in terms of production, or line, supervisors. When production is done on a one-shift basis, the company may need three supervisors. As a second shift is added, more supervisors have to be added. They are usually hired on a salary basis and can supervise a certain range of production. It is also possible that on the first shift output volumes may increase so much that a fourth supervisor might need to be added. In either case, a "complete" supervisor has to be hired; they seldom will work on a part-time, hourly basis.

Stepped costs vary with changes in the **range** of production, but not on a one-to-one basis with incremental volume. If one input unit of the resource can support a small number of outputs, the cost is called a **stepped variable cost;** conversely, if a large range of production is possible with the purchase of one more unit of input, it is called a **stepped fixed** cost. Stepped costs have a smaller **relevant range** of production than true fixed costs.

Returning to Lawnmasters

"Absorption of overhead" is one of the most obscene terms I have ever heard.

Peter Drucker (1)

Looking at Lawnmasters' cost numbers for making TurfMaster, the figure that immediately grabs attention is the amount of overhead each bag has to **absorb** to make sure all the dollars spent in production are attached to units of finished goods. What does this number mean, and what can the company do to decrease its impact?

The overhead number reflects the dollars spent on overhead for every hour of labor. The common term for this figure is **burden rate.** For Lawnmasters, each hour of direct labor is "burdened with" $38.00 in overhead cost. From another angle, for every $1.00 of labor cost in the product, there is approximately $2.40 of overhead incurred. This is, in common terminology, a 240-percent burden rate.[2] In using direct labor hours as its allocation basis, Lawnmasters' management is assuming that overhead is *causally related* to the number of direct labor hours used.

Decreasing the impact of overhead on product costs, though, is not a simple process. The numbers might lead you to think that simply reducing labor will reduce overhead, but there's no real proof of this. The answer lies in looking at the individual line items in the cost list. Are they all as low as they can be? Could changes be made to reduce the need for these overhead items? Removing cost from overhead is always the first path for reducing their impact on product costs.

The list for Lawnmasters, though, looks fairly lean. While some small improvements might be made, management doesn't really know

---

[2]A word of caution needs to be voiced at this point. One of the ongoing controversies in companies is what this overhead vs. labor relationship really means. In reality, it simply says that every hour of labor is going to bring with it $38.00 of overhead; there's no proof that the labor causes the overhead, though. It is wrong, then, to look at the costs listed and leap to the conclusion that the way to reduce overhead is to cut back on labor. Labor DOES NOT cost $53.00 per hour [$15.00 labor rate + $38.00 overhead], it costs $15.00 per hour. Overhead will not go away simply by eliminating labor; the rate per hour will simply go up (e.g., $38,912/900 hours = $43.24 per hour).

how it can make a major impact in this area. They are already redeploying idle direct labor to indirect tasks, such as loading trucks with finished goods as needed (this is the basis for the indirect labor charge in the overhead account). In reality, most of the costs in the overhead pool are fixed costs. Utilities and indirect labor probably have more of a stepped fixed nature, but this doesn't really simplify the situation that much; the costs in the overhead pool are very "sticky" with respect to changes in manufacturing volume.

While these sticky costs can be bad if production volumes drop off (i.e., fixed costs will be spread over fewer units), volume upswings can greatly reduce the cost per unit. Looking ahead to 1993, we remember that Lawnmasters is projecting sales of $250,000 (see Figure 4–5). At a cost of $25.00 per bag of TurfMaster, this represents 100,000 bags sold (1,000 batches made). What happens to the fixed cost for overhead when this volume change is factored in? The impact is marked:

Total overhead:	$38,912
Total labor hours for 1,000 batches:	16,000
Overhead per direct labor hour:	$ 2.43

New cost per 25# of TurfMaster:

Materials...	$ 7.15
Labor...	2.40
Overhead...	2.43
Total product cost.................................	$11.98

This $3.65 reduction in cost per bag of TurfMaster arises from the behavior of the fixed cost component of the product: Fixed costs are spread over more units, reducing their total impact on the cost per good unit produced.[3] This phenomenon underlies the complex world of product costing.

---

[3]Obviously, Lawnmasters would probably incur some increases in its stepped costs with this large an increase in production output, and might even have to move to larger facilities. But it provides a target for management to shoot for; the more fixed costs can be kept under control, the less their impact on product costs. In this case, management is achieving a higher productivity from these fixed resources.

ACTUAL COST, STANDARD COSTS, AND MANUFACTURING SETTINGS

The improvement of understanding is for two ends: first, our own increase of knowledge; secondly, to enable us to deliver that knowledge to others.

John Locke (2)

The example worked through for Lawnmasters provides a basic idea of what types of calculations underlie the cost-accounting process. In deriving these numbers, the **actual costs** of production were used from the financial statements and applied to the known level of production. These numbers were developed after the process of making TurfMaster. The "game" was over, and the tally of the final score made.

Such *ex post* calculations provide adequate detail and rigor to meet the demands of GAAP, but have far less value for management. Why? Because they are ex post. In order for information to have value for decision making (management's concern), it has to arrive before actions occur, or ex ante. The need to have reliable **estimates** of the projected cost for various levels of production is the basis for developing **standard cost** approaches to cost accounting.

Basics of Standard Costing

Standard cost models were developed in the early 1900s by the scientific management group, as they sought to bring regularity to the shop floor. Based on detailed time-and-motion studies, the allowable time, and hence cost, for various steps in the production process were painstakingly detailed in the attempt to remove the need for the worker to think, as suggested by the following statement:

All possible brain work should be removed from the shop and centered in the planning or laying-out department, leaving for the foreman and gang bosses work strictly executive in its nature . . . . There is no question that the cost of production is lowered by separating the work of planning and the brain work as much as possible from the manual labor.[4]

---

[4]If this sounds a bit strange, you can verify this position by returning to some of Taylor's original writings, in which he repeatedly takes this stance. Suggested works include *Shop Management* and *The Principles of Scientific Management*, both contained in a collection of Taylor's works published in 1911 by Harper and Row. These books are readily accessible in most business libraries, and may be found in used book stores—they were widely published and distributed. The quotation here is from *Shop Management*, pages 98 and 121.

Taylor's work led to the development of elaborate methods for breaking down each and every part of the organization's work into small, well-defined pieces that were then studied to determine the "optimal" method and time for their performance. Taylor's views brought him into direct conflict with fledgling labor unions, and led to a full congressional investigation of the techniques and approaches of Scientific Management in 1912.

The scientific management methods survived the controversy and formed the basis for many common industrial engineering techniques still in use. Standard cost accounting also owes its existence to this group, which developed time and cost estimates for performing various jobs. The estimates were fed into the accounting system to provide a way to record (in a "scientific" manner) the allowable cost for a job and to identify deviations from these standards (called *variances*). As has been detailed in many of the current books on the shortcomings of the FMIS for internal decision making, these costing approaches have remained relatively unchanged since their inception more than 80 years ago.

The development of standard costs begins with a study of the actual production of a part or product. The *process flow* is detailed, timed, and evaluated, looking for a "best time" or "best method" to support the development of a standard operation procedure for each of the tasks performed *on the plant floor.* Once these estimated time and material standards are set, they are adjusted to allow for an *acceptable* level of scrap and down time for the job. In other words, an engineered standard builds in an assumption of an acceptable level of waste.

These physical standards are then used to develop cost standards, using current knowledge about pay rates, material costs, and related items. This is the standard cost used from that point on to evaluate the efficiency and effectiveness of the production process. The standards are reviewed periodically (usually annually) to see if they need to be adjusted. Once set, the standards serve as the basis for the majority of internal FMIS-based information.

Going back to the Lawnmasters example, the material and labor used in 1991 to make a batch of TurfMaster could be seen as a standard of sorts. In fact, this section could just as easily have been introduced as the standards preset for making TurfMaster. Doing so would have suggested that industrial engineering studies had been completed and that these figures represented the estimate of the expected performance in the plant under normal operating conditions.

Using Standards for Costing and Control

When standard costing is used in place of actual costs, the cost accounting process changes significantly. Specifically, each and every time a unit of output is produced, the *standard* costs for the labor and material are entered in the finished goods inventory account. At the same time, the overhead is attached. This full cost number is used to value inventory for the period and to establish projected profitability levels.

Using the standard costs numbers in this way does raise some interesting problems, though: Reality seldom comes in at standard. It is less common for production to take place using the standard quantity of materials and labor than it is to hit the mark. The gap between reality (actual cost) and expected cost (standard) is the *variance from standard*. It can be positive or negative (company spent more or less than expected) and can be the result of a multitude of factors occuring during the operating period.

These numbers are all collected on a monthly basis in a traditional FMIS; individual product runs are usually not tracked to determine their variances. At the end of the month the books are closed, the total costs assigned to inventory based on the preset standards are tallied, and the actual costs of production recorded for the period are summed. These results are then put into a report that lists actual costs of production versus standard and the variances that have accumulated over the month (see Figure 5–3 for an example of Lawnmasters' results in February of 1991).

The variances are categorized as either **spending** (more dollars were spent than allowed for the quantity of the resource used) or **efficiency** (more of the resource was used than expected). In the case of overhead variances, another twist is added. Because it is calculated using one of the other factors of production (e.g., labor), and it is subject to volume effects due to its high component of fixed costs, a **volume** variance is generated (i.e., overhead was under- or over-absorbed due to volume fluctuations).

Once these variances are reported to management, with suitable explanations obtained from the plant manager, they disappear from view. The FMIS, in fact, takes these variances and creates an accounting transaction around them, which is then used to adjust the value of the recorded inventories and cost of goods sold to *actual cost*. In the end, the cost accounting process goes full swing,

FIGURE 5–3

Lawnmasters, Inc.—February, 1991

Basic Variance Analysis

Quantity produced: 620 bags of TurfMaster

	Actual Quantity	Actual Price	Standard Quantity	Standard Price	Quantity* Variance	Price† Variance
Materials:						
Fertilizer	7600 #	$0.35/#	7440 #	$0.30/#	$56.00(U)‡	$372.00(U)
Grass seed	290 #	$1.50/#	310 #	$1.50/#	$30.00(F)	–0–
Weed killer	4600 #	$0.18/#	4650 #	$0.20/#	$ 9.00(F)	$ 93.00(F)
"Secret" ingredient	3200 #	$0.25/#	3100 #	$0.25/#	$25.00(U)	–0–
Bags	650	$5.10/100	620 bgs	$5.00/100	$ 1.53(U)	$0.62(U)
Labor:	105 hrs	$14.75/hr	96 hrs	$15.00/hr	$132.75(U)	$24.00(F)

*The quantity variance is the result of taking the actual price and multiplying it by (actual quantity − standard quantity) of the material or labor at the actual level of production.

†The price variance is the result of multiplying the standard quantity for the actual level of production by (actual price − standard price).

‡Whenever the price or quantity actually used is greater than that suggested by the standard, the variances is called "unfavorable", and is denoted by a (U) after the number. Conversely, the term "favorable" (F) is used whenever actual price or quantity is *less than* the preset standard. The terms only refer to directionality, not whether the difference is inherently good or bad. In fact, given the importance of Lawnmasters' balanced formula to the success of the product, all the quantity variances are undesirable. In the arena of price variances, lower price can translate to poorer quality, which, while triggering a "favorable" price variance would hardly be preferred, or valued by customers. In a related vein, the labor variances often reflect a problem with the raw materials or process, rather than the productivity of the workers.

FIGURE 5-3
(Continued)

Overhead:

Actual overhead expense...	$3,248
Budgeted overhead for 600 units of output.........................	3,648
Overhead spending variance..	$ 400
Applied to products: 105 hrs @ $38.00..............................	$3,990
*Applied if labor at standard; 99.2 hrs @ $38.00.................	3,770
Over-absorbed overhead due to excess labor......................	$ 220
Budgeted overhead for 600 units......................................	$3,648
*Overhead—standard cost at actual volume.........................	3,770
Overhead volume variance...	$ 122

Volume variances arise with respect to the fixed-cost portion of overhead. Given that the entire list of overhead items is being treated as fixed for the sake of this problem, the question that arises is, what overhead should have been spent if production had been at 600 bags, the scheduled output, and not 620?

recording production at its actual cost in order to make the books balance. This is the major purpose served by variances in the accounting model.

On the plant floor, though, the variances are not quite so benign. Because they flag nonstandard performance, they generate a defensive game in which the operating manager looks across the broad range of things that have happened during the period in question, picks an event that appears to justify the "miss," and then returns to the more critical demands of managing the production floor. The report comes as little surprise to the plant manager; the ongoing production problems have been a daily reminder of the need to improve.

If the game stopped with this rationalization of the fact that reality is seldom predictable between operations and accounting, there would probably be little cause for concern. But these numbers enter into the evaluation process higher in the organization. Top managers, in fact, use these numbers as though they have some hidden meaning, some value above and beyond balancing the general ledger. They want to know the *cause* of the variance, looking for one clean reason for the problems. That is what is supplied by the plant manager, then, even though everyone knows a million things went right and another quarter million went wrong during the period in question.

When the standard cost system is used for management control purposes, the flaws in its design and execution are exaggerated. It generates a *meet standard* mentality among the operating managers, who seek to avoid the monthly call (four weeks removed from the end of the period) questioning their management ability. The most frustrating part of this game is that it can actually reinforce mediocrity and ineffective performance.

When the goal of *meeting standard* replaces the real objective — maximize the value created in the plant by making things better, faster, and cheaper every day — the result can be devastating. Poor quality goods are pushed through to the next station, or on to the customer, in order to meet standard. Excess work-in-process and finished goods inventory is run to absorb overhead. The use of the standard costs for control can create a nonproductive game that takes on a life of its own, making it difficult to initiate the continuous improvement philosophy and the tools it has spawned. This is the reality and battleground of modern financial management. The tool that is being used to keep an accurate tally of the ongoing costs of production is creating havoc inside the organization because it is poorly suited to the goals of World-Class Manufacturing.

THE ENVIRONMENT MEETS ACCOUNTING

What an absurd amount of energy I have been wasting all my life trying to figure out how things "really are," when all the time they weren't.

Hugh Prather, *Notes to Myself (4)*

Dealing with the complexities of different manufacturing environments and varying management objectives is the challenge facing the cost accounting field today. In coming to grips with these demands, some old tools can be brought back into use, and some new ones will be developed. There is precedence for creating different types of accountings for different manufacturing settings; two very different approaches to the costing problem—**job order costing** and **process costing**—represent the end points in this continuum of solutions, as suggested in Figure 5–4.

Job Order Costing

Job order costing is usually done in a job shop or some other setting where each and every order is different, using unique materials and methods to complete. It is based on a detailed set of records that lists materials used, labor and machine time consumed, and all other traceable direct costs *caused by* the job (e.g., new dies) to the specific order. Often estimates are made of these costs in order to secure the job (through a bidding process), but the conventional term *standard cost* is difficult to apply in these settings. If there is little or no *regularity* in the types of jobs run, it is hard to conceive of how an elaborate standard costing system could be effectively used.

Overhead in most traditional job order costing systems is applied using a preset rate, like the one developed for Lawnmasters. Each job is allocated a share of the common costs based on its usage of more easily identifiable resources (e.g., labor or materials). The key

---

FIGURE 5–4
Approaches to Cost System Design

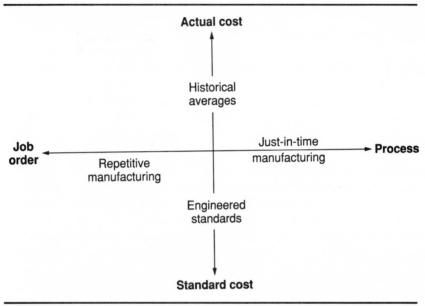

Actual cost

Historical
averages

**Job
order** — Just-in-time
manufacturing — **Process**

Repetitive
manufacturing

Engineered
standards

Standard cost

---

factor in job order systems is the assumed uniqueness of each job run. Actual costs are usually the best way to track these systems, providing a profitability analysis for each job and critical information for making future bids.

Process Costing

At the other end of the spectrum is process costing. In this approach, the focus shifts from individual, countable units of product assigned to a unique job to the ongoing production of a uniform product, such as paper. In process costing, the units of output can be difficult to count, the tie between materials and labor used in a period and the units produced can be quite fuzzy, and hence the cost of any one unit of output can be close to impossible to determine with any accuracy. Process costing is a system based on the use of **averages.** The cost of production for the period is the average of all the dollars spent for materials and conversion (machine costs usually become the defining characteristic of the production and costing system) over the entire range of good units produced.

Process costing lends itself more readily to a standard cost model because of its very nature: Averages are the best numbers available. Because standards are one type of average based on a predefined set of operating characteristics, they can be quite compatible for costing ongoing production. The hard part of process costing is deciding exactly how much work was done in a period; the productive process seldom shuts down, and individual output units are difficult to count (are all rolls of paper equal?), so the use of **equivalent units of production** is required. Equivalent units incorporate all of the work that has been done on beginning work-in-process, completed units, and ending work-in-process to develop a "completed goods" proxy to drive the rest of the costing process. Costs are applied to equivalent units first, then distributed to the various units finished and in-process to support inventory valuation and the determination of the period's net income.

New Environments, New Demands

Job order and process costing are traditional ways that the FMIS has attempted to reflect the various characteristics of the manufacturing environment. **Repetitive manufacturing** hybrid models have also been developed, following many of the basic elements of standard costing. Repetitive manufacturing, where the same general mix of products is made on a regular basis, is the dominant type of production environment. In using standard costing in this arena, which is the *de facto* accounting model of choice, heroic assumptions are made about the stability of production. In repetitive manufacturing environments, operations is often at odds with accounting (who ask unanswerable questions about causality) and marketing (who can't seem to get the forecast right).

The major changes occurring today in manufacturing methods and the costing models used to support them are taking place in repetitive manufacturing settings. It is probably because the needs of this group have never been adequately addressed with a standard cost model that focuses solely on direct materials and direct labor that are variable on a per unit basis. Many of the costs in a repetitive manufacturing setting are triggered by the production of a **batch**, not one unit. Setup costs are the most visible example of batch costs that impact the effectiveness of operations and hence the cost of carrying them out. But the standard cost model of the 1920s does not have any provisions for batch costs. So these costs, like many others that could be traced to some aspect of the production process on a regular basis, are dumped into the overhead account and charged out on direct labor hours or material dollars.

Activity-based product costing is one of the tools that have been developed to replace standard cost models in repetitive manufacturing. Described as "two stage allocation" by its developers,[5] activity-based costing sets up an intermediary pool of costs, driven by some activity *indirectly* caused by the production of a unit of output, and then identifies a countable way to measure the use of the resources contained in this activity pool (e.g., the cost **driver**). In simple terms, activity-based costing attempts to attach more of the costs of production directly to the process itself, rather than relying on extensive allocations that blur these relationships. The details of this approach can be found in Chapter 8.

The shortcomings of cost accounting for repetitive manufacturing settings are beginning to be addressed, and those systems are undergoing radical changes. Just-in-time manufacturing is one example of a new approach to this setting that is reaping major improvements. Obviously, if the standard costing system in use for repetitive manufacturing settings is already mismatched to reality, they are totally unsuited for this major shift in production philosophies. In fact, many of the JIT accounting systems emerging today are returning to actual costs as a more effective tool to track ongoing performance and improvements.

In designing a cost accounting system, the underlying features of the manufacturing process need to be taken into account. The design choices reflect two basic decisions: (1) whether to use actual costs, historical standards, or engineered standards as the costing approach; and (2) what type of process flow assumptions (job order, process, repetitive, or reality) will be used to structure the costing process. In the past, these decisions have been made around a dominant concern for the reliability of the cost figures for inventory valuation and external reporting. Today, the criterion and focus of the cost-

---

[5]Robin Cooper, formerly of the Harvard Business School, and Robert Kaplan, currently on faculty at Harvard, have provided the major impetus for the development of activity-based product costing models. Their efforts have spawned the rebirth of the management accounting discipline, leading others to question various aspects of existing practice and to develop more effective tools and techniques. These changes are the basis for the discussions in the second half of this book.

accounting system is changing, reflecting the fact that internal decision support is just as critical, if not more so, than putting the "right" price tag on goods and services (e.g., full costs, fully absorbed) for the auditor.

In matching accounting to the production process, the basic design features that need to be taken into account are as follows.

1. **Regularity.** Are the same products made on a consistent basis? If so, the costing problem is simplified, and stable estimates of costs can be created.

2. **Complexity.** What level of interdependence is there between the production of the various component parts and final goods? Interdependence translates to shared resources, which create complexity in the costing process. How many different parts and products are made? Product proliferation, using unique parts for every design, makes it increasingly difficult to cost the process and to track whether continuous improvement goals are being made. In fact, increasing levels of complexity cause cost, as more and more resources are dedicated to coordinating and controlling the production process and the flow of resources through it. Complex manufacturing requires complex accounting.

3. **Linearity.** Are products flowing on a smooth basis through the plant, yielding predictable output of good units on a daily or weekly basis? The more stable the output, in terms of good units produced, from the manufacturing process, the easier it is to assign costs accurately.

4. **Flow characteristics.** Are products made singly, in batches, or continuously? The way product flows through a plant determines the types of costs that are caused and defines the optimal structure for the cost system itself. The cost-accounting system should *mirror* the production process.

5. **Variability.** The resources consumed in the productive process provide a range of productive capacity. A few items, such as direct materials, can be said to vary directly with the level of output, but it is quite difficult to make this claim for most of the resources used. Determining how variable, or responsive, the various resources are to changes in activity volumes is a critical element in the design process. It

guides the types of assumptions and estimates that have to be employed and creates a realistic focus on the capacity of resources in the management process.

6. **Capacity.** The effective versus utilized capacity of the plant is a critical aspect for designing the cost system. Outside of traditional concerns about whether a theoretical optimum or average activity level should be used, management is beginning to understand that capacity is a systemic, or "whole plant," concept that can be impacted only by properly managing the bottlenecks. In designing the cost accounting system, the impact of bottleneck resources on total available capacity needs to be isolated and factored into cost estimates. All resources are not equal.

7. **Controllability.** If a decision is made, which costs are readily eliminated? A cost system has to reflect, in a realistic manner, the degree to which various costs can be affected, or changed. If a cost is basically uncontrollable at a certain level of the process, it is counterproductive to include it in the ongoing cost estimates. Additionally, if a resource and its associated costs will not go away, no matter what decisions are made, then it has to be clearly labeled as an unavoidable cost of production.

8. **Capability.** While many of the above design characteristics reflect current operations, an effective cost accounting system has to move beyond existing assumptions to signal *resource capability.* One way this can be done is to identify the degree of idle resources in the plant and put a cost on them, thereby encouraging management to find new ways to use them or to eliminate them if possible. This is the most difficult concept to apply in the design process. Knowledge about how to capture and report resource capability is just beginning to be developed. It is the major challenge facing the FMIS today.

9. **Type and proliferation of automation.** As new forms of technology are implemented, they radically change the manufacturing process and the cost structure of the company. Fixed costs increase as automation is introduced; this creates significant costing distortions if it is not clearly reflected in the costing estimates.

10. **Structure of the support systems.** How is manufacturing supported by other areas of the company? What characteristics of the manufacturing process drive activity and costs in these nonmanufacturing areas? What is the support structure of the firm? What are its costs and value to internal and external customers? Internal service departments are a major part of the total cost of running a company. When these costs are allocated to productive units on an indiscriminate basis, they not only distort product costs but can actually make a product or product family uncompetitive. Value has to be identified, tracked, and maximized in the support areas as well as on the plant floor. Allocations hide this fact and are to be minimized.

This list (which is an incomplete catalog of the features of the manufacturing process that affect the cost of doing business, and hence the system designed to capture these costs) gives a realistic picture of how complex the costing problem really is. Simple cost systems, which may serve external users adequately, simply do not have the capability to track and support ongoing production. As manufacturing and service companies evolve, so must the systems used to record and evaluate their performance.

The Financial Cycle

The financial planning process is a cycle, as suggested in Figure 5–5. Its value lies in setting the objectives for the coming year (or several years), placing financial estimates around these objectives, and creating a database of potential costs for a range of activities. In creating this plan, marketing and production play the pivotal role. Marketing provides the sales forecast; production determines how those projected demands will be met. Other factors feeding the budget process include general economic trends, new product information from the research and development group, corporate plans for acquisitions and divestitures, and financial market characteristics.

Going full circle, it would appear that the managerial FMIS should feed the financial FMIS, serving as the set of cost estimates that actual costs can be compared against. This is not reality in many companies today, but there is increasing recognition that the budget is the link between these two aspects of the FMIS. As suggested in the

FIGURE 5–5
The FMIS Cycle

Traditional/Current cycle:

A constructive alternative:

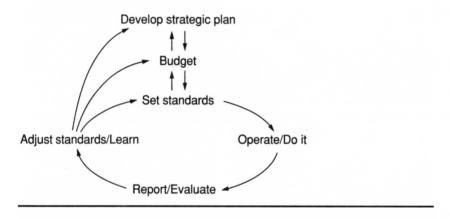

bottom panel of Figure 5–5, it is possible to combine these two sub-systems. The key is to abandon traditional engineered standard costs as the basis for costing products and establishing goals, and substitute some form of historical cost in its place.

What this would accomplish is obvious; the budget could be directly built on actual cost performance from prior periods, and the variances in a current period could be used to adjust these "standards" on a real-time basis. Suggesting that this move be taken, though, flies in the face of traditional advice in the financial arena; engineered standards are usually suggested to be more objective and reliable than history as the basis for setting goals and evaluating performance.

In a competitive arena focused on continuous improvement as defined by the customer, it is difficult to understand why a static standard, such as an engineered standard cost estimate, should be preferred. If an objective "goal" is desired, some form of theoretically optimum performance can be estimated by the engineers familiar with the process. This objective benchmark does not do away with the need to have a set of cost numbers that give an accurate estimate of how well the company is currently performing against this goal. Accepting the fact that actual cost is a better metric is not easy, or natural, for most financial managers. Yet this is one of the few available approaches that will support continuous improvement, provide a means to merge the financial and managerial aspects of the FMIS, and support the development of activity-based cost management systems for internal decision making.

Recapping the Chapter

This chapter has detailed the basic characteristics of both traditional and modern cost-accounting practices. A cost is defined as *the resources used up in making a product, performing a service, or supporting operations over a defined period of time.* Cost accounting is the branch of the FMIS that records, tallies, and reports these facts to the organization. It is focused on the internal customer, following the core assumption that there are *different costs for different purposes.*

While internally focused, cost accounting has not always delivered on its obligation to the internal customer. For the past 75 years, in fact, the cost-accounting process has been driven by the *full costing* mentality: All costs have to be attached to some final product or service. This led to the proliferation of arbitrary allocation methods that have tended to obscure the cost of many of the underlying activities inside the value chain. The discussion pointed out that many of the costs in a cost accounting system are *fixed* with respect to changes in output volume, a fact that adds complexity and potential distortions to the costing process.

The chapter ends by suggesting that different organizational settings require different cost accounting models. Once this transition is made, the FMIS can begin to use data from the rest of the organization to create value-adding cost analyses. Regaining relevance in cost accounting, therefore, requires a complete overhaul of the tools and beliefs that have led to the current crisis. Only if every plant and every company is producing one item, over and over, does the standard costing model really fit. In this case, the degree of regularity is so high that preset standards can actually be of some use. The real world of management, though, is a complex muddle of a million parts, processes, and services that change constantly in the search for higher profits, sustainable competitive advantage, and long-term survival of the organization. The very concept of a "standard cost" is the antithesis to this reality. Flexibility and change, not stability, is the key to effective cost accounting and FMIS design.

> *There are men who would quickly love each other if once they were to speak to each other; for when they spoke they would discover that their souls ... had only been separated by phantoms and diabolic delusions.*
>
> Ernest Hello, *Life, Science and Art* (4)

SUGGESTED READINGS

Belkaoui, A. *Conceptual Foundations of Management Accounting.* Reading, Mass.: Addison-Wesley, 1980.

Churchman, C. West. "Managerial Acceptance of Scientific Recommendations." In *Information for Decision Making: Quantitative and Behavioral Dimensions,* ed. A. Rappaport. Englewood Cliffs, N.J.: Prentice Hall, 1970, pp. 435–444. The rest of this text may prove useful for the entire CIRM education process.

Coda, Bernard A., and Barry G. King. "Manufacturing Decision-Making Tools." *Journal of Cost Management for the Manufacturing Industry,* Spring 1989, p. 31.

Dearden, John. "Time-Span in Management Control." *Financial Executive,* August 1988. Reprinted in *Readings in Cost Accounting, Budgeting and Control,* ed. William E. Thomas. Cincinnati, Ohio: Southwestern, 1988, pp. 368–381.

Drucker, Peter. "The Coming of the New Organization." *Harvard Business Review,* January-February 1988.

Drucker, Peter. "What Business Can Learn from Nonprofits." *Harvard Business Review,* July-August 1989, pp. 88–93.

Etzioni, A. "Humble Decision-Making." *Harvard Business Review* July–August 1989, pp. 122–126.

Fasci, Martha A., T. Weiss, and R. Worrall. "Everyone Can Use This Cost-Benefit Analysis System." *Management Accounting,* January 1987, pp. 44–47.

Johnson, Thomas. "Activity-Based Information: Blue Print for World-Class Management." *Management Accounting,* June 1988, pp. 23–30.

Kammlade, J., P. Mehra, and T. Ozan. "A Process Approach to Overhead Management." *Emerging Practices in Cost Management,* ed. Barry Brinker. New York: Warren, Gorham and Lamont, 1990, pp. 193–198.

Mintzberg, H. *Impediments to the Use of Management Information.* Montvale, N.J.: National Association of Accountants, 1975.

Sathe, V. *Controller Involvement in Management.* Englewood Cliffs, N.J.: Prentice Hall, 1982.

Staubus, George. *Activity Costing and Input-Output Accounting.* Homewood, Ill.: Richard D. Irwin, 1971.

CHAPTER 6

NUMBERS FOR
MANAGING OVERHEAD

*If you want the present and the future to be different from the past,
Spinoza tells us, study the past, find out the causes that made it what
it was and bring different causes to bear.*

Will and Ariel Durant (1)

Understanding and controlling the use of overhead is by far the most troubling of the challenges facing modern financial managers. Overhead is the pool of indirect cost that is not attached to any specific value-adding output. This portion of the total cost of doing business has grown rapidly in the last 40 years, leaping from a modest 5 to 10 percent in the 1930s and 1940s to over 50 percent in many companies today. What has caused this change? Have companies become so bureaucratic that they now look more like government than the lean, entrepeneurial firms that spawned them? The truth lies somewhere in between.

Overhead is the lump of cost that is not understood; it is a blob of mixed resources purchased for a multitude of purposes, and it is controlled only through budget line item accountability. It includes all the indirect costs of manufacturing, as well as the selling, general, and administrative costs that are reported separately in financial statements. Even this massive dollar amount is understated, though. Every time a meeting takes place, overhead is incurred. Each time paperwork is completed that does not directly benefit a customer, overhead is incurred.

The focal issue underlying a company's ability to understand and control overhead is value. Does the customer perceive that the work being performed is required? If so, then the overhead is a vital part of doing business. Could the tasks be done more effectively? Without a doubt they could, but at least the customer in general is willing to pay for them. Costs that cannot pass the "value" screen are waste. No one is willing to pay for waste, let alone a customer with a broad range of alternative uses for his or her funds.

The need to assess the value-adding potential of any cost appears quite logical, so what is the problem? Because overhead is a heterogeneous mix of poorly understood costs, it is uncontrolled and, in many cases, invisible. The resources are pooled together, not on the basis of any specific criteria, but rather by the fact that they cannot be tied to one specific unit of output. These outputs, or directly identifiable products, are a small part of the activity chain that ultimately delivers product to customer. Does a customer value the order entry department? Given that no product can be received if an order is never entered, it seems likely that this activity would be valued. Does a customer value endless check sheets that slow down the completion of the order-entry task? Probably not.

Overhead that creates value for the customer isn't overhead. It's value-adding service and support cost. Overhead that creates value for no one is waste. It's to be eliminated. Applying this simple rule is the first step in creating an FMIS that supports management decision making and the attainment of long-term strategic goals. Ignoring it can lead to loss of competitiveness and the corporate decline that follows closely on its heels.

ALLOCATIONS—SHIFTING VIEWS OF REALITY

It is obvious that to be in earnest in seeking the truth is an indispensable requisite for finding it.

John Henry Cardinal Newman, *Oxford University Sermons*(4)

Overhead is that pool of costs that no one owns or understands. It is, in many ways, a force all its own within the organization, growing like a cancer, eating up profits as it goes. What are the issues in the overhead area, and what solutions have been attempted to date? The journey begins in the area of overhead allocation and its impact on the perceived profitability of various products, services, and divisions within a corporation.

Basic Approaches to Overhead Allocation

One of the best ways to think about overhead allocation is as an "unnatural act." Why? Because the very basis of allocation is the assumption that little is known about what actually caused the cost. An allocation is an *arbitrary assignment of indirect costs to a unit of final product or service.*[1] It is a process that takes place every day, in every company, whether manufacturing or service oriented. As part of accepted FMIS practice, the use of allocations is seldom questioned. All of the dollars have to be charged somewhere if all costs are to be covered, right? That question will be addressed as this discussion of overhead allocation unfolds.

The most commonly used form of allocation involves the charging of manufacturing overhead to the units produced in a period. In developing a standard cost for Lawnmasters in Chapter 5, the calculations were:

Overhead cost per direct labor hour:

$$\frac{\text{Total overhead cost}}{\text{Total direct labor hours}} = \frac{\$38,912}{1,024} \text{ or } \$38.00 \text{ per direct labor hour}$$

Overhead cost per bag:

Batch overhead cost (100 bags): $38.00/hour × 16 hours/batch = $608.00
Overhead cost per bag: $608.00/100 or $6.08 per bag

1991 cost per 25# of TurfMaster:

Materials	$ 7.15
Labor	2.40
Overhead	6.08
Total cost/bag....	$15.63

The use of direct labor hours as the overhead basis means that every time a direct labor hour is used, overhead will be charged at a rate of $38.00. This is probably fine for our simple company, producing one main product (TurfMaster) on a repetitive basis, but does the approach have flaws that might make it less suitable in more complex settings?

---

[1]When some bit of forethought goes into this process of attaching overhead costs to their causes, the terms *apportionment* (attachment using gross estimates) and *assignment* (attachment based on causal relationships) are more appropriate.

There are a number of problems with using direct labor hours as the basis for charging out overhead, as succinctly stated by Moxie in his *1913* treatise on factory cost keeping:

> This method has few advantages, and many disadvantages. The chief advantage is found in the fact that almost certainly the calculations made upon this basis will absorb the whole expense in a given time. Its weaknesses are, however, manifold. In the manufacture of many articles there is one operation dependent upon hand labor, and many other operations performed almost entirely by machinery. If the indirect expenses are distributed by . . . labor . . . the process dependent upon hand labor is charged far more heavily than is the process involving machinery.[2]

Moxie goes on to note that in the case where two machines have different purchase and operating costs, the use of direct labor basis will consistently misstate the cost accounting process. Finally, Moxie suggests that if one machine requires more labor than another, this fact will also translate to distorted product costs.

Projecting Moxie's statements into a modern context, the problems surrounding the current use of direct labor as the basis for overhead allocation should not be a surprise. Increasing levels of automation, the development of numerical control machines that need little or no direct intervention by an operator, and the presence of a broad range of high- and low-technology machines in one facility are realities today. Using direct labor to distribute overhead, when overhead is caused by demands and activities that have almost no relationship to labor, incorrectly leads management to believe that eliminating labor content in a product—or eliminating the product itself—will reduce overhead costs. Rather than tackling the growing pool of indirect costs and bringing its growth under control, attention is directed toward getting rid of the products and services that are the "dogs" of the line—those with a high labor content.

The problems with direct labor hours as an allocation base have been well-documented. Some have suggested that sloppy cost accounting practices in this area are to blame for competitive problems

---

[2]E. Moxie, *The Principles of Factory Cost Keeping* (New York: The Ronald Press Company, 1913), pp. 65–66.

in Western companies.[3] Some state that accountants have actually regressed, showing less sophistication in their techniques than they showed in the 1920s.[4] Others argue that management accountants "lifted" standard costing techniques from a warring group of industrial engineers and, having picked up these tools without understanding what they meant, have been unable to adapt them to the changing needs of management. Finally, a growing number of concerned practitioners and academics suggest that the root cause of the obsolescence of the FMIS is an education process that is out of touch with the issues affecting modern organizations.[5]

Whatever the causal factors are for this shortfall in FMIS practice, the fact is that a large majority (some estimate up to 90%) of the existing cost-accounting systems in place apply full cost concepts with one driver or allocation base: direct labor hours. Few companies today are heavily populated with direct labor employees, so this practice has to change. Its presence causes excessive outsourcing of components and products as "high labor rates" (which translate to "fully loaded" labor, or labor plus its share of overhead) make in-house operations appear unprofitable.[6]

Alternative Simple Bases and Issues

If direct labor is an inadequate basis for allocating overhead, are other simple, or one-level, drivers any better? The options readily avail-

---

[3]The list here would be quite long, but the primary critics are Eli Goldratt and Thomas Vollmann. Both have published several books based on the premise that existing measurement processes in companies focus attention on the wrong things, turning eyes away from improving the manufacturing process itself while encouraging activities and investments that impair long-term growth. See, for example, *The Goal: A Process of Ongoing Improvement,* by E. Goldratt and J. Cox, Cronton-on-Hudson: North River Press, 1986; and "The Hidden Factory" by J. Miller and T. Vollmann, *Harvard Business Review,* Sept-Oct 1985.

[4]The best source of these arguments can be found in the stream of work performed by Robert Kaplan, Robin Cooper, and H. Thomas Johnson, most notably *Relevance Lost: The Rise and Fall of Management Accounting* (Boston, Mass: Harvard Business School Press, 1987).

[5]This initial argument was made by P. Armstrong in his article "Changing Management Control Strategies: The Role of Competition Between Accountancy and Other Organizational Professions," in *Accounting, Organizations and Society,* 1985, pp. 129–148. It is also one of several arguments at times used by Johnson in his discussions (Kaplan et al., *Relevance Lost*).

[6]A case written by Robin Cooper in the Harvard Business School case series, called *Camelback Communications,* is an interesting exercise for anyone who wishes to understand what a direct labor hour allocation process can do to a company.

able for most companies include direct labor dollars (Moxie already negated this basis), material dollars, machine hours, prime costs, and good units produced. What happens when these are used in the costing process?

Direct labor dollars provide little relief from the problems with direct labor hours as an allocation basis. While it can be argued that they may give a better handle on the complexity of making a product (high labor rates for more highly skilled workers), it is hard to make a case that anything is gained by substituting a dollarized version of this measure. What of the other options?

Material dollars are one of the increasingly popular allocation bases being used by many companies to attach all the costs associated with inventory management, logistics, and purchasing. Here there is some hope, one would think. The costs being distributed by material dollars should have some relationship to these overhead areas, so an improvement is being made, right? Minimally. There is very little reason to believe that the cost of an item has a strong bearing on the amount of purchasing effort or logistics entailed. In fact, high-cost items usually bring with them tighter overall control, reducing the total costs needed to maintain the inventory.

One example of the inherent problems in using material dollar allocation schemes lies in the area of logistics. Logistics costs are more often than not related to the bulkiness of an item and the number of times it is moved. Caterpillar, Inc., in fact, uses pounds of steel moved as the basis for charging out these costs, because they firmly believe that most of the costs in this area are *driven by* the weight of the part or product. Purchasing costs, on the other hand, are driven by a multitude of factors, including the number of times an item is ordered, whether or not expediting has to occur to attain it, and the ease of purchase (e.g., is it a repeat purchase from an approved vendor?).

Using material dollars to allocate overhead can unfairly tax high-cost components, irrespective of other key operating concerns. It can lead to part proliferation, as design engineers are encouraged to develop products that use many cheap parts that may make ongoing production of the product more difficult. This runs counter to the efforts to simplify the process, which suggests that integrated components that are easily assembled are preferred, because they improve quality and decrease production cost. Moxie provides us with a view of the problems this single-driver allocation approach can create:

The result would be to charge the manufacture of bolts, in which the material cost is high, with an amount of indirect expense wholly disproportionate to the machine use required (vs. making nuts)...But this method is unsatisfactory for other reasons. Under its operation the large-size bolts bear a heavier amount of expense than would bolts of the smaller sizes, in which the amount of material used is considerably less. The machine work for the production of different size bolts is, however, exactly the same.[7]

Material dollars as an allocation basis create a different kind of distortion in the cost-accounting process, one that is actually more counterproductive to World-Class manufacturing than labor hours. Because it encourages part proliferation and reflects little of the underlying complexity that is actually causing the overhead costs, it counters many of the benefits gained through design for manufacturability and product simplification.

Machine hours can provide a better basis for overhead allocation, but only if a large number of machine classes and overhead rates are maintained. It does provide a clearer tie between most indirect manufacturing costs and the charging basis than direct labor, especially in a high-technology environment. Indiscriminately used, though, machine hours can lead to a cross-subsidization of expensive technology by cheaper, simpler alternatives.

For instance, if machines are placed into classes based on *function*, a fully depreciated punch press will bear the same overhead cost per hour as the expensive numerical control (NC) machine sitting next to it on the plant floor. The likely outcome of this situation is that the company will (not surprisingly) win all of the bids requiring the sophisticated NC technology, while losing more and more of its traditional business that is run through the older machinery. In the long run, this type of distortion can be as dangerous as that caused by using direct labor or material dollars bases.

What of the remaining approaches? Prime cost (the total of direct labor and direct materials) as an overhead base simply multiplies the problems caused by using one of these costs alone. All the weaknesses remain, and no benefits are gained. That leaves good units produced

---

[7]E. Moxie, *The Principles of Factory Cost Keeping* (New York: The Ronald Press Company, 1913), p. 70.

as the only single-driver allocation approach available. How can attaching the diverse mix of overhead to units produced on a flat basis provide a realistic estimate of the amount of indirect resources consumed? A complex and costly to produce product would bear exactly the same overhead charge as a simple product. The probability that the customer of the simpler product will be willing to pay for the extra costs caused by the complex product is slim; quite likely easy business will be lost, and the company won't be able to keep up with the demand for its more complex items. The outcome in the long run looks no more promising than that obtained using other methods.

Multiple Basis and Causality

To get around some of the problems with a single overhead rate, companies often develop a different rate for different departments, use a combination of several different approaches for various parts of the overhead pool (e.g., machine costs by machine hour), or develop two-stage allocation procedures. Each of these methods provides a clearer tie between the overhead rate and the causes of the cost in an area. In the overhead area, any change that incorporates causality in a more precise way is an improvement, reducing the distortions in the costing process.

Departmental versus plant-wide overhead rates is a first-pass modification on traditional overhead allocation methods. It does have a marked impact on product costs in multiproduct settings, as suggested by Figure 6–1. Lawnmasters' operations have now been changed to reflect the fact that it not only makes TurfMaster, but also blends and repackages other common lawn care products. With this increase in product variety, it now matters how costs are allocated, because these different final products put different demands on the company.

The two departments at Lawnmasters have different levels of labor and capital intensity, as suggested by the high overhead rate per direct labor hour in the mixing versus packaging departments ($50.42 versus $20.43). When these rates are applied to the products Lawnmasters is currently making, the difference in these two approaches really strikes home. Turfmaster, which is a heavy user of the mixing department, is moderately undercharged using one overhead rate. Vita-Grow, though, which only requires repackaging for final distribution

---

FIGURE 6–1
Lawnmasters—An Expanded Analysis

Relative overhead costs, total labor hours, and departmental costs for the two-stage operation:

	Plantwide total	Dept. A— mixing	Dept. B— packaging
Overhead costs	$38,912	$30,250	$8,662
Total labor hrs.	1,024	600	424
Overhead/DLH	$38.00	$50.42	$20.43

The overhead assigned to three different products based on a single versus multiple rate would become:

	Plantwide total	Dept. A— mixing	Dept. B— packaging
Total labor hours used:			
TurfMaster (100 bags)	16 hrs	14 hrs	2 hrs
Feed & Grow (100 bags)	6 hrs	2 hrs	4 hrs
VitaGrow (50 cases)	8 hrs	None	8 hrs
Cost assigned to batch:			
TurfMaster (100 bags)	$608	$706	$ 41
Feed & Grow (100 bags)	$228	$101	$ 82
VitaGrow (50 cases)	$304	$-0-	$163

Overhead per unit sold	Plantwide rate	Departmental rates
TurfMaster (100 bags)	$608/100 = $6.08	($706 + 41)/100 = $7.47
Feed & Grow (100 bags)	$228/100 = $2.28	($101 + 82)/100 = $1.83
VitaGrow (50 cases)	$304/50 = $6.08	$163/50 = $3.26

---

is severely overcosted when one plantwide rate is used (a $2.76 difference, or an 85% error). By simply adopting departmental rates, it appears that Lawnmasters can make a significant improvement in the accuracy of its costing process.

Multiple Drivers

Another way Lawnmasters might go at this problem is to use more than one overhead basis. Keeping the same three products, what would happen if the costs associated with materials are now separated from the labor-driven overhead pools and assigned to the items offered? Looking at Figure 6–2, the costs now shift markedly toward VitaGrow and away from Feed & Grow. The materials cost for VitaGrow are significant.

FIGURE 6–2
Lawnmasters—Multiple Overhead Drivers

Relative overhead costs, total labor hours, and departmental costs for the two-stage operation, as well as materials-related overhead:

	Plantwide total	Labor-based Dept. A— mixing	Dept. B— packaging	Materials- based
Overhead costs	$27,238	$21,700	$5,538	$11,674
Total hrs/$	1,024	600	424	$45,750
Overhead/driver	N/A	$36.17/DLH	$13.06/DLH	$0.25/Mat. $

The overhead assigned to three different products based on a single versus multiple rate would become:

Total drivers used	Dept. A— mixing	Dept. B— packaging	Material dollars
TurfMaster (100 bags)	14 hrs	2 hrs	$ 715
Feed & Grow (100 bags)	2 hrs	4 hrs	$ 950
VitaGrow (50 cases)	None	8 hrs	$2,500

	Labor-based		
Overhead/batch	Dept. A— mixing	Dept. B— packaging	Materials-based
TurfMaster (100 bags)	$506	$ 26	$179
Feed & Grow (100 bags)	$ 72	$ 52	$237
VitaGrow (50 cases)	$-0-	$104	$625

Overhead per unit sold	
TurfMaster	($506 + 26 + 170) = $711/100 = $7.11
Feed & Grow	($72 + 52 + 237) = $361/100 = $3.61
VitaGrow	($104 + 625) = $729/50 = $14.58

Do any of these numbers really make that much sense? Is there any indication that the costs suggested in Figure 6–1 are any better or worse than those in Figure 6–2? From the standpoint of getting the overhead dollars into the right basic cost pool, there is obvious movement in the right direction. But does it make sense to charge out the machine-intensive costs in mixing on labor hours, or the costs of handling materials on material dollars? It is doubtful that a sound argument could be made here.

The implication of these analyses is that changing the basis of allocation does change product costs (sometimes to a great degree, sometimes minimally). But as long as the choice of allocation bases, or *cost drivers,* remains poorly defined, the refinements in the cost pools has little bearing on improving the accuracy of the product costs generated by the system.

Homogeneity: Like Costs in Like Places

An allocation rate is the result of dividing a cost pool, such as materials-related costs, by a prechosen activity measure (e.g., material dollars). Errors in calculating or combining costs to develop the cost pool (the numerator), or failure to apply causality to the choice of activity (the driver, or denominator) render this cost estimate useless. Yet given the way that these numbers are used to support ongoing decision making, product costing and profitability analysis, and strategy development and deployment, it is critical that they more closely reflect the linkage between the consumption of resources (costs) and the products and services produced (benefits) within a company.

The concepts of an "input–output" matrix can be applied directly to the costing area, as suggested in Figure 6–3. In this case, the inputs and outputs aren't data, but instead are the actual resources obtained and consumed by the organization. In developing a cost model of the organization, it is useful to place costs that support an activity into the same cost "pool." When this is done, the concept of **homogeneity** is being applied. In a well-defined cost system, costs are summed together only if they are homogeneous (i.e., support one, and only one, type of activity).

Material and labor represent two common homogeneous pools of cost in a manufacturing environment. The cost object—the production of a specified unit of product or output—is the basis for defining and including the various resources consumed in these two categories. The other major piece of product cost, **overhead,** consists of everything else. Putting these diverse costs into one pool violates the homogeneity concept. It is of little wonder to accounting theorists that the "glob" called overhead creates confusion and conflict in an organization. No one knows what it really is, why it exists, or what value it adds. It simply sits, simmering and growing, as everyone watches in consternation.

Homogeneity is a key cost-accounting principle. It guides the analysis and construction of the various cost pools contained within

FIGURE 6–3
Costing: An Input–Output Approach

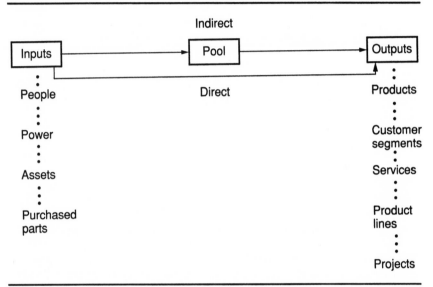

the overhead glob. Putting like costs in one pool, though, does not mean putting all the rent expenses or indirect materials together. This would be a pool with homogeneous *inputs,* defined by type of resource. The cost pool, to provide decision-relevant information, needs to be *homogeneous with respect to use,* not input. The costs contained in the cost pool have to support one activity, or use. If this fact is overlooked, there is absolutely no way to choose a cost driver that makes any sense at all. Once the cost pool is pulled together by **use,** identifying a usable activity basis becomes a more focused and productive process.

Summing up the discussion to this point, single-driver cost allocation schemes are flawed, by definition. Except in some very unusual situations, the indirect costs of meeting customer expectations are seldom driven by one activity or demand (e.g., labor). Expanding the allocation process to include multiple rates for departments, or to reflect material versus labor-driven costs, is an improvement, but only minimally. The development of useful information about the cause and benefit of indirect costs requires the following.

1. The creation of homogeneous cost pools defined by the **use** made of the resources in the pool; common use defines the boundaries for including resources.
2. Identification of a logical activity measure, or driver, to charge this homogeneous pool of costs out to those products, services, and customers that are served by them.

This creates a causally based (e.g., activity-based costing) costing process that will meet the needs of short-term operational decision making and development of product cost estimates.[8]

SHARED RESOURCES AND CAPACITY CONSTRAINTS

Everything that enlarges the sphere of human powers, that shows man he could do what he thought he could not do, is valuable.

Samuel Johnson, *Life of Samuel Johnson*, by James Boswell

Few companies have the luxury of having dedicated plants and personnel for each product produced. Instead, a factory turns out a broad range of products (using a common pool of resources) that are sold to a large variety of customers in different configurations through different distribution channels. What is the profitability of an order, then? With all these layers of interdependence and shared resources, the truth is impossible to determine. The best that can be done is to estimate the profits from any one order or generated by a specific customer relationship or market segment.

Understanding and controlling shared resources starts with their assignment to the products, customers, and services that consume them. The caveat in this process is **causality**: There must be a clear linkage between the assignment of these costs and the product, customer, or service. If this relationship doesn't exist, the attachment of these shared costs is an **arbitrary allocation**. It provides little useful information, and it can, in fact, distort the decision process. Resources that cannot be traced, exactly or in some estimated manner,

---

[8]The usefulness of these data for intermediate and long-term decision making is still being debated. Causality requires an in-depth knowledge of a system and relative stability in the relationship between inputs and outputs. This is difficult to achieve beyond the short term.

to a product, customer, or market segment, *should not* be attached to them. Doing so violates the basic tenets of the costing exercise, muddies the decision-making process, and hides more information than it reveals.

Unfortunately, most of the resources owned by a company are shared by its products and customers. With so few directly traceable resources to deal with, can the costing exercise ever hope to achieve accurate estimates and product costs? Yes. Because accuracy means that the estimates are close to, or reflect, actual resource consumption: Estimates that approximate the relationship between the various activities undertaken in the organization and the resources they consume are value-adding. Can this number ever equal a "true" cost of making a product, selling it, or providing a service? No, because there are too many factors (including projected product life cycle, economic cost of capital, and related concepts) that affect actual resource consumption patterns or that enter into the analysis of costs and cost behavior.

The impossibility of arriving at a "true cost" does not mean that it is acceptable for the financial function to continue to provide only full cost numbers based on traditional assumptions and management philosophies. There are better ways to design and operate a costing system available. Activity-based cost management is one potential avenue for improvement. The objective, whatever tool or system is used, is to more closely match resources consumed to their causes, whether those are products, service bundles, customer orders, or market segments. Costs have to be segmented based on the type of service they provide. Each such cost system will be unique, because each company acquires different resources, arranges them in a different manner, and uses them to provide a different range of products and services.

> *American business can out-think, out-work, out-perform any nation in the world. But we can't beat the competition if we don't get in the ball game.*
>
> President George Bush

Capacity: An Overarching Concern

In a factory, the total amount of production is limited by the physical size and throughput capabilities of the building that houses the plant. It may also be constrained by an expensive, or perhaps excessively large, machine that paces the production of the entire facility (the **bottleneck resource**, also called **pacing**).[9] When a facility is operating at its optimum (e.g., no more production is possible with the given resources, and there is no slack, or down time, for breaks, shift changes, or other disturbances) the term **theoretical capacity**, denoting the highest volume that could ever be achieved, is used.

Most facilities don't operate at their theoretical level, though. Instead, most companies use **practical capacity** or **normal capacity** as their baseline for defining the potential range of production. Practical capacity is "the full utilization of resources that can be sustained under attainable operating conditions."[10] Normal capacity is usually defined as the average level of production. Finally, **budgeted capacity** is what management expects to produce within the facility over the next year, or fiscal period, while **actual capacity utilization** is what comes to pass.

Why do we care about all of these different concepts of capacity? Because fixed costs spread over more or less units has a marked effect on unit costs. When a company states that it is operating "at capacity," the question that should follow is, "What does capacity mean?" Management may feel they're at practical capacity, but if they improved the process flow within the factory, or found a way to improve the throughput potential for the bottleneck resource, this number would change. More capacity, or throughput, means lower potential cost per unit.

A second question that should accompany any discussion of capacity is, "How much could we make?" This baseline, or practical capacity, is the goal; until the plant is running at this level, capital assets are being wasted. The traditional term for this waste is **idle capacity.** Prior to the mandate for absorption costing by the SEC in 1933, many companies booked an idle capacity charge directly against the reported net income. This loss, which could only be avoided by fully utilizing the plant, was a net expense of the operating period

---

[9]The pacing work center is a concept discussed in the article "Excess Capacity Costs" by M. Ostrenga, in the *Journal of Cost Management for the Manufacturing Industry*, Summer 1988, pp. 39–44. Bottleneck approaches have been heavily promoted by Eli Goldratt (*The Goal: A Process of Ongoing Improvement*, E. Goldratt and J. Cox, Croton-on-Hudson, N.Y.: North River Press, 1986) as a way to improve the throughput, and hence effectiveness and usable capacity, of a system.

[10]C. Horngren, *Cost Accounting: A Managerial Emphasis*. 5th ed. (Englewood Cliffs, N.J.: Prentice Hall, 1982), p. 248. (Note: This is the same cite used by Ostrenga in the previously cited article.)

that could only be avoided if management secured more orders. Idle capacity concepts faded from usage in the 1940s, but they are beginning to resurface as Western companies begin to look for ways to bring costs down by minimizing waste.

Shared Resources and Accountability

Shared resources are a problem for many reasons, not the least of which is the difficulty they create for identifying potential capacity for a plant. Shared resources create the need to develop charging schemes that adequately attach their costs to those activities, products, services, departments, and customers that benefit from them. Dealing with shared resources requires a clear understanding of the existing service provided by the resource, the areas benefiting from it, and some relative estimate of usage.

The field of cost accounting has developed myriad approaches, with varying degrees of complexity, to charge shared resources to productive departments.[11] There are few companies today that don't employ elaborate **cross-allocation** calculations to spread the costs from burgeoning support groups to those areas actually producing products and services for customers. It is an area of constant controversy.

Charging out service costs through cross-allocation schemes goes one step beyond the problems with allocation methods described above; productive departments can be potentially "tolled" for services they often don't desire or use. The impact of this problem is most easily seen in multiplant firms, where controllable overhead is often a minor element of the total overhead cost the area is required to absorb into ongoing production. Problems begin to emerge as the magnitude of these uncontrolled and growing costs begin to make internal production uncompetitive with external vendors.

One area where the impact of the distortions from cross-allocations and the full-cost accounting model come to bear is in the area of make versus buy decisions. Often made using full-cost assumptions, these decisions are tipped toward outsourcing in many

---

[11]These techniques include direct charges to productive departments, cross-allocations, and sequential allocations. As long as relative use is part of the process of arriving at these costs, the outcome has some value. But the real question of import is never asked: would the "customer" (e.g., paying department) freely purchase the service or pay the required price for it? This is where the discussions should begin.

cases where, in reality, internal production is more efficient and effective. In a World-Class organization, every department, whether "productive" or not, should provide a cost-effective, high-quality level of service as required by *the customer*. For internal support groups, the customer is the using department. If the customer's needs aren't being met, or are being met but with excess cost (e.g., waste), then *that area* of service should be considered for outsourcing.

The competitive gains that can be made from more effective management of overhead areas begins with abandoning the full-cost accounting model. Costs are not to be covered; they should be providing value that the customer is willing to pay for. Companies like Weyerhauser and Dennison are opening up discussions and procedures that allow internal customers to buy their support services from the outside, if a better price can be obtained. This is a wake-up call for many parts of the company that have forgotten the relationship between cost and value.

Shared resources and the issue surrounding them will continue to draw attention and create controversy within organizations. The essence of an organization is found in these areas; without shared resources a company does not really exist. The more decentralized a corporation becomes, the less integrated its efforts become. At some point, the corporation becomes a holding company, exerting little influence on the independent divisions that comprise it.

Within a company, this type of treatment of shared resource problems is more troubling. Effectively meeting customer requirements is the result of well-coordinated efforts of individuals across the organization. Splintering these coordinated efforts through outsourcing shared resource requirements will undoubtedly create other problems, unforeseen in the short term, but critical in the long term. Sustainable competitive advantage comes, not from divvying up shared expenses in order to find creative ways of "covering" them, but from expecting the same level of performance and value-added activity from all areas of the firm. Shared resources are an area of opportunity and challenge for the World-Class corporation.

COSTING PRODUCTS AND SETTING PRICES

> *The consumer, so it is said, is the king . . . each is a voter who uses his money as votes to get the things done that he wants done.*
>
> Paul Anthony Samuelson, *Economics* (3)

The most common application of costing concepts today is in valuing inventory and setting prices. In the United States, companies base most of their pricing on some form of "cost-plus" scheme, a two-stage process in which target profits for a specific product or product line are determined (using an ROI, or targeted return on investment basis), and then the markup needed to reach that level of profitability is calculated as follows.

1. Target profit calculation:

[Average invested capital] × [Target ROI] = Target profit

2. Markup calculation:

$$\frac{\text{Target profit}}{\text{Annual volume} \times \text{Total cost per unit}} = \frac{\text{Markup percentage}}{\text{on total cost}}$$

Total cost approaches include the selling and administrative costs in the cost base, which indicates that the markup is, in reality, the desired profit percentage. Other cost constructions can be used in this analysis, including full cost and variable cost. Each time the **base cost** (i.e., full cost versus total cost) is reduced, or covers a smaller portion of the total costs, the markup percentage has to increase. Why? Because more items (e.g., profit plus selling costs) have to be recovered in the markup over "cost."

This cost-based approach to pricing is an established practice in the United States. It can be used to identify the desired price, but the market actually sets the selling price in all but a few instances. The cost-plus approaches often serve as a way to determine which products appear to be the best performers for the company. *Cost-plus pricing is not the correct way to evaluate the relative profitabilities of different products.* Unless a variable cost basis is used in the calculations, and the number of "errors" in establishing these costs are minimal, using cost-plus concepts in product-line decisions can lead to disaster.

The Japanese do not use cost-based pricing schemes. Instead, they focus on determining what price they need to put on a product to gain maximum market penetration, or market share. This price, with a profit factored in, sets the ceiling on allowable costs. Actual costs are then compared to this desired cost; if actuals are greater than desired, a **target cost** is identified. Target costs are excess costs that are targeted for elimination. More time will be spent exploring the concept of target costing in Chapter 9.

The key factors to keep in mind in understanding and utilizing various pricing schemes and concepts are as follows: (1) in cost-plus pricing, the cost base chosen will also dictate the desired markup percentage; (2) these calculations should not be used in making decisions to add or drop product lines; and (3) the Japanese look to the market to set the limit on cost, and then work to push actual costs below this ceiling. In the Japanese setting, prices are taken as given, and costs are targeted for improvement; American approaches tend to take costs as a given, and target specific markups and profitabilities. These two approaches set up markedly different dynamics inside the organization; the two sides are not playing the same game.

Technology, Costs, Prices, and the Market

Inherent in the costing process is an underlying organizational structure, strategy, and set of processes that provide products and services to the market. Each combination of these elements of production leads to a different clustering of costs and a different value-adding capacity for the organization. Competitive advantage accrues to those companies that find the most effective, efficient, and innovative ways to combine the limited resources at their disposal to create value for the customer.

Technology plays a major role in defining the organization's feasible set of structures, strategies, and products. If a company uses a modern technology, such as just-in-time manufacturing, it can reduce the time to market for its products, cut the costs of providing the same products, and create a strategic advantage. Yet these technologies are not free. They bring with them a range of acquisition, maintenance, and people costs that can offset the market advantages they provide. More technology is not always good. Intelligent application of technologies within the existing structure of the organization is.

This is perhaps the hardest lesson for American managers to learn. Technology has always been the optimal solution for ongoing productivity problems. Replacing a "recalcitrant" workforce with a submissive machine seemed the best alternative. But each machine brings with it a range of hidden costs that adds to the total overhead of the company. If costing systems were refocused onto machines and away from labor, the full impact of new technology on the costs of doing business could be determined. But when labor remains the central focus in the FMIS, machine- and technology-based costs have the potential to spin out of control. Why? Once again, because lumping these costs into the heterogeneous overhead pool and spreading them out on direct labor (in other words, violating the causality principle) makes these incremental costs invisible.

The theme of this chapter is simple. To be an effective management tool, the FMIS must mirror the organization—its structure, strategy, technology, and processes. This mirror needs to reflect the value chains that knit the organization together, pulling resources from different areas in the process of meeting customer expectations. Meeting this objective requires the careful analysis of the various paths that exist to fill customer needs, the identification of activities and their separation into value-adding and non-value-adding groups, and the development of cost estimates for these various activities, wherever they may occur in the value chain.

Redesigning the FMIS is not an effort that can begin in a vacuum, without attachment to the history of cost theory or the organizations it serves. The concepts and techniques necessary to transform the FMIS into a value-adding tool already exist; applying the logic of causality, traceability, homogeneity, and variability is the starting point. Understanding the difference between history (financial accounting) and the future (managerial accounting) is the ultimate goal.

Recapping the Chapter

This chapter has focused on the issues surrounding overhead management and control in companies today. Overhead is a broad mix of heterogeneous resources used for many purposes throughout the many value chains making up an organization. It has been a poorly understood and managed part of the company, often neglected in the search for cost improvements and more effective management.

There are a series of overhead allocation schemes that are commonly used in companies, including direct labor hours or dollars, material dollars, machine hours, and good units produced. Each of these approaches were detailed, and their weaknesses identified, in the discussion. The overriding point was that any single *driver* allocation scheme distorts the costing process. Several multidriver examples were then pursued, but to no avail. The key point made in this section: Costs have to be charged out to the products and processes using them. Causality is the key to effective short-term cost accounting.

Having detailed traditional views of the costing process, more realistic input–output models for understanding and controlling costs were reviewed. Built on the concept of causality, these *activity-based* systems promise to provide clearer information for internal users. Whereas traditional accounting systems are built around output volumes, activity based accounting factors in inputs from across the organization. The information to create these systems comes from the managers who are going to use them. These systems retain a fairly short-term focus because they fail to factor in strategic concerns and the more difficult issues surrounding shared resources.

In the Long Run...

The reasonable man adapts himself to the world: the unreasonable one persists in trying to adapt the world to himself. Therefore all progress depends on the unreasonable man.

George Bernard Shaw, *Reason* (3)

The issues surrounding developing short-term estimates of long-term costs have been examined from many perspectives in this chapter. It is not an issue for accountants alone; in fact, cost theory is the basis for management decision making and the potential profitability of an organization. At its essence, cost theory is based in economic theory, but it operates in the real world. That means that the niceties of economics, where all costs can be examined in terms of long-run and short-run implications, are simply not available or practical to employ in creating a functioning FMIS.

Cost theory attempts to close the gap between economic rationality and the practical constraints of daily operating conditions. When properly applied, through careful choice of the right cost construction for the decision being made, it can provide reasonable estimates of the economic costs and benefits of various decisions. Poorly applied, through adherence to full-cost models, poor design, or improper execution, cost systems can impair the competitiveness of an organization. In that case, there may be no long run.

Increasing attention is being brought to bear in this important area of financial management. Financial managers are returning to the classroom to update their knowledge, learn new techniques, and fine-tune their skills. As they become better suppliers of information, they must also take on the role of educating their customers—both internal and external to the firm—on what numbers are available, when to use them, and the strengths and shortcomings of the various cost analyses they provide. The changes needed to convert financial management from a watchdog function to a competitive-team orientation will begin with this open exchange of information, and a clear understanding, on both sides of the desk, of the various assumptions and options that guide costing practice.

> *One aspect of the dawning information era, an aspect which may catch most accounting and information executives by surprise, is that the new information technology will prove to be the battlefield where the forces of traditional management meet those of industrial democracy. . . . Accounting and information system designers generally are unversed in such matters. They are well advised to do their homework for they will be in the middle of the fray.*
>
> Norman MacIntosh,
> *The Social Software of Accounting & Information Systems*

SUGGESTED READINGS

Armstrong, Peter. "Changing Mangement Control Strategies: The Role of Competition Between Accountancy and Other Organizational Professions." *Accounting, Organizations and Society,* 1985, pp. 129–148.

Arnstein, W., and F. Gilabert. *Direct Costing.* New York: AMACOM, 1980.

Beaujon, G., and V. Singhal. "Understanding the Activity Costs in an Activity-Based Cost System." *Journal of Cost Management,* Spring 1990, pp. 51–72.

Berliner, C., and J. Brimson. *Cost Management for Today's Advanced Manufacturing: The CAM-I Conceptual Design.* Boston, Mass.: Harvard Business School Press, 1988.

Campbell, R., M. Janson, and J. Bush. "Developing Strategic Cost Standards in a Machine-Paced Environment." *Journal of Cost Management,* Winter 1991, pp. 18–28.

Dixon, J. R., A. Nanni, and T. Vollmann. *The New Performance Challenge: Measuring Operations for World-Class Competition.* Homewood, Ill.: Business One Irwin, 1990.

Edersheim, E. H., and B. Vandenbosch. "How to Make Accounting Count: Causal-Based Accounting," *Journal of Cost Management,* Winter 1991, pp. 5–17.

Emore, J., and J. Ness. "The Slow Pace of Meaningful Change in Cost Systems." *Journal of Cost Management,* Winter 1991, pp. 36–45.

Ferrara, W. "The New Cost/Management Accounting: More Questions than Answers." *Management Accounting,* October 1990, pp. 48–52.

Garner, P. *Evolution of Cost Accounting.* New York: Garland, 1988.

Goldratt, E., and J. Cox. *The Goal: A Process of Ongoing Improvement.* Croton-on-Hudson: North River Press, 1986

Hilton, R. *Managerial Accounting.* New York: McGraw Hill, 1991.

Johnson, H. T., and R. Kaplan. *Relevance Lost: The Rise and Fall of Management Accounting.* Boston, Mass.: Harvard Business School Press, 1987.

Johnson, H. T., and D. Loewe. "How Weyerhaeuser Manages Corporate Overhead Cost." *Management Accounting,* August 1987, pp. 20-21.

Kammlade, J., P. Mehra, and T. Ozan. "A Process Approach to Overhead Management." *Journal of Cost Managment,* Fall 1989, pp. 5–10.

MacIntosh, Norman. *The Social Software of Accounting and Information Systems.* New York: Wiley, 1985.

National Association of Accountants, Research Report #19, 20, and 21. *Analysis of Non-Manufacturing Costs for Managerial Decisions.* New York: National Association of Accountants, 1951. This group published a broad series of reports and bulletins on the various aspects of cost accounting, which can be obtained by contacting the Institute of Management Accountants, Montvale, N.J.

National Association of Cost Accountants, Research Bulletin #23. *Direct Costing.* New York, 1953.

———. Research Bulletin, Section Three. *The Analysis of Cost-Volume-Profit Relationships.* New York, 1949.

———. Research Bulletin, Vol. 28, No. 1. *Developing Basic Cost Information for Material and Labor.* New York, 1946.

Ostrenga, Michael R. "A Methodology for Identifiying Your Excess Capacity Costs." *Journal of Cost Management,* Summer 1988, pp. 39–44.

Parent, Andre. *Distribution Costs: Their Control and Analysis.* Ontario, Canada: The Society of Industrial and Cost Accountants of Canada, Special Study #3, 1962.

Staubus, G. "Activity Costing: Twenty Years On." *Management Accounting Research,* 1990: Volume 1, pp. 249–264.

———. *Activity Costing for Decisions.* New York: Garland, 1988.

Weber, Charles. *The Evolution of Direct Costing.* University of Illinois: Center for International Education and Research in Accounting, 1966.

Weisman, Dennis. "How Cost Allocation Systems Can Lead Managers Astray." *Journal of Cost Management,* Spring 1991, pp. 4–10.

CHAPTER 7

NUMBERS FOR
SHORT-TERM DECISIONS

Learn to reason forward and backward on both sides of a question.

Thomas Blandi (1)

There's a mighty big difference between good, sound reasons and reasons that sound good.

Burton Hillis (1)

Decisions about current operating conditions, the best way to manage or utilize existing resources, and a host of other **ad hoc** problems and opportunities are part of every day's menu of events for the operating manager. In approaching these decisions, the manager has to examine both the financial and nonfinancial implications of each opportunity or solution, with a constant eye toward ensuring long-term profitability through effective management of short-term events. This is an area critical for every operating manager to understand; asking the right questions is the first step in making sure the full set of alternatives available to the company is considered when decision analysis is performed.

The FMIS plays a significant role in the analysis of short-term decisions (those that affect one year or less of operations). In a traditional FMIS, though, much of this support is gathered on a case-by-case basis. Many of the costs that are affected in these situations are normally bundled with similar costs in an overhead pool, or are treated as joint or shared resources that are seldom queried on a piecemeal basis. An activity-based FMIS can provide more of this information on an ongoing basis, but the nature of short-term decision making—with its focus on choosing among one-time opportunities for obtaining incremental profits—means that no matter what numbers are available, the key issue will always be, "What are the implications of this decision?" If the numbers look good, but the strategic implications of a decision are troubling, the short-term gain may simply not be worth the long-term price.

The characteristics of short-term decision making that set it apart from other activities performed by an operating manager include the following:

- They affect costs, resources, or activities that have been obtained, and are normally used, for other purposes.
- They generate **incremental** costs or revenues.
- They represent situations that can be modified or reversed, as well as completed, within a short time period.
- They are normally considered to be **nonstrategic** in nature, although at times this perception may be misleading.
- Analysis of the impact of these decisions is done on an **ad hoc** basis.
- Managers in the affected areas usually oversee or guide the decision process—few of these decisions involve top-level management.
- Availability of idle capacity in the affected areas is a key criterion in the decision process.

Other factors shape these decisions, but the essence of this class of decisions is that they are nonstrategic, short-term, often one-time opportunities that generate incremental costs and revenues. The criterion that is used in making these decisions is quite simple: The incremental revenues from the action or opportunity must exceed the incremental costs.

The types of decisions that are included in this short-term classification include cost-volume-profit analysis (CVP), make-versus-buy decisions, product line add or drop decisions, one-time offers of incremental business at reduced prices, sell-or-process further analysis for joint products, and optimizing the use of scarce resources. A quick review of these topics suggests that they cover the entire range of managerial decision making, encompassing most of the short-term "changes" that can be accommodated without a major investment in new fixed assets, radical changes in existing resources, processes, or policies, or any other long-term structural or strategic concerns. They are, for the most part, decisions made only occasionally that affect only a limited aspect of the company's operations.

Identifying the Costs that Matter

What costs affect this decision process? The key question asked when short-term decisions are analyzed is, "What changes?" The objective is to isolate those costs that will be *changed* by the decision; those that don't are irrelevant to the decision. The focus is on identifying the **relevant costs**, those that are affected by the change or opportunity that is being considered. In looking for these costs, the financial manager is constantly assessing whether the decision can be made within existing capacity constraints.

A second major factor to consider in assessing which costs matter and which don't is to remember that choosing one alternative screens out others. If both alternatives are sound investments and can be managed with existing resources, both should be pursued: A choice need not be made. In most cases, though, deploying resources for one set of activities closes out their availability for other uses. This is called an *opportunity cost*: The potential benefits (e.g., revenues) foregone by choosing one course of action over another. In developing the decision analysis, it is everyone's responsibility to search for and name potential opportunity costs; they may change a decision process markedly.

There is a need for honesty in the decision process. Often a short-term decision is made, such as a make-versus-buy decision that results in outsourcing an existing product or component, with an assumption that resources currently dedicated to that product will no longer be needed. That fact alone is probably true, but if the resource is not eliminated, or taken out of the total cost package, it isn't correct to include it in the analysis. In other words, if a cost could be eliminated, and is, it is an **avoidable** cost and is therefore relevant to the decision being made. If the resource is retained, or shifted to other uses, it is an **unavoidable** cost and is *irrelevant* to the current decision.

Before going into further detail on several of the ways this type of analysis can be done, one other warning needs to be discussed. While short-term decisions supposedly include only those that are nonstrategic in nature, in reality many of them have significant strategic implications. When a decision is made, for instance, to accept a one-time order from a large department store for one or more of the company's products, the actual costs and profits are not the only issue. What if other customers find out about the price break awarded to this customer? Will they contently continue to pay the usual selling price, or will they also lobby for price reductions? If these price breaks are granted to everyone, can the company stay in business? These issues are real but often overlooked concerns when short-term decisions are made.

The analysis of short-term decisions is heavily dependent on financial estimates of the projected relevant and incremental (new, or added) costs of a proposal. These costs are compared to the projected revenues. If the numbers look good, the decision isn't made; it simply moves to the next stage, in which qualitative issues, such as the possibility that this one-time deal will upset existing market arrangements, are added. These qualitative factors may not seem as "hard" or reliable as the numbers, but a poor strategic decision can be more fatal than simply undercosting one customer or overcharging another. Qualitative factors capture the **risk** the decision bears for the long-term success of the organization. Whether or not dollar signs can be attached to these factors, they're important.

CVP ANALYSIS

> *We all know how the size of sums of money appears to vary in a remarkable way according as they are being paid in or paid out.*
>
> Julian Huxley

Cost-volume-profit (CVP) analysis is a technique for evaluating the impact of changes in the expected volume of sales on the costs and profits those sales will generate for the company. At its core, CVP analysis is simply a reflection of the following equation:

Total revenues − Total costs = Net income before tax (NIBT)

When we expand this equation to incorporate the fact that some costs **vary** directly with changes in volume (variable costs) while others provide service over an extended range of production volume (fixed costs), the equation becomes

Total revenues − Total variable costs − Total fixed costs = NIBT

One more transition places the formula in reasonable form for analyzing a broad range of profitability questions. In this final form, the equation reflects very precisely the **unit-based** nature of most revenues and costs:

Total revenue = Selling price per unit × Volume sold, or $(S/P_u)V_s$

Total fixed costs = TFC

Total variable costs = $VC_u \times V_s$

Profit = Net income before tax, or I_B

This results in the formula

$$(S/P_u)V_s - [(VC_u X V_s) + TFC] = I_B$$

The CVP formulas simply capture the impact of volume changes on the total costs and profits of the firm. As can be seen, swings in volume directly affect the total revenues and the total variable cost amounts. For every new unit sold, a constant and predictable revenue and variable cost will be generated. The fact that the selling price and variable cost per unit are fairly constant, no matter what volume of goods is sold, leads to the following useful number:

$$S/P_u - VC_u = \textbf{Unit contribution margin, or } CM_u$$

The unit contribution margin is the amount of money left over, after paying the costs directly related to the sale (e.g., variable cost), to cover fixed costs and provide the company with a profit. It is called the contribution margin because it represents the dollars each unit sold contributes to the company for other uses. (e.g. fixed costs and profits).

These formulas can be used as they are, or manipulated to yield the **break-even** formula. This equation gives an indication—for a one-product situation—what level of sales a company will need to generate in order to break even (total revenues equal total costs, or profit is zero). The equation is directly derived from the general equation when profit is set equal to zero:

$$\textbf{Break-even volume} = \frac{\text{Total fixed costs}}{\text{Contribution margin per unit}}$$

If a company wants to factor a profit into this calculation, it simply has to add the desired profit (I_B) to the fixed costs on top of the equation and re-solve it. The break-even volume of sales is a way for a company to gauge the riskiness of a course of action.

A CVP Example

An example may help here. Anderson Manufacturing, a medium-sized manufacturer of dress shoes, is considering expanding its line to include exercise shoes. To be able to support this new product, equipment will have to be leased at an annual cost of $500,000 per year. Other fixed costs associated with the new line of shoes, including new personnel, advertising, and promotion are estimated at $350,000 per year. In looking at the product, management estimates that it will cost $10.00 to make each pair of athletic shoes, and that it can sell them through their existing distribution channels for $20.00 per pair. Management would like to know what volume it will need to break even as well as what volume will be needed to generate $150,000 in profit. The solution?

Anderson will need to sell 85,000 pairs of athletic shoes to break even [($500,000 + $350,000) / ($20 − 10)], and 100,000 pairs to generate $150,000 in profit [($500,000 + $350,000 + $150,000) / ($20 − $10)]. As can be seen, above the break-even sales level of 85,000 pairs (or 85,000 × $20.00 = $1,700,000 in revenues), the entire contribution margin, or $10.00 per pair of shoes sold, drops through to profit. Above break-even, the company begins to earn a profit equivalent to the contribution margin per unit.

Because every unit sold above break-even generates profit at a constant rate, CVP analysis is often called profitability analysis. It identifies that point at which profits begin to be made. The other interesting fact about CVP analysis is that it markedly demonstrates the impact of high levels of fixed costs on the company. Because most companies are **price takers** in the marketplace, there is little a company can do to increase its selling price, even if it wants to. Instead, a company has to trade off the fixed and variable costs of production under different production settings (e.g., high labor content versus machine-paced) to identify the optional mix of resources given expected sales levels.

Providing this type of information is one of the key roles played by the financial manager in a company considering the implementation of advanced manufacturing technologies. Most of these technology-intensive systems generate higher levels of fixed costs than more traditional, labor-intensive manufacturing methods. If projected sales volumes are low, or the riskiness of the line of business is high, these fixed costs can become a major problem. They won't go away (in other words, are unavoidable) if volumes fall off in the short run. In making many ongoing decisions, an operating manager needs to consider the impact of the decision on the *cost structure* (ratio of fixed to variable cost) of the firm.

CVP and Multiple Product Settings

CVP analysis can be expanded to include multiple products by utilizing the **sales mix** expected for the group of products. Each product's contribution margin per unit is multiplied by its percentage of the total sales in the mix. Returning to Anderson: They believe that their sales mix for the coming year will be six pairs of dress shoes for every four pairs of athletic shoes sold. This means that, to use CVP analysis, they have to develop a **weighted average contribution margin** for the projected mix (e.g., a 60-percent weighting of the contribution margin for dress shoes and a 40-percent weight attached to athletic shoes contribution). If the unit contribution margin for dress shoes is $15.00 per pair, the weighted contribution would be

$$(\$15.00 \times 60\%) + (\$10.00 \times 40\%) = \$13.00$$

This is the *average* contribution margin per pair of shoes sold. How is this number used?

To show this, let's complete the analysis for Anderson by noting that, in addition to the fixed costs for athletic shoes, it incurs $1,200,000 per year in fixed costs for dress shoes. It also wants, in total, to generate $400,000 in profit for the coming year. The analysis reveals that

$$\text{Break-even volume} = \frac{(\$1,200,000 + \$500,000 + \$350,000)}{\$13.00}$$

or

$$\$2,050,000/\$13.00 = 157,693 \text{ pairs of shoes}$$

The sales needed to generate $400,000 in profits are

$$(\$2,050,000 + \$400,000)/\$13.00 = 188,461 \text{ pairs}$$

Of this total of 188,461 pairs, 60 percent are dress shoes (113,077 pairs) and 40 percent are athletic shoes (75,384 pairs). This may seem odd, as it seems to suggest that the company needs to sell fewer athletic shoes to break even. In reality, if there are no interdependencies between sales of dress and athletic shoes, the 85,000 pairs of athletic shoes will need to be sold to break even as a free-standing enterprise. What this analysis is suggesting, though, is that because the dress shoes have a higher contribution margin than athletic shoes, they help cover some of the *joint costs*. In looking at a sales mix approach to CVP analysis, the complementary nature of sales of one product versus the other is factored in through the weighted average contribution margin. The answer suggests what mix of sales is needed to reach the total profit objective, not what level of sales are needed for each line to break even independently.

Does asking dress shoes to bear some of the freight for athletic shoes make good business sense? That depends on what the market, or customer, wants. If Anderson is afraid of losing out on a big department store account because it can't offer the athletic shoes, then it will go ahead with its decision to add the line if it projects that it can sell at least the 75,384 pairs the second analysis indicates is the critical level. The decision comes down to understanding the market, understanding customer expectations, and gauging the reliability of the estimates management generates.

Unless the marketing department is convinced it can meet the sales levels suggested in the second analysis, Anderson will have to rethink its entire strategy. Looking solely at the dress shoes for a minute, we see Anderson has to sell 80,000 pairs of dress shoes to break even ($1,200,000/$15.00) and 106,667 pairs to generate the $400,000 profit it desires [($1,200,000 + $400,000) / $15.00]. If, without the athletic shoes, management believes it can only sell a little more than 90,000 pairs of dress shoes (80% of the 113,000 pairs in the mix analysis), but with them could sell the 113,000 pairs, it is better off selling the athletic shoes. Why? As suggested below, total profits are $150,000 if only dress shoes are sold, and $400,000 if both are offered:

Formula: (Projected volume − Break-even volume) × CM_u = Profits
   Dress shoes only: (90,000 − 80,000) × $15.00 = $150,000
   Dress and athletic: (188,462 − 157,693) × $13.00 = $399,997

It seems obvious that, even if the athletic shoes don't really pay their own way, it certainly makes sense, in total, to offer the complete product line of dress and athletic shoes.

Related Issues

CVP analysis can be expanded to a number of different settings and, with modifications, cover a broad range of problems. It is especially useful when new products are being launched. The technique has its limits, though, not the least of which is the fact that it is based on the assumption that the fixed and variable components of the cost puzzle can be reasonably estimated (most companies do make these estimates).

When using CVP analysis management needs to be very careful about its projected sales, price, and cost patterns. The technique is very sensitive to fairly minor shifts in these assumptions, leading the company into trouble rather than out of it. In addition, CVP analysis is only one quantitative tool available to analyze this class of decisions, can often omit critical variables, and ignores the qualitative issues that may color the value of the calculations in general. That doesn't mean the tool should be tossed away; it is useful for gauging the baseline sales volumes needed to cover a period's costs, to get a handle on how increased fixed or variable costs will affect the company's profitability, and related issues. CVP analysis is the starting point in understanding the impact of various sales and cost patterns on profits.

DIFFERENTIAL ANALYSIS AND THE FMIS

It is futile to linger endlessly over differences; the fruitful research is to look for points of contact.

A. G. Sertillanges, *The Intellectual Life* (4)

CVP analysis is useful when the question being asked by management is, "What impact will changing volumes have on profitability?" By examining the profitability issues from the perspective of a break-even or baseline of operations, it provides a clear signal to management about the impact of fixed costs on the bottom line, as well as the impact of incremental sales on this measure of performance. Maximizing profitability in a CVP setting is equivalent to maximizing the total contribution margin available given existing products, market conditions (e.g., selling prices), and production constraints.

Not all decisions made by management tie so directly to volume-based profitability. In many cases the questions being asked are not, "How can we maximize profit?" but rather, "Which one of these available options makes the most sense?" When the decisions management is attempting to make deal with alternative courses of action, the potential for investing in a variety of assets, or the decision to continue to add value to a product or not, the analytic approach used is **differential analysis**. The focus is on what changes (e.g., costs or revenues) if one course of action is pursued instead of another.

Differential analysis requires the following:

- A recognized need to change existing policies, processes, or tactics.
- The development of more than one alternative approach to meet this perceived demand for change.
- Selection, or availability of, a *status quo*, or baseline level of operations that the alternatives can be compared to.
- Mutual exclusivity within the set of options—only one approach can be pursued. Once a choice is made the other options are no longer viable at the current point in time.
- An ability to estimate the **incremental**, or decision-caused, costs and revenues each alternative will generate.
- The ability, authority, and willingness to make a choice among the competing alternatives.
- Assessment that this decision will have minimal impact on other aspects of the business, strategy, or operations.

To employ this set of techniques, management has to be able to clearly identify a core problem, develop a set of options for dealing with this problem, and then, through the use of existing and ad hoc data available through the FMIS and other sources, create an economic analysis, and comparison of, the alternatives. The term *differential analysis* comes from a recognition that the technique revolves around the ability to identify differences in the cost and revenue potential for the various options identified in the decision-making process.

The decision rule in choosing among the options is, at first glance, quite simple: Choose the alternative that minimizes total cost (i.e., maximizes total profits). Yet there are a broad number of ways to improve profitability, ranging from negotiating price breaks for individual materials through redesigning the product or process to decrease its cost profile. In differential analysis, then, the objective is **choice**, not risk assessment (e.g., CVP). If the analysis ends up impacting multiple periods, the technique can be modified to incorporate the **time value of money**, or the effect of interest on long-term cash flows.

The most difficult part in coming to a full understanding of differential analysis is the fact that only those costs that **change** will be factored into the computations. The most natural thing to do is to include all the costs and revenues of every feasible approach, but if a cost or revenue remains unchanged from one scenario to the next, it adds no value to the decision process to include it. All it can do is muddy the waters, making the decision more difficult to make. Once again, operating managers have to take an active role in helping identify, honestly and openly, what resources really will be affected by the decision. It is not a financial exercise, devoid of internal realities. It is the lifeline for every manager and every department in a company; these short-term decisions lay the path for the future.

Resources that have already been committed or money that has already been spent are, by definition, irrelevant to the differential analysis. These prior costs, or **sunk costs**, cannot be changed no matter what is done in the future. It may be hard to abandon a project that has already been started (and consumed significant resources), but if its projected future benefits to the company are less than those offered by another project or approach, the decision to abandon the existing work may well be the best course of action. Alternatively, when undertaking a differential analysis, we try to estimate the cost of foregone profits, or **opportunity costs**, to factor in the realization that dedicating resources to one course of action will prevent us from pursuing another.

Decisions involving differential analysis can at times appear to be counter-intuitive; companies are hard-pressed to abandon a project that has been previously judged to be a good idea. In fact, a suggestion to abandon can be seen as a "career limiting move" (CLM) by the powers that be. And attempts to factor into the analysis cash flows that, by definition, won't exist if the decision is made (opportunity costs) can be seen as "featherbedding." It seems unnatural to include things that will never come to pass, while throwing away the harsh reality of sunk costs that may even be recorded in the general ledger as assets. Yet the economic rationale for eliminating sunk costs and factoring in opportunity costs remains; all a manager can affect is the present and future—the past is a closed book that cannot be reopened.

Differential Analysis and "Special" Orders

One of the easiest ways to understand differential analysis is to actually apply it to several common decisions that face most companies at least once a year, if not more often. While these decisions are ad hoc in nature, they are often recurring; the customer or product may change, but the underlying dynamics do not. To understand this type of decision, we can look at a small company faced with a common problem.[1]

Management at Western Soap Company, a medium size manufacturer of different types of bar soap, has been asked by a major corporation to consider renting out one of its soap-making lines for $200,000 per month. Western is currently using this line for its own production, with an average before tax profit of $125,000 per month.

This may look like a straightforward decision for management, but there are **differential costs** under each of the two scenarios. If Western Soap rents out the line, it will have to incur overtime on its other machines to make up for the lost production time. Management has determined that this will amount to $50,000 per month. Even with this overtime, management estimates that it will have to turn away business if it rents out this much of its capacity.

John Andrews, V.P. of operations, estimates that $250,000 of existing business will be lost (before-tax profits are averaging 20 percent of sales) because of the decision. The rented line will also bring with it additional crewing and maintenance costs, estimated at $21,600 and $48,000 per month, respectively; this is in addition to the $50,000 of overtime that will be needed to get existing work done on time. Finally, if it rents out the line, Western will incur about $10,000 a month in additional overhead costs for laboratory testing and other required support. Summarizing, Western Soap's management projects the differential revenues and expenses from the proposal as follows:

---

[1] These materials were developed by the author for the textbook *Accounting Principles,* by P. Fess and C. Warren, published by SouthWestern Publishing (Cincinnati, Ohio). While they were not directly used in that text, the support of these authors is gratefully recognized in the development of the materials and arguments.

Western Soap—analysis of incremental profitability

Rental revenues		$200,000
Less additional costs:		
Lost profits on line	$50,000*	
Labor on line	21,600	
Machine maintenance	48,000	
Additional overtime	50,000	
Additional laboratory costs	10,000	179,600
Additional profits from rental		$20,400

*(20% of $250,000) = $50,000.

Other factors management has to consider in making this decision include whether or not this decision will permanently affect its business in any way, as well as the risk that the rental arrangement may be only a short-term agreement. After weighing these and other factors, the rental option still appears favorable. In the end, Western's management decides that the $20,400 in additional profits for the rental option makes sense, and agrees to the contract.

In this simple case, the company is faced with limited capacity, and an offer to buy line time that will displace ongoing business. The **opportunity cost** of the decision is the $50,000 in foregone profits that the line could have generated if normal products were made. Western Soap, though, would need to be very careful about the precedent that this sets up. Is management completely sure that the lost business will not come back to haunt it? If the line becomes free again (e.g., the rental agreement is cancelled), can Western refill this idled capacity, or will the business that was turned away be permanently lost? These and related questions temper the decision process. The dollar estimates of potential cash flows are the beginning of the decision analysis, not the end.

In accepting special orders, special production arrangements, or similar types of proposals, there are a series of issues that must be addressed:

- Will the order displace existing business or utilize idle capacity?
- Will the precedence set by a decision to take the business lead to potential problems with existing customers or future orders?
- Could this "special" deal eventually become regular business? If so, would it still be profitable if it had to help cover the larger costs of actually running the business?
- Does everyone promise this is a one-time deal? Are they willing to stand behind this claim?

- What other factors (such as resources not normally included in the costing of a product) or costs might be impacted by this decision? Should those factors be added to the analysis?

In other words, the incremental, or special order, is evaluated based on the direct impact it will have on profitability, but the assumptions underlying the use of the approach is that the decision will not lead to a long-term practice of accepting orders from this customer, or any customer, at the specified price or arrangement. Western Soap cannot consistently rent out its soap-making facilities to other companies without eventually losing all of its established customers for finished goods. And if it turns into a facilities rental company, what will happen if its renters change their mind? Incremental business is a short-term decision that can lead to long-term disasters if not carefully monitored and controlled.

For the operating manager faced with a series of daily decisions, differential analysis provides a tool for pushing the limits on expected costs and benefits of new business, provides a forum for discussing current and future business plans, and brings to light discrepancies in current practices that could lead to long-term problems. Knowing what is assumed in making a decision, and what is left out, needs to be carefully spelled out. Everyone has to take an active role in making sure all feasible options are considered and that a realistic estimate of the total costs and benefits of the decision are developed.

Make versus Buy: A Common Decision and Its Impact

Accepting incremental business represents the use of existing capacity; make versus buy decisions affect the company's own products and processes on an ongoing basis. In these settings, the decision is usually triggered by an offer from another firm to produce a component or product at what appears to be a reduced cost to the company. Often the offer will be sweetened with free transportation, free inventory carrying costs, guaranteed quality or delivery levels, and related options.

In approaching this type of decision, management has to identify those costs that will be **avoided** if the outsourcing takes place. Calculating the labor savings alone, which is common practice, is an inappropriate approach. Labor may be freed up if the outsourcing takes place, but will it be laid off? And what about the facilities that are currently used to make the product or component? Can they be redirected to other uses at minimal cost, or will they remain idle, silently eating away at ongoing profits?

These decisions are made on a daily or monthly basis in many large companies, and they are one of the most dangerous, and most often incorrectly performed, calculations undertaken using the FMIS. Why? Because these analyses seldom incorporate all of the real costs of making the change to outsourcing, usually fail to ensure that the "savings" will really be attained (e.g., that the costs are truly avoidable), and often fail to incorporate the qualitative factors, such as quality, timeliness of delivery, and technology transfer concerns, that can create new problems for the company and its management.

In approaching a make-versus-buy analysis, then, the following factors have to be clearly identified.

- What is the quoted price?
- Does it leave out any important costs, such as (1) the expense of providing one of our engineers to help train their workforce; (2) the cost of providing our machinery or material to complete the work; (3) the cost of capital from the extension of our operating cycle; or (4) will it create additional paperwork, incoming inspection, material handling, or related support costs?
- For those resources freed up by the outsourcing, will their costs really be eliminated, or are they simply going to be shifted onto other products or processes?
- If we lose the capability to make this component or product, will it cause any long-term problems in product modifications, new designs, or other demands to emerge downstream?
- If we transfer this technological capability to the vendor, what impact will it have on our competitive capability now and in the future?

This list suggests that this "simple" decision is actually quite complex. How is it normally made? Unfortunately, common practice is to compare the quoted price for the component to the "full cost" of making it internally. The problems with this approach should be evident given the above discussion. First, many hidden costs can be caused by the outsourcing. Usually the quote is approached as if it represents a scenario where the component is delivered, in usable form, to the production line. It ignores incoming inspection, incremental costs in the support group, and all of the related hidden costs noted above.

Second, the "full cost" of the internal operation is *not* the correct number to use. This is a decision calling for differential analysis of *all* projected costs and revenues. A full cost number does not factor in the concept of *avoidable* costs at all; it is usually a very rough calculation of the materials, labor, and some portion of the overhead "glob" that has been assigned to the component. If the labor isn't eliminated or the overhead reduced, the costs won't go away. Instead, a smaller level of internal activity will be made to bear a larger pool of costs with no added value to the customer to justify a price increase to offset this loss. Continuously conducting make-versus-buy analysis with this flawed set of numbers can set up a dynamic that results in the closing of a plant due to excessive "labor rates" (e.g., fully burdened direct labor costs).

Third, this type of decision can have long-term implications as the firm gives away a piece of its productive capability, whether by physically reducing its asset base or by transferring its technology to another company. The future is built on productive capability, not current capacity utilization. Capability given away today can be very costly to repurchase downstream. Technology transfers can lead to irreclaimable long-term losses, as the outside source begins providing competitors with the same "deal" that it has now secured with your firm.

What if the technology, or ability, given away is part of the firm's *core competencies*? The impact of this decision on a company's sustainable competitive advantage could end up being fatal, as the ripple effects to other products made by the company accelerate the losses. The point being made here should be clear: Make-versus-buy analysis is a dangerous and ever-shifting decision process that cannot be done in isolation by a purchasing department intent on attaining its cost reduction goals, or a financial manager concerned with only the numbers. Make-versus-buy analysis, though deceptively simple and often repeated, is a future-constraining decision.

Placing Estimates around Avoidable and Incremental Costs

People who dislike doubt often get into worse trouble by committing themselves to an immature and untenable decision.

Charles Horton Cooley, *Life and the Student* (4)

It is easiest to understand these issues if some numbers are brought to bear. Johnson Electronics is a medium-sized manufacturer of computer systems. One of the critical components used by Johnson is a small printed circuit board. It uses three of these boards in every computer it builds. Planned production for the coming year is 180,000 computers, so that means that 540,000 circuit boards will be needed.

Johnson has made these circuit boards in their own manufacturing plant in the past, but the purchasing manager has just received an inquiry from a Japanese firm offering to begin making the boards for $4.50 each, including materials. Johnson would pay all shipping costs for the boards. Currently, the full cost of making the board is $5.00, consisting of $3.00 in materials and $2.00 as a fully burdened labor rate (overhead is 300 percent of labor cost, or $.50 in labor and $1.50 in overhead). This makes it appear that there will be a $.50 reduction in the cost per board if it is outsourced, which translates to a $270,000 decrease in Johnson's costs. It looks like an opportunity that is too good to pass up. Or is it?

The purchasing manager contacts Sally Rogers, plant controller, to discuss the opportunity. Sally agrees that the quoted price sounds like an excellent cost reduction opportunity, but is curious about several of the details. After detailed discussions with the plant manager and other operating managers throughout the company, it becomes apparent to Sally that the $5.00 is not the appropriate number to use to reflect avoidable internal costs, and the $4.50 leaves out a lot of costs the outsourcing will cause. With these facts in mind, Sally decides to determine what costs will be caused by the outsourcing, and what real costs will be avoided if the internal production of circuit boards is discontinued.

Johnson Electronics
Proposal to Purchase Circuit Board
Incremental Indirect Costs

Engineering support: Trips to vendor site (12 at $5000 each; $60,000); one "engineer equivalent" at $70,000 per year; other engineering costs: $15,000 per year.

Purchasing: Trips to vendor (12 at $5000 each); one half-time purchasing agent at $40,000/year; additional administration: $25,000 per year.

Shipping: Boards are F.O.B. Japan. Estimate $.10/board shipping.

Incoming inspection: Two full-time employees: $28,800 per year total additional salaries.

Projected rework labor: Two full-time employees: $38,400 per year.

Inventory carrying cost: 15% estimated cost of capital on an average daily inventory of an incremental 90,000 boards at $4.50/board cost = $60,750/year.

If the production is moved out of the main plant, there are obviously some costs that will be avoided. These are estimated to be all direct materials, 33 percent of the overhead currently charged to the product (33% of $1.50, or $.50), and 40 percent of the direct labor currently dedicated to making the circuit boards (40% of $.50, or $.20), or a total of $3.70 in cost ($3.00 + $.50 + $.20 = $3.70). According to the plant manager, the other direct labor people will be used on other products. There will be no foreseeable reduction in other plant support costs (e.g., fixed overhead), supervision costs, or machining. So, while the volume of boards made in the plant may be reduced, only $3.70 of the cost they are currently covering will be avoided. The remaining $1.30 of the current board's cost will still be incurred, bringing the final estimate of the actual cost of the purchase option to $6.63 ($5.33 + $1.30), as shown here:

Johnson Electronics Proposal to Purchase Circuit Board "All-in" Board Cost Analyis	
Quoted price per board	$4.50
Engineering support ($60,000 + $70,000 + $15,000) divided by 540,000 boards	.27
Purchasing support ($60,000 + $40,000 + $25,000) divided by 540,000 boards	.23
Shipping	.10
Incoming inspection ($28,800/540,000 boards)	.05
Planned rework ($38,400/540,000 boards)	.07
Carrying cost ($60,750/540,000 boards)	.11
Estimated incremental cost per board	$5.33
Nonavoidable costs	1.30
Total "all-in" purchased board cost	$6.63

The "all-in" board cost summary report indicates that continuing to make the board is the best alternative available to Johnson Electronics. Using information provided by various managers around the company, Sally was able to determine that additional inspection would be caused by the outsourcing, that the direct labor costs would be only partially eliminated, and a series of other key facts, all leading to a much different decision than the "facts" might originally have suggested.

In many companies this analysis would have led to outsourcing. Why? Because the incremental creep in the cost of other products, and long-term problems that are likely to be created by the decision, are often ignored. When all of the costs caused by the two alternatives were recognized by the company, it was clear that outsourcing would actually increase total costs, not decrease them.

Expanding the decision analysis in this manner is logical and not very difficult, yet it is seldom undertaken. Why? It would be easy to argue that it is because the numbers aren't easily obtained, but that would be only part of the story. What really undermines the development of comprehensive analysis in situations such as these is the fact that the individuals responsible (and thus rewarded) for price "savings" are often detached from the FMIS and the operating environment. The very presence of a "purchase price variance" account, and its use to reward purchasing, can lead to outsourcing that actually increases rather than decreases total cost.

To correctly analyze these types of decisions, all of the affected resources have to be identified, costs attached to them, and the harsh realities of what costs will really be avoided faced. It doesn't make good business sense to give away production that is actually being done cheaper inside than it can be done outside, but if many of the costs that go into the analysis are hidden from view or ignored, then these types of problems can occur. Only one fact can be relied on in every situation: The *full cost* estimate used to value inventory for external reporting is *not* the right number to use.

EXPANDING THE LENS: DECISIONS THAT AFFECT MULTIPLE TIME PERIODS

It is a cheap generosity which promises the future in compensation for the present.

J. A. Spender, *The Comments of Bagshot* (4)

Before leaving the concept of short-termed decisions, it is important to recognize that many of these proposals actually have impact over multiple periods. These costs and benefits may simply repeat period after period, but many of them, if carefully analyzed, may be different each period. It is always important to analyze *when* the various cash inflows and outflows associated with a decision are going to occur, as well as what their potential magnitude will be. To do this, the financial manager employs a special tool, called **discounted cash flow analysis,** that factors in the time value of money for decisions that span more than one-period. What are the issues in these multiperiod settings?

Attributable Costs and the Decision Process

Some "short-term" decisions actually affect long-term operations. Chief among these are decisions made to add or drop a product line, customer segment, develop a new product or redesign a process. These decisions span more than one period; they are usually discussed in conjunction with make-versus-buy and related decisions because they use the same basic technique to develop the cash flow estimates that drive the analysis.

The concept of "differential" cost is as applicable to multi-period problems as to one-period ones, but a new term is used to capture the avoidable nature of some of the costs affected by the decision: **attributable cost.** Attributable costs are those that will go away, in time, if a decision is made to discontinue a product, segment, or division. It captures the fact that these costs may be eliminated over a lengthy period of time, rather than all at once. When combined with the fact that the underlying cash flows from the costs and revenues in these decision contexts also extend over multiple periods, this redefinition assists the financial manager in properly matching projected inflows and outflows for the alternatives being examined.

Factoring in the Time Value of Money

Once the long-term cash inflows and outflows are assigned to the appropriate period, the **present value,** or estimate of the worth of those cash flows in terms of today's dollar, is calculated. The way this is set up is illustrated in Figure 7–1. As can be seen, the objective is to restate the future cash flows to a constant dollar. Each period's present value is an indication of how much money would have to be invested today, at the prescribed interest rate, to yield that cash flow in the future. Present value calculations simply recognize the impact of interest on the decision process in multiperiod contexts.

Reviewing Figure 7–1, it is clear that the farther away in time a cash inflow or outflow occurs, the less value it has to a decision being made today. The discounting factors represented in the table come from the following formula:

$$\frac{1 - (1 + i)^{-n}}{i}$$

FIGURE 7–1
Present Value and Project Analysis

Western Soap Company is continually receiving inquiries about available capacity. Since it recently rented out one of its soap lines on an ongoing basis, it has been having to turn a lot of this business down. Faced with a high class problem, the CFO, Fran Gammell, has decided to explore the possibility of adding another line. Two companies have quoted on systems, each having different startup costs and run capabilities (e.g., speed and capacity). Fran feels a good return, or cost of capital percentage, is 15% for this type of investment. The breakout of the two alternatives is:

Year	Cash flow line A	PV_f	PV_A	Cash flow line B	PV_f	PV_B
0	($350,000)	1.00	($350,000)	($450,000)	1.00	($450,000)
1	75,000	.870	65,250	100,000	.870	87,000
2	125,000	.756	94,500	150,000	.756	113,400
3	150,000	.658	98,700	200,000	.658	131,600
4	150,000	.567	85,050	200,000	.567	113,400
5	200,000*	.507	101,400	250,000*	.507	126,750
Totals	$350,000		$ 94,900	$450,000		$122,150

Based on these calculations, Fran decides to purchase the second line. Although it has a higher initial cost, it will yield an additional $27,250 in incremental cash flows over its lifetime than its less expensive competitor.

NPV_f = The net present value factor, or discounting rate, that will make a dollar in the future equivalent to a dollar today.
NPV_A = The net present value of the projected stream of cash inflows. It is derived by multiplying the net cash flows by the present value factor.
*The final year's cash flows include the projected salvage value of the assets.
**In making a decision in a present value framework, the project with the highest *net present value* (total of the present value column) is the one chosen, given everything else is equal.

---

where i = the interest rate and n = the number of periods the discounting process actually occurs. If you look at the formula, you can see that it reflects the fact that an implicit interest is earned on every dollar invested in an asset. Another way to think about the net present value (NPV) of an investment is

$$NPV = \frac{F}{(1 + i)^n} - \frac{I}{I}$$

Or, the sum of all the discounted [future value divided by (1 + interest rate) over the number of periods of interest], less the initial investment.

This calculation is easily done with most calculators. In addition, the **discounting factors** that are developed from this formula can be found in tables that make the application of the present value calculations straightforward. Whenever possible, the discounted cash flow approach should be used; it provides a more accurate view of the costs and benefits of a project, allowing multiple opportunities to be analyzed on an equivalent basis.

This is very cursory examination of present value concepts. The objective is not to detail all the major characteristics and considerations that go into its use, but rather to illustrate the basic concepts and provide the basis for understanding how decisions that affect multiple periods differ from those that have a one-period impact. If present value concepts are not incorporated into the analysis, it is difficult to compare different alternatives that affect multiple periods. On the other hand, it is always important to remember that present value concepts are built from a broad range of assumptions and estimates. Cash flow estimates made for a period five years from now are probably less reliable than those made for next week or next year. NPV is one more tool to use in conducting a comprehensive analysis of short-term decisions.

Risk, Short-Term Decisions, and Other Considerations

Throughout this chapter a range of short-term decisions, the issues that have to be addressed in making them, and the key financial methods used to develop the analysis have been presented. In each case, one theme has remained constant: The financial analysis is only the starting point in making a decision. Obviously, if the numbers don't bear out further consideration of an alternative, the analysis can be discontinued at that point, but positive cash flows do not necessarily translate to good decisions.

One of the hardest things to factor into decision analysis is the concept of risk. Many different calculations, such as **expected value,** can be done to provide some insight into how uncertainty about the cash flow estimates affects the analysis, but in the long run, judgment is required. No matter how thoroughly numbers are developed, they cannot incorporate everything that needs to be considered before the decision is made. Strategic factors, precedence, internal concerns, "gut feelings," history, and a range of other behavioral concerns color the decision process in organizations, moving them far afield from the rational process described in most books on the topic.

When all is said and done, numbers can make a decision look more rational, ease a bit of anxiety about the judgments being made, and perhaps even eliminate some alternatives on the solid facts alone, but they cannot be relied on as the sole criterion in decision making. Management's objective is usually clear: Generate the activities needed to support long-term sustainable advantage through increased profitability, reduced cost, and improved operations. What is important to keep in mind is that the numbers are not the whole story, but they should not be ignored. Otherwise, decisions may continue to follow flawed patterns, being made because "we've always done it that way."

For the practicing manager, the impact of the organization's culture and history on the range of feasible decisions is no secret. When that individual's own career aspirations are built into the process, it becomes clear that these very rational short-term decisions may not always be made in such a clear-cut and defensible manner. A special order may be taken because it will help a special customer, who just happens to be related to the CEO. A proposal will be passed because the top manager really likes the idea and is willing to place the company's money where his interests are. And many a project that has outlived its usefulness is continued because no one wants to take the risk of being fired by pointing out that the "Emperor has no clothes."

THE WHYS . . . AND WHO CARES?

It is easy to shrug off information, to back away from controversial decisions, and to continue playing the corporate game using traditional rules. Unfortunately, what is easy can often lead to fatal strategic errors—cumulative problems that eat away at profits, slowly sinking the firm. The material in this chapter has been focused on the different issues surrounding short-term decisions and the need to factor long-term concerns and qualitative issues into the decision process.

Every manager in an organization can and should play a role in generating alternatives for problems as they occur, raising issues and concerns about a "great" piece of incremental business, and assessing long-term implications of a course of action. Even if a decision is being made higher in the organization, the input of everyone who could shed light on key issues and concerns needs to be gathered. The reason is clear. Short-term decisions cumulate, creating long-term patterns and ways of thinking that can lead to deteriorating performance and lost profitability. They are not decisions to be made lightly, or by one functional area. The long-term, after all, is made up of many short-term events.

World-Class performance is built on daily decisions, made using numbers that reflect long-term strategic concerns. Sustainable competitive advantage is not a buzzword, or a grand ideal never to be reached. It comes from having a clear view of where advantage lies, and then crafting short-term decisions to support the attainment of long-term goals. Making minor changes in daily operating procedures, implementing JIT manufacturing, redesigning process flows, and analyzing make-versus-buy opportunities have one thing in common: They require a clear understanding of the concepts that surround the application of numbers to short-term decisions. They must embody the notion of *different costs for different purposes*.

Each short-term decision has to incorporate immediate and long-range concerns, reflect the firm's overall strategy, and model in both quantitative and qualitative factors. If a JIT cell is being planned based on cost savings from eliminating inspection, rework, or some other activity (and hence, resources), in the manufacturing process, these assumably *avoidable* costs have to be removed. If faulty assumptions are allowed to shape short-term decisions, everyone loses. Understanding the issues and approaches to short-term decisions applies to every manager in every type of organization—high tech, low tech, service, manufacturing. Making sure sound decisions are arrived at is everyone's responsibility.

Decision making in organizations is a very human art that, if done well, can lead to competitive success; if done poorly over extended periods, it can lead to disaster. What has been suggested throughout these pages is that numbers can at least provide a common language for discussing the options available to the company, can attempt to factor in many of the intangibles that give management that queasy gut feeling, and they can help identify alternatives that may sound good on the first pass but have undesirable long-term consequences. The key is to make sure that the very best financial estimates possible are used, that every resource affected is honestly reviewed for the impact the decision may have on it, and that history not be allowed to rule the day.

> *Rational decisions do not always provide a good basis for appropriate and successful action. . . . Making a decision means accepting responsibility for the performance of the action and for its appropriateness.*
>
> Nils Brunsson, *The Irrational Organization*

SUGGESTED READINGS

Brunsson, Nils. *The Irrational Organization*. New York: Wiley, 1985.

Curtis, Donald. *Management Rediscovered: How Companies Can Escape the Numbers Trap*. Homewood, Ill.: Business One Irwin, 1990.

Fess, P., and C. Warren. *Accounting Principles*. 16th ed. Cincinnati, Ohio: SouthWestern, 1990.

Shillinglaw, G., and P. Meyer. *Accounting: A Management Approach*. Homewood, Ill.: Richard D. Irwin, 1986.

Weston, J., and E. Brigham. *Managerial Finance*. Hinsdale, Ill.: The Dryden Press, 1981. There are newer versions of this book available.

PART THREE

PUTTING NUMBERS TO WORK TO CREATE LONG-TERM VALUE

CHAPTER 8

NUMBERS TO SUPPORT VALUE CREATION: THE CUSTOMER PERSPECTIVE

It is not enough to be busy; so are the ants. The question is: What are we busy about?

Henry David Thoreau (2)

Keeping an eye on customer expectations, and delivering products and services that meet them, is the focus of emerging management practices in every business discipline. To meet these needs effectively, efficiently, and consistently is the challenge that underlies this upsurge in focus on the customer as the central point in designing and managing a company. Value is delivered through the coordinated efforts of individuals scattered across the organization, performing a diverse set of activities, on both an ongoing and an ad hoc basis. Each customer-defined value chain consumes its own unique set of resources and shares in the use of common resources.

Meeting and exceeding customer demands is based on a sound understanding of existing resource capabilities, how these resources are currently being used, and what the approximate cost is of delivering a complete, and unique, **product-service bundle** to a customer. The knowledge needed to make these assessments has not always been available in the FMIS. This shortfall, though, was not due to lack of ability but to lack of demand. When the corporate playing field was redefined by global competition and the adoption of *systemic* (interdependent or linked) management techniques, such as just-in-time manufacturing, the core assumptions about what needed to be measured, when, and how were radically altered.

The structure of the traditional FMIS is being revamped. This process, called **activity-based cost management system** (ACMS), is gathering momentum; it has gone from an interesting tool to the engine driving the restructuring of the FMIS and financial management. Not every company is finding activity accounting to be the answer to its needs, but examining this technique triggers productive discussions about what type of information is needed to effectively manage ongoing and strategic activities. No matter what name describes these systems in the future, one fact is clear: Traditional FMIS structures and practices must be modified if they are to support value creation through continuous improvement.

BASIC ACMS CONCEPTS

Accounting systems become rigid when their primary goal is to satisfy GAAP and financial reporting requirements.

Bill Turk, *Handbook of Cost Management*

While ACMS is a more comprehensive concept, most managers are familiar with ABC (activity-based costing). This is probably due to the fact that ABC was used to describe the first wave of FMIS change; it focused on improving the product costing process in companies saddled with archaic direct labor-driven allocation processes. Whatever name is used by an author or consultant to set their approach apart from the pack, the basic building blocks of these refocused systems don't change. What are these common characteristics?

1. The systems focus on activities, or what is actually done in an organization, as their starting point. In doing so, they merge financial and nonfinancial measurement and control systems.

2. Resources consumed by these activities are approximated, creating **cost pools** that match the natural structure of the organization rather than the traditional accounting focus on lines of responsibility and natural expense categories (e.g., direct labor).

3. The cause of these costs, called a **cost driver**, is identified and used to attach the resources consumed to the various activities, products, and services that benefit from them.

4. These **activity-based costs** are bundled together in a **bill of activities** that provides a semidetailed listing of the activities performed within a specific value chain or setting, creating a cost estimate for that value chain.

5. In performing these analyses, *actual costs* or budgeted costs are the starting point, rather than engineered standards.

An activity-based cost management system attempts to match the resources consumed within an organization with their causes. An ACMS thus supports the continuous improvement process:

> Cost drivers are factors that affect subsequent activities; they cause costs to be incurred. The foundation of any continuous improvement process is built on the identification of root causes or sources of a cost. This procedure involves identifying cost drivers to avoid the suboptimal approach of treating a symptom of the cost. Activities highlight the factors that drive cost and indicate where action or change is required.[1]

Developing these cost estimates marries the FMIS with the operating control system; most of the drivers used are actually measurements maintained in these areas. In designing an ACMS, the objective is to mirror the structure of the organization's process flows, or value chains. In achieving this "match" between the FMIS and the organization's structure and processes, the ACMS is able to provide more accurate estimates of the cost of various products and alternative approaches to organizing work. It is also a more adequate basis for decision making, as the costs affected when a decision is made are already visible, or measured, by the system. It is a decision support tool that can easily factor in continuous improvement or other strategic objectives.

ABC AND PRODUCT COSTING

Even a stopped clock is right twice a day.

Anonymous

As the weaknesses of the traditional FMIS surfaced, the resounding cry became, "These numbers are irrelevant!" The key issue discussed as solutions were sought was how to add relevance in a world where even being approximately right was a triumph. It was clearly understood that trying to develop a "true cost" for a product or service is like searching for the Holy Grail: Its existence is unquestioned, its possession unlikely.

---

[1] J. Brimson and M. Burtha, "Activity Accounting," in *Handbook of Cost Management*, ed. Barry Brinker (New York: Warren, Gorham and Lamont, 1991), pp. C1–5.

In reality, the FMIS can only claim to have all the "costs" in the right bucket two times in the life of an organization—when it first opens its doors for business and when those doors finally close for the last time. In between? The FMIS attempts to freeze time (the period close), shuffles reality into definable clusters (the chart of accounts), adjusts the scoreboard if mistakes are found (issue and analyze financial statements), and then blows the whistle for the next round of play. Since *economic value* is an ever-changing, illusory concept, and the FMIS is an approximation of that roiling pot of inputs and outputs, the estimates it produces are unlikely to be precisely correct.

Relevance does not mean that the numbers are precise, but that they are at least reasonable approximations of reality. In simple terms, relevance means usefulness for the designated purpose. If the FMIS is designed to support management decisions, then its relevance is defined by the types of decisions made in that organization. These costed estimates have to be free of bias (point in the right direction), accurate (be at least in the general area of the right number), germane to the common classes of decisions made (focus on the same game plan as the rest of the team), and timely (get there before the game is over).

Relevance comes from accepting the ambiguity of the costing process—the inability of the financial system to track, on a real-time basis, resource value and utilization—and the *uselessness* of any information that arrives after a decision is made. Gaining relevance is the challenge facing the FMIS; it means revamping existing approaches to reflect the strategy, structure, decision-making needs, constraints, and process characteristics unique to each company.

The Building Blocks of Activity-Based Approaches

Knowledge of means without knowledge of ends is animal training.

Everett Dean Martin

One of the most confusing things about the ACMS design process is coming to an understanding of what an *activity* is. It seems pretty straightforward—an activity is what is actually done in the organization. But should this effort, or work, be parceled into large or small bundles? The final answer is always a judgment call. Cost centers are usually larger than an activity; an engineering-based time and motion study that identifies each task performed to complete a job is too small. When the activity measure is too global, the numbers hide as much information as they reveal. When they are defined too low in the organization, the FMIS gets bogged down in pointless levels of detail that add unnecessary complexity to the system, and that draw attention to aspects of the job or activity that simply do not matter that much.

The FMIS has to be flexible to be useful; this flexibility is curtailed when the activity focus is pushed too low in the organization. Consider purchasing. It is usually defined as a cost center within an organization, providing necessary services to support the materials flow, capital asset acquisition, and any other event that requires significant financial outlays by the company. It is obvious that the purchasing group buys goods (its primary mission) but there is a series of activities performed under this umbrella. For instance, purchasing is charged with obtaining and qualifying vendors for the various materials used. This group also expedites orders whenever shortages occur and the materials have not yet arrived. Included among its other activities are placing orders, interfacing with accounts payable, verifying receipt of the goods in usable form, supporting or maintaining the MRP (materials requirement planning) system, and attending forecast and production meetings. These activities are detailed in Figure 8–1, along with a breakdown of the resources that are estimated to be dedicated to each of these activities.

Notice that an activity was not defined as "answering the phone." Answering the phone is a task that is performed for any number of reasons. The phone call may actually serve as a trigger for other types of activities to be performed, but the task of answering it is not a primary feature of the "work" called purchasing. In fact, even if the department was called "Customer Service" instead of purchasing, answering the phone would not be an activity. The activity would be the work, or response, that the phone call would set in motion. The phone call *drives*, or precipitates, the activity that follows. An activity is a bundle of tasks leading to a value-added unit of service or production that can either be provided directly to a customer, or be bundled with other activities to form a complete product-service bundle.

FIGURE 8–1

Activities and Their Resource Demands

		Area Analyzed: PURCHASING			
Activity	Time spent, %	Driver	Frequency	$ Affected	Cost per Occurrence
Process routine orders	15%	# POs	25,000/yr	$37,500	$ 1.50
Process special/ new orders	15%	# POs	250/yr	37,500	150.00
Vendor qualification/ negotiation	10%	# done	25/yr	25,000	1,000.00
Expediting	25%	Various	Daily	62,500	312.50
Acct. payable reconciliation	10%	# POs	25,250/yr	25,000	.99
Verifying receipts	10%	# POs	25,250/yr	25,000	.99
Support MRP	5%	N/A	N/A	12,500	N/A
Meetings	10%	N/A	N/A	25,000	N/A
TOTALS	100%			$250,000	

The bundled set of activities that yields a value-added product or service for the customer is what was identified earlier as a bill of activities. It is a primary component of any activity-based costing system. It aggregates the work that is performed to yield a final product or service, thereby providing a means of costing and analyzing both the content and necessity of each activity. The time required to complete each activity can be added to the analysis, supporting process-flow improvements and related analytics. In general, a bill of activities is a complete routing of the company's response to a customer request for a product-service bundle. It is comparable to a bill of materials, reflecting the flow of the conversion process from the moment an order is received until a satisfied customer provides payment.

What is interesting about this approach to the FMIS, in addition to the fact that the financial system mirrors the horizontal value chains that comprise the organization, is that the financial and operational managers begin talking the same language, focusing on the same problems, and dealing with comparable numbers and performance statistics. The closeness of these two systems is the measuring stick for determining the efficacy of the activity-based FMIS. The two systems are brought together through the identification of activities and the choice of drivers used as the trigger, or signal, that a unit of work has been set in motion.

Most of the literature in this area denotes drivers as the **cause of cost**. In reality, they are the trigger points for the activities that then consume resources, which become part of the costs of meeting customer expectations. The underlying cause may be difficult to identify, but the operational **proxy**, or the measurable event that puts in motion the tasks leading to the completion of the activity, is usually part of the ongoing measurements in the operational control system. In many cases, a good driver turns out to be a piece of paper that is passed along to track the progress of an order. For instance, the driver of logistics costs is the decision to move material, but what can be seen and touched are the move tickets attached to a pallet designating its next location. Each move ticket is a countable proxy for the activity "moving materials." The tickets are much easier to count than the actual movements.

Mapping, or performing a process analysis on, the flow of the product through the system is a valuable way to get a handle on many of the activities performed, as suggested in Figure 8–2. It is a powerful tool, and is particularly useful if the customer's use of the product is included. Formally incorporating the customer's view helps identify value-added activities (those that help meet customer needs) and the less desirable non-value-added ones (those the customer will not pay for). Improvements are often easy to make once the flow of goods and services through the company is clearly detailed.

As can be seen, a defined sequence of events occurs—including moving materials, setting up machines, and initiating the order itself—that all factor into shipping the goods to the customer on time, in the right amount, and at an acceptable level of quality. Some of these activities are part of a traditional costing system, but many are not. Many of the noted activities are buried somewhere in an overhead pool, being charged indiscriminately both to products that benefit from them and products that don't.

The fine points of constructing an activity-based FMIS would fill a book. The list of suggested readings at the end of the chapter provides a starting point for understanding the subtleties of designing and using these systems. It is more important at this stage to look at why companies are using these systems.

FIGURE 8–2
A Typical Process Flow

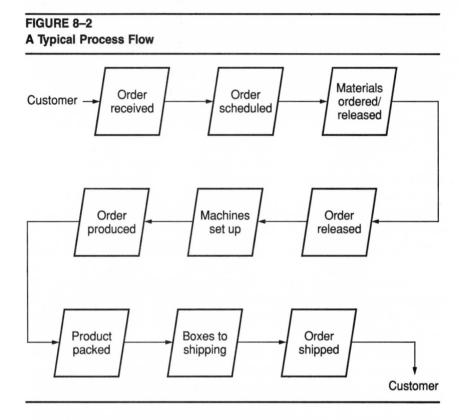

Revising Costs and Correcting Mistakes

ABC was the first attempt made by financial managers to add relevance to the FMIS. Focused on product costing, its objective was to break down the **overhead pool** of the company into chunks that more clearly reflected the type of value those resources provided to the final product. The goal was not to develop better inventory numbers for external reporting, though, but to provide a more realistic estimate of a product's contribution to the overall profitability of the company. Products that caused excessive costs (in other words, cost more to provide to the customer than the customer was willing to pay for them) were highlighted in this analysis. The focal point was not merely attaching costs to products, but costs to causes; inserting this buffer between the product and indirect costs provided a mechanism for querying the value-adding nature of the work being done, rather than solely focusing on reported profits under a full-cost accounting system.

In the earliest stages, these systems focused solely on manufacturing costs, as suggested by the following list, or hierarchy, of activities detailed by Robin Cooper, one of the strongest proponents in this area:

1. *Unit-level* activities, which are performed each time a unit is produced
2. *Batch-level* activities, which are performed each time a batch of goods is produced
3. *Product-sustaining* activities, which are performed as needed to support the production of each different type of product
4. *Facility-sustaining* activities, which support a facility's general manufacturing process[2]

As can be seen, each of these activity clusters takes place on the plant floor. This fact led many companies and financial managers to ignore the ABC message simply because they didn't manufacture a product. This was an early misstep that is currently being righted as it becomes clear that the technique is actually of more value for the service side of a manufacturing business (or any other white-collar type of setting, including a pure service company) than it is for a traditional manufacturing setting. But what was done with ABC, and what benefits were obtained?[3]

---

[2] Robin Cooper, "Activity-Based Costing for Improved Product Costing," in *Handbook of Cost Management,* ed. Barry Brinker (New York: Warren, Gorham and Lamont, 1991), pp. B1–3. Much of this work was developed in tandem with Professor Robert Kaplan of the Harvard Business School.

[3] Surveys conducted by the Manufacturing Roundtable at Boston University suggest that ABC is one of the most disappointing modern management tools. Many of the reasons for these problems lie in the hype that went along with early implementations, and the fact that most of these initial systems were built from the general ledger, simply providing new ways of allocating the same poorly understood costs. A tremendous debt is owed to individuals like Robert Kaplan and Robin Cooper for getting this change process underway; it is time to move beyond these early systems. Given that the costs of building new data collection systems are not trivial, these projects have to be carefully planned with one overriding concern in mind: will this system provide the type of information needed to make sound decisions on an ongoing basis? If an FMIS doesn't support internal decision making, it has little value for operating managers.

The key message delivered by the ABC models is that direct labor-based overhead allocations can distort costs unless direct labor is the *major* cost incurred by a company. As the technological intensity of companies has escalated, the focus on direct labor continues to make less and less sense. This unfocused approach to product costing becomes especially troubling when its impact is realized: Labor-intensive jobs are absorbing the cost of new technology while utilizing little, if any, of these assets' capacity. This cross-charging of costs has created a recurring phenomenon in companies across the country: Labor-intensive jobs have become the "dogs" of the product line, to be outsourced or discontinued whenever possible, while technology-intensive products continue to be touted as the sweethearts of the company because of *perceived* high levels of profitability.

When the ABC process is applied in these companies, a more realistic picture of product profitability emerges: Many technology-intensive products begin to look quite unappealing as they are assigned the costs they actually cause. The long-pondered question, "Why do we always win the bids for the complicated jobs and lose them on the simple ones?" finally has an answer, it seems: The costing process is distorting the numbers. Fixing the FMIS at this preliminary level does help companies stem the flood of activity out of their plants. In fact, Lifeline Systems in Cambridge, Massachusetts, has actually brought production back from the Far East to its Boston plant based on an ABC-based analysis of the underlying economics of the outsourcing process.

ABC for product costing is still being implemented at companies, following the model detailed in Figure 8–3. Unfortunately, its focus on manufacturing overhead alone, and its failure to pick up the entire horizontal value chain from the customer's perspective, is proving to be a weakness. Activity-based product costing, if solely focused on the plant floor, cannot answer the hard questions surrounding the effective utilization of the company's less tangible assets (e.g., its management group). It is, though, a good starting point for understanding how distorted product cost estimates can lead to market disaster.

The information for creating an ACMS starts with understanding the daily routines of doing business: the horizontal linkages of individuals all focused on creating value for the customer (implicitly, at least). This information cannot be found in a book, nor does a financial manager automatically receive a magic wand when gaining

FIGURE 8–3
Typical Structure of an ABC System

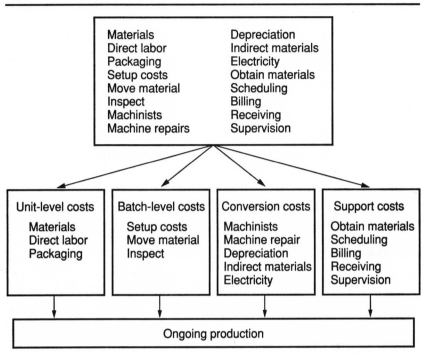

a professional certification (CMA or CPA). It is knowledge resident in the workforce itself. An ACMS is built by the individuals inside the organization, is designed to meet their decision-making needs, and is revised whenever it fails to deliver on a timely basis. Unlike traditional financial systems, an ACMS is built by and for its customer: the individuals who populate the corporation.

What this translates to in practice is the very real need for everyone to be actively involved when an ACMS is designed, as well as to take responsibility for reporting its shortcomings and suggesting potential improvements that will help it meet its customer's expectations in a more reliable, relevant manner. It is an information system that should make sense to the individuals down in the trenches of the organization, whether in productive or service areas. It is *not* a top-management tool; an ACMS is an internal information system that has to make sense to its users and reflect their needs.

The ACMS has to reflect the objectives of the company and the changing nature of the work performed throughout the value chain. When a company dedicates itself to the philosophy of continuous improvement, it cannot continue to use an FMIS built around a goal of *meeting the stated standard* (i.e., traditional, or standard, costing). If the technologies used to make a product or deliver a service are changed, the FMIS has to incorporate these new characteristics, starting with a new process analysis and continuing on through the development of new cost pools and drivers. If a different strategic objective is adopted, the numbers have to be recast to provide realistic, accurate, relevant, and timely information that can support the attainment of these goals (if they continue to make sense given ongoing results). An ACMS consists of a changeable mix of numbers and measures designed to fit the fluid organizations it serves.

Expanding the View: Accounting for the Black Hole

The art of progress is to preserve order amid change and to preserve change amid order.

Alfred North Whitehead (2)

When the techniques inherent in ABC systems began to be mastered, it became clear that opportunities for improvement were to be found throughout the company. Realizing that value was not only added on the plant floor, companies began to look for ways to capture the value created in that mystical world of the white-collar worker, an area that had become the "black hole" in the annual profit plan. Under the banner of activity-based cost management, these expanded approaches to revising the FMIS began to focus on customer-driven costs.

Value creation is the most important concept being discussed in the management literature today. As defined by the customer, value is that bit of "extra" beyond the physical material or movements in a product or service that makes it worthwhile. Value creation is not confined to the plant floor, though. Every individual in the organization should be supporting the value-creation process for the customer. Even if tying a support group to the customer requires an immense leap of faith, it isn't hard to understand how failures in a support group's activities can lead to customer dissatisfaction.

Activities that do not support customer needs, now or in the future, are non-value-adding. No customer will ever be willing to pay for them; their cost has to be covered out of allowable profits. Activities that cause dissatisfaction are service, or value-creation, *failures* that create excess costs (noncomformance costs) and inhibit the overall ability of the company to meet customer expectations. If a customer is only willing to pay for value creation, it is critical for a company to understand how its current activities measure up against this exacting standard.

The underlying logic for designing an ACMS differs very little from its predecessor, ABC, so the challenge lies in actually developing useful cost estimates that everyone can buy into, without creating a monstrous record-keeping system in the process. In fact, tackling white-collar productivity measurement is part and parcel of the design process. Whereas the ABC system can build on existing measurements (drivers), the ACMS often cannot. This is because traditionally very little time has been spent finding out what support groups really *do*. They are controlled through a budget negotiated annually to supply a range of services, none of which are totally understood.

It's clear that there is ample room for improvement in this area; if factories were run the way the back office is in most companies, there wouldn't be any company, period. Following procedures that have often outlived their usefulness, pushing paper with no ties to the customers or other departments, the back office often functions more as a bureaucracy that frustrates and thwarts action than as a support group to enhance the efforts of others. There is really no one to blame for this state of affairs; it is the result of years of neglect as everyone focused on keeping the manufacturing process rolling smoothly. In discussions of value creation, the normal approach is to focus on marketing and manufacturing—everyone else simply adds cost to the final product.

In reality, the support services often are a critical element of the value chain. The customer may not directly interface with the purchasing department or accounts payable, but if these functions are handled poorly the customer will be affected. There are very few areas of the company that do not add value to the final customer. That doesn't mean there isn't rampant waste, unnecessary work, and excessive staffing levels in the support areas, but rather that this non-value-adding work is only a part of the total efforts that make up the activity matrix for these groups.

In constructing a customer-driven FMIS, every aspect of the company must be examined. Each individual needs to be asked the basic question, "What do you do and why do you do it?" No matter what part of the company the individual works in, it is important to understand what they are doing, how it does or does not affect the delivery of value to the customer, and what can be done to eliminate the non-value-adding work that is consuming excess resources and hurting profits. A complete value chain incorporates the work completed in the back room as well as that done on the physical product itself.

Customer-Driven Support Costs

As can be seen in Figure 8–4, when a customer focus is taken, the cost hierarchy is expanded to include costs traceable to orders, to customers, to channels, to markets, and to the enterprise in general. This expanded view allows a company to analyze, and estimate the cost of, the activities performed to actually get the product to the customer. What has to be determined in the analysis and design stage for a customer-driven FMIS is how deeply the underlying system should be explored. The figure suggests one driver for fairly major cost centers in the company. This may be an improvement over the existing approach, but it really doesn't help the company focus on areas that need improvement.

If the FMIS is to provide information to support decision making, it has to have an adequate level of detail. It may be enough to note that each shipment costs $150.00 in handling and related activities, but that doesn't give any indication if that number is too big or too small, or where improvements could be made in either the process or the costs of performing these activities. To gain insights into an area, such as shipping, it is often useful to do a **benchmarking** study to establish how other companies are performing this task, and what their apparent costs are. This analysis can help focus attention on areas that need improvement, prioritizing the ongoing efforts of management to enhance the value creation process throughout the organization.

But to support this analysis, the underlying activities that make up the shipping function need to be understood. How many people are used to do what part of the job? Does paperwork unnecessarily

FIGURE 8–4
A Cost Hierarchy

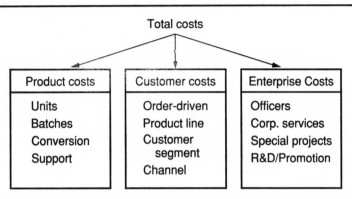

Total costs		
Product costs	**Customer costs**	**Enterprise Costs**
Units	Order-driven	Officers
Batches	Product line	Corp. services
Conversion	Customer	Special projects
Support	segment	R&D/Promotion
	Channel	

burden the group, requiring additional personnel and slowing down the process of moving materials to internal or external customers? Are material handling methods inefficient? Does the area provide maximum value for the dollars of resources it consumes? These questions cannot be answered if the FMIS is focused too high in the activity chain. On at least an annual basis, it is probably a good idea for every individual to detail what they do and why. The best time to do this is when budgets are being prepared; the resources and workload are matched during this period.

Creating Relevance by Predicting the Future

This leads to the final, but perhaps most critical, concept to keep in mind when designing an ACMS addition to, or focus for, the FMIS. These systems consist of a series of **cost estimates**. The estimates can be employed in any number of decison settings and should be verified on at least an annual basis for their correctness, but they are not intimately tied to the general ledger. In fact, the ACMS system, as a reflection of the budget, is only as close to the general ledger structure as the budget itself is. If the budget really doesn't match the ledger, neither will the ACMS. This is perhaps the least understood aspect of these new approaches to financial management: The numbers are estimated costs for future work, not actual costs for completed work. That's why they are relevant—the dollarized estimates are available *before* the decision is made.

ABC estimates are cousins to traditional standard costs, but they are based on the actual process and costs planned by the company, rather than an engineering cost model. Also, the estimates span a much larger arena of action than the engineered standards, including support as well as manufacturing processes. This relationship, while close at times, does not mean that the engineering group can devise an ACMS; unfortunately, engineering appears to be as locked into their costing models as traditional financial managers can be to theirs.

The tools and techniques for developing an ACMS may at times come directly from industrial engineering practice, and at others bear no relationship to them. The process analysis phase, if done through an engineer's eyes, would focus on time-and-motion, or excessively detailed, methods. An effective FMIS does not need this level of detail. An engineer would build waste and down-time factors into the estimates created, establishing a *static* measurement system and a "meet standard" mentality within the firm. An effective FMIS encourages continuous improvement, reflects the level of waste against some theoretically optimum level of operation, and creates the *dynamic* metric critical to the learning organization. The systems are much different in intent, and in the details of their construction and use, from engineering models. As with continuous improvement, designing and using a relevant FMIS requires a change in mindset, not just methods.

NEW APPROACHES TO ONGOING PROBLEMS

Social advance depends as much upon the process through which it is secured as upon the result itself.

Jane Addams (2)

Updating the FMIS to include activity-based concepts provides a company with a set of numbers that can be put to work on traditional, ongoing problems that were often addressed through ad hoc analysis. For instance, when an activity-based FMIS is in use, the make-versus-buy decisions faced by the company can easily be completed in the comprehensive manner suggested in Chapter 7. Many of the activities that are affected in a make-versus-buy scenario are recorded in the activity-based system already; the trick is identifying those that will "go away" (are avoidable) should the outsourcing occur. In addition, though, an activity framework can help the company look at the *new*, or incremental, costs that will accompany the outsourcing process, such as increased shipping and incoming inspection expenses.

A well-known model used in manufacturing, the **economic order quantity** (EOQ) method for managing inventory levels, cannot be completed without many of the estimates that are an integral part of an activity-based FMIS, as underscored by the following formula:

$$Q^* = (2FS/CP)^{0.5}$$

where

$Q^* = $ the optimal order/production quantity

$F = $ the cost of ordering, or setting up the process to make, the good

$S = $ the projected demand for the product per period

$C = $ carrying cost per dollar of inventory held per period

$P = $ the price, or cost, of the product

Perusing the list of information needed suggests that the carrying cost and cost to order the goods are critical elements of the EOQ model, yet neither is reported on an ongoing basis in the FMIS. The carrying cost itself is an enigma—it contains the cost of holding the goods (cost of capital), moving them, throwing some away as obsolescence or damage occurs, and all related costs caused by the decision to inventory products.

Conversely, the cost of ordering a product, whether it be the cost to place an outside order or to communicate and set up the production process to make the good, is not available in a traditional FMIS. To effectively use this model for decision making, the operating manager requires activity-based cost estimates. Revising the FMIS to incorporate these estimates is not a game with a limited payoff; it provides vital information for supporting ongoing decision making. If relevant numbers were easier to obtain, these sophisticated decision models might see more use.[4]

---

[4]The EOQ model is well-known and often criticized in the manufacturing literature. By building in such things as an expected, or accepted, cost for carrying inventory, setting up a machine, or related items, it builds in an expectation or tolerance for non-value-adding activities and other forms of waste in much the same manner as the standard costing model does. This has led many experts to discount, perhaps even scorn, this model. Yet it has relevance as long as its assumptions are understood and addressed.

For instance, in a JIT manufacturing setting, the solution of "zero inventories" comes from challenging the belief that set-up time has to be greater than zero (this is the same belief that quick changeover methods challenge) as well as increasing the cost of carrying inventory to a more realistic (or much higher) level. When coupled with the cost of decreased velocity in getting material through the plant, these adjustments drive the optimal order quantity to that required now (the right quantity at the right time and in the right place). Zero inventories are the result of changing the assumptions about how to manufacture; they do not result from an arbitrary decision to eliminate inventories.

Cost of Quality: The Debate

An activity-based FMIS provides a series of numbers that can be useful for ongoing decisions, but its value does not stop there. The information, or set of estimates, contained in the system support a broad number of ad hoc and ongoing reporting capabilities. Cost-of-quality reporting is proving to be one of the most valuable of these. As companies continue to implement total quality management programs, there is a growing recognition of the need to track the economic, as well as operational, improvements being gained.

Cost-of-quality reports usually categorize the various expenditures made by a company to improve or track product quality as conformance and nonconformance costs. The former refers to costs generated by *planned* activities; the latter reflects all the fire-fighting and rescue efforts undertaken when a "handoff" along the value chain is fumbled. These two categories of quality costs are often further divided into the following categories:

1. **Prevention costs:** The expenditures made to build a quality consciousness within the company, or to design quality into the product at inception. Items in this category include TQM training classes, design for manufacturability, vendor certification for zero-defect delivery of materials, and related before-action events.

2. **Detection costs:** Any activity that focuses on isolating defects as they occur, to prevent them from being passed along the value chain. Costs usually included here are off-line inspection, statistical process control costs, and incoming inspection of raw materials.

3. **Internal failure costs:** When a unit has been completed, and is then subjected to a series of tests for functionality, failures can occur. These testing, rejection, rework, and scrap costs are part of the internal failure quality costs for a company.

4. **External failure costs:** If a customer receives faulty merchandise, it is classified as an external failure. These costs are often recorded on an ongoing basis as warranty, field repairs, returns, and replacements. While these are definitely external failure costs, the more important issue is what impact external failures have on future sales. Some companies, such as Polaroid Corporation, are beginning to factor the

market costs of external failure into their cost-of-quality models. It is often the largest cost of all.

These four categories of cost include all the missteps, fumbles, and failures the company experiences in delivering products and services through the value chain. Not all of these costs are incurred on the plant floor; a mistake in accounts receivable is just as critical to the delivery of a complete product-service bundle as one on the plant floor—in fact, maybe more so. The mistakes on the plant floor may not directly affect a customer, but a mistake in accounts receivable quite likely will.

A customer won't forget getting a "pay up or else" phone call from a supplier, especially if they don't deserve it. If this mistake results in the loss of the customer, the downstream costs of back-office mistakes may actually prove to be larger than those made on the plant floor. And if the internal customer is factored into the quality analysis, even more interesting questions arise. For instance, when a schedule change has to be rapidly implemented due to errors in marketing or some other area of the company, is a quality cost generated? Without a doubt. Responding to schedule changes is often a major source of non-value-added work in planning and purchasing groups.

There are obviously grounds for classifying these nonconformance costs as external failures of the department that caused the problem to occur. How many people in a company, when asked, would classify a major portion of their work into the expediting category? If expediting has to occur, it isn't time to award a medal to the people who did the impossible and responded to the emergency; it's time to isolate and eliminate the problems that caused the emergency. Any organization that depends on heroics to save the day can learn a lot from simply recognizing that heroes are needed because a mistake or fumble has occured somewhere else in the company. Some emergencies may be caused by the external customer, but these are often the exception rather than the rule. Many "customer-caused" emergencies are the result of missing customer deadlines or product shortfalls, once again a failure that stems from the company itself.

In designing an activity-based FMIS, the activities that are going to be clustered into the cost-of-quality report should be thought through and built into the system wherever possible. The goal is to create a database of costed activities that fold naturally into a series of reports that support the other improvement efforts taking place inside the firm. As activity clusters are created, it is easy to put a "tag" on that data element that says, "put this in the cost-of-quality report." When it comes time to generate the report, the number of occurrences of each tracked activity, multiplied by the activity-based cost estimate of what that type of activity costs, on average, will yield the cost-of-quality report.

This report can be generated as soon as the **operating details** are known. There's no need to wait for the general ledger closing—which can take two weeks or longer—to get this information. It can be pulled up any time for any period desired and presented on an as-needed basis, because it builds from operating details and financial estimates, not actual costs. This raises the question: What if actual costs for a specific category exceed the activity-based estimate? Obviously, there is a need to signal this event to management, but the reporting takes place on an *exception* basis only. There's no need to generate the report unless there's a major shift in actual costs versus planned expenditures.

Cost-of-quality reports build naturally from an activity-based FMIS. The numbers needed, though, are not readily available in the general ledger. Some accounts can be tracked from the general ledger to a cost-of-quality format, but in reality few of the traditional accounting numbers prove to be readily usable in a quality module. That means that most cost-of-quality reporting is currently being done on an ad hoc basis, with the financial manager actively having to seek out and estimate much of the information that would be readily available in an activity-based system. The benefits, though, do not stop there.

Supporting the Just-in-Time Effort

One of the biggest roadblocks to implementing just-in-time manufacturing often proves to be the FMIS. Specifically, the labor efficiency and volume variances reported in a traditional system give exactly the *opposite* signal about performance effectiveness as the operating system. For example, if a just-in-time process is operating effectively, it will produce only enough units to meet demand, whether that is customer-driven or derived from a calculation of uniform plant load. That may result in lower production levels for a period, and a "volume variance" red flag from the accounting system.

Taking the just-in-time message one step further, it is common knowledge that any mistake found in a product will shut down a just-in-time line. The logic is clear: The system is designed to turn out only good product. Instead of the traditional "run and sort" model of manufacturing, it is a "stop and fix" world. That is better all the way around, as continuing to make a product when there are known defects is a far cry from value-added manufacturing. But when the line stops, so does the accounting "ticker" that absorbs overhead into the product. The absorption process is put on hold while the quality problem is fixed or other adjustments made to the process. Once again, operating managers, doing the "right thing" when total quality is their goal, are at odds with the traditional FMIS.

Another interesting facet of JIT manufacturing is the blurring of direct and indirect labor. The JIT cell is designed to effectively utilize resources for the entire range of activities that have to occur to produce a product or subcomponent. The concepts of "direct" and "indirect" labor become untenable when the operating objective is to have everyone pitch in to keep the cell running. The impact of this objective is simple: Whoever is free at the moment runs to get the materials from the loading dock. Waiting for an indirect laborer to move the raw materials could end up shutting down the line. If a direct laborer has time to spare, he or she will do the indirect task.

Indirect and direct labor categories lose their meaning in a JIT manufacturing setting. Yet the FMIS continues to track these elements. The result? It is likely that a direct labor "efficiency" variance will be generated on an ongoing basis, as individuals rotate through the cells doing what needs to be done. The very strength of JIT manufacturing, the flexibility and reliability of production, can trigger "red flags" in the FMIS. Which signal is correct? If product is getting out on time and in the right quantity, does it really matter who did what, when?

In designing a JIT manufacturing accounting system, the objective is to expand the cost pool to include every individual, activity, and material that is in some way tied to the production of the cell. This **conversion cost pool** is charged out to good units produced by the cell. It's a very simple accounting process; it eliminates detailed direct labor tracking, the endless inventory transactions as materials move through the plant, and the need to develop detailed labor standards for each aspect of the productive process. JIT manufacturing accounting systems, which were developed in the late 1980s, appear to be precursors to the ACMS. The primary driver of costs in the cell are the units made. If no production is needed, the cell does not operate. Simplicity in the production process is mirrored by simplicity in the accounting system, which divides total cost to support a cell by the number of good units produced to obtain the cost per good unit estimate.

The term **backflushing** has become a very popular way to describe the accounting cycle in a JIT setting. The basic concept in this approach is that no accounting transactions are recorded until the finished goods emerge from the cell. At this point, the raw material inventory is checked for the amount of materials used per unit (a standard, or estimate) as well as the value-added, or conversion, cost occuring within the cell. Instead of multiple transactions for each time materials or labor are added during the conversion process, one generic entry is made when a unit is completed. The term *backflushing* reflects the fact that the inventory transactions are recorded when production is done; they lag behind the actual movement of material from raw materials to work in process to finished goods.

In a 1987 study of the types of accounting and performance measurement systems being used by leading JIT manufacturing companies, several interesting facts were uncovered:

- Many companies have begun using rolling averages of historical actual costs as the costing standard. This number, when trended, provides information on whether the cell is achieving its continuous improvement goals.
- Time-based performance measures are a critical element in JIT manufacturing. Cycle time measures (e.g., elapsed time between units coming out of the cell) are used to track improvement, the linearity of production, and to attach costs to units produced when several different products in a product family are manufactured in the same cell.
- Move and queue, previously unmeasured aspects of the process flow, have become clearly recognized as non-value-adding activities and are often assigned their approximate costs.[5]

In other words, companies adopting JIT manufacturing have had to make significant changes in their FMIS to support the cellular concept and the continuous improvement philosophy. When these changes are not made, the effectiveness of the JIT implementation can be drastically impaired, as the conflicting messages from the operating and financial measurement systems muddy the water.

One final point is important to make before leaving the JIT manufacturing concept. In many companies, putting JIT into place has

---

[5]C. McNair, W. Mosconi, and T. Norris, *Meeting the Technology Challenge: Cost Accounting in a JIT Environment* (Montvale, N.J.: National Association of Accountants, 1987).

resulted in drastic reductions in inventory and in the physical space needed for the manufacturing process. Both of these happy events have a downside; vacant floor space is excess capacity. One of the troubling problems in the JIT setting is the fact that the improvements may be easy to see, but unless the resources that have been idled by these gains are eliminated or redeployed for making another product, total costs will not go down. In this situation, the FMIS is giving the right signal. Idle capacity is an expensive waste of productive resources. If the JIT implementation is successful, idle capacity will be created. It is management's job to find new uses for this capacity or to get rid of it; otherwise costs haven't changed. No improvement is noted by the FMIS because no economic benefit has been gained. That is a hard fact for an operating manager to face up to, but a necessary one.

VALUE-ADDED AND THE ACMS

Man's judgments of value follow directly his wishes for happiness — they are an attempt to support his illusions with arguments.

Sigmund Freud (1)

One of the most interesting and yet troubling uses being made of the ACMS system in many companies today is to identify, and put a price tag on, the value added by the firm to its products and services. It is a concept that builds from an understanding that the customer is willing to pay only for products and services that he or she values. Customers look at the company as a black box, as suggested in Figure 8–5. They come in contact with the organization when an order or request for service is placed, and again when the contracted service is completed. In between? The customer could not care less, in most instances, how the company gets to the final product; a customer's concern is focused on the cost, timeliness of delivery, and quality of the good or service. If the company provides this good or service in the desired way, on time, and for the price the customer feels is reasonable, the customer's expectations have been satisfied.

Inside the organizational black box, management plays a resource deployment game. It is a very complex game, requiring the coordinated efforts of individuals throughout the company. As the order flows horizontally across the organization, moving from one functional area to the next, value is added. This value, though, seldom equals the cost that is recorded in the FMIS. Because many of the tasks or activities performed are nonessential in the customer's eyes (e.g., a

FIGURE 8–5
A Customer's Viewpoint

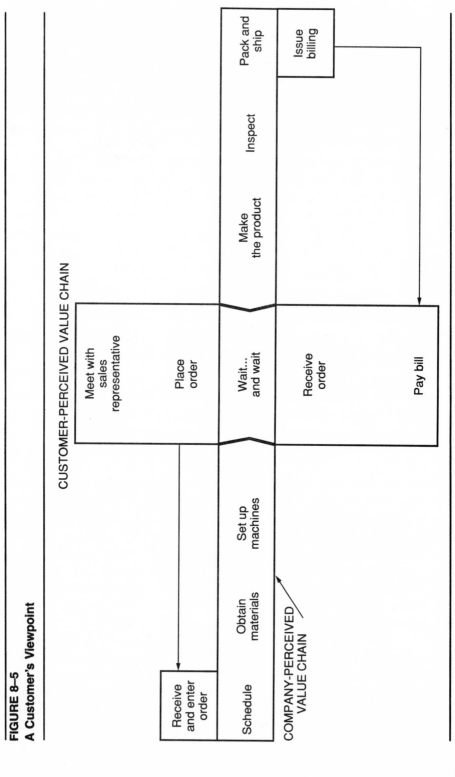

customer is seldom willing to pay for scrap and rework), they don't add value to the final good or service; instead, they increase its cost.

In designing an activity-based FMIS, it is often helpful to map out the process flow for the good or service. This flow includes every activity or task performed from the time the order is received until it is deemed acceptable by the customer. By definition, many of these tasks will be service or support based. For instance, if order entry doesn't complete its tasks, the customer's expectations are unlikely to be met. These costs are recorded in the overhead account in a traditional FMIS, yet they can be directly tied to the value chain. If an activity is a necessary part of meeting customer expectations, it doesn't really matter whether it is paper, people, or machine based in nature: Value is added when customer needs are met efficiently and effectively.

Assessing Value Creation—Potential versus Actual

Waste is present in every organization. Those that excel in the marketplace, though, find ways to trim this waste to its minimum. That is what sets Japanese organizations apart from their Western counterparts: Waste is present, but it is not an accepted part of doing business. The continuous improvement philosophy reflects the Japanese intolerance for imperfection. It has become more than a cultural phenomenon, though; it has become a source of competitive advantage.

In a perfect world, plants would run at theoretical capacity, every company would be operating at "six sigma" quality levels, and responsive service channels would be the norm rather than the exception. Given that few individuals or companies have reached this stage of perfection, how can they assess their relative performance against their World-Class competitors?

Several approaches are currently in use. The first, developed by Computer-Aided Manufacturing International (CAM-I), focuses on measuring the **manufacturing cycle efficiency** (MCE), or the effectiveness of current capacity utilization.[6] The structure of the formula is

$$MCE = \frac{\text{Processing time}}{\text{Processing time} + \text{Inspection time} + \text{Wait time} + \text{Move time}}$$

---

[6]C. Berliner and J. Brimson, eds., *Cost Management for Today's Advanced Manufacturing: The CAM-I Conceptual Design* (Cambridge, Mass.: Harvard Business School Press, 1988), pp. 4–5.

This measurement captures the value-added time in manufacturing as a percentage of the total throughput time for that item. Few customers place value on moving, queueing, or inspecting activities. These activities add cost but no value, and in fact impair the firm's ability to meet customer expectations on the cost and responsiveness dimension.

This same type of measurement can be developed for service, or support, areas of a company. For instance, when an activity analysis is performed for an individual or small group in an area, the activities can be segmented into value-adding versus non-value-adding segments quite easily. How? By looking at the listed activities with a critical eye and a simple question: Would the customer be willing to pay for this?

For instance, most managers spend at least 15 percent of their time in meetings. Is this a value-adding activity? While meetings can be value-adding, especially in an era of increasing reliance on team-based decision making, it is hard to dispute the fact that many ongoing meetings are difficult to justify if "value" is the metric used. Are they part of the organizational "dance" that keeps products flowing smoothly through the facility? Rarely. They are, for the most part, firefighting events or rationalization mechanisms. These are not value-adding activities.

Once all of the organization's activities have been identified, the total percentage of time spent on value-adding activities versus the total time available yields a support efficiency measure comparable to the MCE for manufacturing. Are you likely to be able to get this information? It depends on the game management is perceived to be playing. If everyone believes that the objective behind the question is a simple effort to improve processes, thereby providing higher service levels to the customer, the information can probably be obtained. On the other hand, if employees believe that the underlying objective is to identify slackards, eliminate jobs, or pin the blame on someone for recurring problems, cooperation will be feigned at best, nonexistent at worst.

This example underscores the most important factor to keep in mind when applying value-added concepts. Management's intent, or the *use* made of information, will affect attitudes, motivation, and the reliability of the data. Value-added measurements, if focused on improving the process, are useful tools for identifying and prioritizing areas of opportunity. If, instead, the information is used as a hammer, or as a device for controlling or punishing *individuals*, the outcome of using value-added metrics may be the destruction of trust in the organization. The message here is simple: Measurement takes place within a social system. The behavior of individuals makes or breaks an organization. If this fact is forgotten, even briefly, assessing value-added can become a destructive exercise.

An activity-based FMIS provides a company with the means to approximate the manufacturing- and non-manufacturing-based value added within the company. This is a tremendous improvement on prior approaches to the age-old problem inherent in trying to establish white-collar productivity measures. Yet, many companies have opted for focusing solely on manfacturing costs when discussing the value added in the firm. In some cases, marketing gets bundled into the analysis, because their role in generating sales is easy to see. It is rare for a company to attempt to assess the value created in the support areas.

In focusing on the complete value chain, the activity-based FMIS expands value creation to include services if they are critical elements in meeting customer expectations. And if these areas generate excessive delays or errors, that is also important to know. For the customer, a day lost in production is no different than a day's delay due to order entry. Both affect the final value of the product-service bundle.

Value-Added and the Service Sector

Many managers active in the service sector tend to ignore activity-based financial systems because many of the early implementations took place in a manufacturing setting. This is unfortunate, because the ACMS techniques are most valuable when the questions revolve around service levels. The "black hole" of overhead for a manufacturing company is often the entire cost structure for a service-related firm.

White-collar productivity, or the assessment of the value created by individuals outside of the manufacturing plant, is a key element of the measures and analysis completed when an ACMS is designed and implemented. Many companies are finding that they are actually beginning to come to some sort of understanding about the capacity of their support/service resources, the impact of process improvements on these areas, and how to control overhead creep through activity analysis. An activity-based FMIS clearly identifies value creation wherever it occurs, whether it can be directly tied to the product-service bundle or not.

A service-oriented company can benefit from the ACMS concepts. As it becomes clear that the value chain in a service organization is as rich, and as subject to measurement and evaluation, as the activities on a manufacturing plant floor, it is likely that greater numbers of service companies will implement the approach. Several large banks, railroads, and health care facilities have already put the systems in place. They are using the activity-based FMIS because it provides vital information about the effectiveness of the service delivery system, its relative cost, and the profitability of various types of services. Value is created any time a customer is willing to pay more for a good or service than the raw materials, labor, or capital required to produce them. That process is not restricted to the "clunk and chunk" manufacturing world.

REDEFINING THE PLAYING FIELD: FINAL NOTES

To err is human, but when the eraser wears out ahead of the pencil, you're overdoing it.

J. Jenkins (1)

The humor in the above quotation is all the more potent because it is so true. Much of what we do in life is a series of missteps, followed by erasures that obscure but do not eliminate the problem. Redefining the FMIS to reflect a customer perspective will involve errors, false starts, and frustration. Many of the changes are so subtle that they appear, at first glance, to be simply "old wine in new bottles."

Taking this stance could prove to be fatal, not just for the profession but for the economy. Many of the core assumptions that underpin existing FMIS techniques subtly but effectively shield important facts and dangerous trends from view. The power contained in a set of numbers that appears to be objective, that bears the weighty mantle of tradition and disclosure demands, and that surrounds itself in a shroud of mystery through arcane calculations understood only by the "anointed," is too real to ignore. As suggested by Anthony Hopwood of the London School of Economics, *accounting shapes reality.*[7] In

---

[7]Anthony Hopwood is one of the most influential and respected accounting scholars. Considering himself an observer of accounting rather than an accountant, he has spent his career illustrating, and supporting efforts to prove, that the hidden power of the accounting model can dramatically impact an individual's perceptions of what is and is not important in an organization. Many of his thoughts are detailed in the journal *Accounting, Organizations and Society,* published by Pergamon Press. His major works are summarized in *Accounting from the Outside: The Collected Papers of Anthony G. Hopwood,* New York: Garland Publishing, 1988.

the numbers that it records, the activities it highlights, and the activities and outcomes it ignores, the FMIS defines the organizational web in which action occurs. This may seem an overly philosophical view of numbers in organizations, but time and again the popular press decries the very same facts. Western management is heavily focused on "the numbers" to direct action, decisions, and strategies. If those numbers are biased, so are the decisions based on them.

The major advantage of redefining the FMIS to incorporate activity-based concepts may flow not only from the fact that more events are made visible, but also from removing the mystery from the accounting process. The flexibility and dynamics of an activity-based FMIS removes the myth of objectivity from the numbers. If anyone can use the numbers, if anyone can see how changing assumptions about the decision or process affects the bottom line, the information is no longer as powerful.

It may seem odd, then, to note that these less power-laden versions of economic "reality" are more valuable for decision making, strategic analysis, and organizational learning. Yet that fact is becoming increasingly clear. Instead of relying on a small squad of specialists to win the competitive war, a company that implements an activity-based FMIS begins to arm the entire organization. In many respects, opening up the FMIS for active use by everyone in the organization *empowers* them. Knowledge is the basis for sound action; a properly constructed FMIS can lead to this knowledge.

Recapping the Chapter

In looking at the FMIS from a customer perspective, the basic notion of activity-based approaches to understanding the organization have been discussed. Starting with a basic definition of activity-based systems (or ACMS for activity-based cost management systems), the chapter presented the common characteristics of these systems as follows.

1. They focus on **activities**, or what is actually done in an organization, as their starting point. In doing so, these systems merge financial and nonfinancial measurement and control systems.

2. Resources consumed by these activities are approximated, creating **cost pools** that match the natural structure of the organization rather than the traditional accounting focus on lines of responsibility and natural expense categories (e.g., direct labor).

3. The cause of these costs, called a **cost driver**, is identified and used to attach the resources consumed to the various activities, products, and services that benefit from them.

4. These **activity-based costs** are bundled together in a **bill of activities** that provides a semidetailed listing of the activities performed within a specific value chain or setting, creating a cost estimate for that value chain.

5. In performing these analyses, actual costs or budgeted costs are the starting point, rather than engineered standards.

The application of these basic steps to the product-costing problem in organizations was reviewed first. As noted, unless expanded, this approach did little more than develop a new way to spread overhead out among existing products; decision-making support was little improved.

Activity-based costing, although not the ultimate answer in the development of relevant FMIS information for decision support, provided the basic framework for current efforts in this area, including the development of ACM systems. An ACMS supports ongoing decision making, as was shown by walking through an example using traditional economic order quantity models, cost-of-quality models, just-in-time accounting, and the development of value-added accounting models. Throughout this period of development, meeting customer requirements, whether external or internal to the firm, is key. Value added doesn't stop on the plant floor.

This chapter provides an overview of what promises to be the backbone of the next generation of financial management tools. Efforts are proceeding on many fronts, as financial managers in the manufacturing and service sectors alike are seeking new ways to meet the challenges of global competition. As new tools are developed for managing ongoing operations, and for achieving sustainable competitive advantage, new forms of accounting have to be adopted. The question that remains is not whether an ACMS is needed in every organization; it is how to structure one to fit the unique demands of each company, each strategy, and each manager that relies on it.

ACMS and The Internal Customer

In many respects, the redesign of the FMIS around activity-based concepts is a step that is required before many of the benefits of World-Class manufacturing and service can be reaped. Because these systems build from a concern with customers and what they value, they transform traditional scorekeeping functions into strategic tools. Based on the knowledge of internal customers (and users) of the information base, an ACMS supports ongoing decision making and the pursuit of continuous improvement.

An ACMS is not a financial reporting system designed for and used by accountants. It is an analytic tool built to match the structure, strategy, technology, and processes of the organization *by the people who will use it*. An ACMS cannot be built without the active involvement of individuals throughout the organization, in every department and in every level of management.

World-Class performance begins with a clear understanding of existing practice and the identification of pockets of opportunity where sustainable competitive advantage can be achieved. This understanding builds from the expertise of management, prior history, sound analysis, and good information. A relevant FMIS is a cornerstone of this understanding; it is a tool that can be of immense help in the competitive arena, or it can, if improperly structured, hide the real game (and risks) from view until it is too late to change course. The FMIS can be a friend or a foe to the company seeking excellence; which result occurs is up to the individuals who use the information.

In formal logic, a contradiction is the signal of a defeat; but in the evolution of real knowledge it marks the first step in progress toward a victory.

Alfred North Whitehead (1)

SUGGESTED READINGS

The Journal of Cost Management for the Manufacturing Industry, published by Warren, Gorham and Lamont, New York. Two collections of articles on these topics are available: *Emerging Practices in Cost Mangement,* ed. B. Brinker (1990), and a forthcoming collection of readings also edited by Mr. Brinker. All can be obtained by contacting Warren, Gorham and Lamont.

Belkaoui, A. *Conceptual Foundations of Management Accounting.* Reading, Mass.: Addison-Wesley, 1980.

Brimson, James. *Activity Accounting: An Activity-Based Costing Approach.* New York: Wiley, 1991.

Brinker, Barry, ed. *Handbook of Cost Management.* New York: Warren, Gorham and Lamont, 1991.

Buitendam, Arend. "The Horizontal Perspective of Organization Design and New Technology." In *New Technology as Organizational Innovation*, eds. J. Pennings and A. Buitendam. Cambridge, Mass.: Ballinger, 1987, pp. 59–86.

Church, A. Hamilton. *The Proper Distribution of Expense Burden*. London: The Engineering Magazine, 1908, and *Manufacturing Costs and Accounts*, New York: McGraw Hill, 1929.

Clark, J. M. *Studies in the Economics of Overhead Costs*. Chicago, Ill.: University of Chicago Press, 1923.

Cooper, Robin. "You Need a New Cost System When . . ." *Harvard Business Review*, January-February 1989, pp. 77–82.

Johnson, H. Thomas. "Reviewing the Past and Future of Cost Management." *Emerging Practices,* pp. 145–148.

Kammlade, J., P. Mehra, and T. Ozan. "A Process Approach to Cost Management." In *Emerging Practices in Cost Mangement,* ed. B. Brinker. New York: Warren, Gorham and Lamont, 1990, pp. 193–198.

McIlhattan, R. "The Path to Total Cost Management." *Journal of Cost Management,* Summer 1987, pp. 5–10.

McNair, C., R. Lynch, and K. Cross. "Do Financial and Nonfinancial Measures Have to Agree?" *Management Accounting,* Fall 1990, pp. 28–36.

Miller, J., and T. Vollmann. "The Hidden Factory." *Harvard Business Review,* September-October 1985.

Staubus, George. *Activity Costing for Decisions: Cost Accounting in the Decision Usefulness Framework*. New York: Garland, 1988.

Turk, William T. "Accounting Simplification." In *Handbook of Cost Management,* ed. B. Brinker, New York: Warren, Gorham and Lamont, 1991: Section F-1.

Yoshikawa, T., J. Innes, and F. Mitchell. "Cost Management through Functional Analysis." *Emerging Practices in Cost Management,* ed B. Brinker. New York: Warren, Gorham and Lamont, pp. 243–248.

CHAPTER 9

NUMBERS FOR
STRATEGIC ANALYSIS

If man has good corn, or wood, or boards, or pigs to sell, or can make better chairs or knives, crucibles, or church organs, than anybody else, you will find a broad, hard-beaten road to his house, tho it be in the woods.

Ralph Waldo Emerson (2)

Understanding and controlling the costs of ongoing business is a prerequisite to competitive survival; strategic advantage is the source of long-run profitability and growth. Strategic advantage, or the exploitation of cost or uniquity as the basis for competition in the marketplace, is what separates top-performing firms from the also rans. It stems from a *systemic view* of the organization and its placement inside the value chain that links the acquisition of raw materials from its source to the ultimate product or service that is delivered to customers. Strategic advantage looks both inside and outside the firm to identify more efficient or effective ways of doing business.

Adopting a long-run perspective allows a manager to see the organization as a kaleidoscope of issues and opportunities. As the length of this forward-looking time frame increases, more and more of the organizational puzzle becomes open to change. The aphorism "In the long run all costs are variable" captures the fact that, if the planning window is pushed out far enough, anything is possible.

This fact, although soothing, can also constrain action as future hopes dominate. Hoping that things will be better tomorrow is, in essence, giving up on the potential of today. As the issues and techniques surrounding the stategic perspective and its impact on the FMIS are discussed, the need to actively work with events in the present in order to support attainment of long-term goals will be emphasized. Sound management in the present is the key; otherwise future plans may never come to fruition. Long-term goals are achieved through incremental daily actions and successes: This is the essence of the continuous philosophy.

GLOBAL STRATEGIES FOR COMPETITIVE ADVANTAGE

The only meaningful concept of competitiveness at the national level is national productivity. . . . Sustained productivity growth requires that an economy continually upgrade itself.

Michael Porter, *The Competitive Advantage of Nations*

The development of a global perspective is no longer an option for a company to debate; it is the essence of survival. The marketplace can no longer be defined within a narrow geographic area. Why? Because at each turn, competitors are emerging, seeking new market opportunities; external pressures are making it impossible for a company to remain isolated. Deciding how to respond to these increasing pressures forms the foundation for the firm's strategic plan. This strategy, set within the constraints of the industry's structure, seeks to identify and exploit areas of competitive advantage for the firm, given its location, the resources at its disposal, and the opportunities arising from changes in industry structures.

The arena of organizational and global strategy is dominated by Michael Porter of the Harvard Business School. In discussing the development of a strategy that can yield competitive advantage, he notes that the key variable is the firm's choice of its *positioning*, or approach to competing, within the industry. Competitive advantage is the first element of this puzzle; the scope of a firm's participation in the industry is the second. In both cases, advantage is based on achieving higher levels of productivity than competitors.[1]

Sources of Competitive Advantage

Interestingly, Porter tightly ties the concept of activities and their organization into a value chain to the firm's ability to attain a competitive advantage. To quote several of his more illuminating thoughts on this topic:

> Competitive advantage grows out of the way firms organize and perform discrete activities. . . . Firms create value for their buyers through performing these activities. . . . Firms gain competitive advantage from

---

[1]Porter has written a number of books on this topic. The material for this chapter is based on his most recent work, *The Competitive Advantage of Nations,* published by the Free Press (New York), 1990. Chapter 2 was used predominantly to frame the arguments in this section, as it summarizes the strategic issues facing companies.

conceiving of new ways to conduct activities, employing new procedures, new technologies or different inputs.[2]

Porter assumes that a firm has a good handle on the activities it
performs within the confines of the value chain, and that the cost of
these activities can be estimated with some degree of accuracy. Yet
this information is not available in most companies. The development
of an activity-based FMIS is not only important for internal decision
making, it is the basis for developing a strong foundation for achieving
competitive advantage.

The value chain is more than a set of discrete activities; it
is a *linked*, or interdependent, array of actions and outcomes that
flows across the organization, resulting in a value-added final product-
service bundle for the customer (see Figure 9–1). There are many ways
to depict this linked series of activities, but one fact remains constant
across them all: Competitive advantage stems from the performance
of the system, not from one specific element of that system. Once
again noting Porter's thoughts on this topic:

> Careful management of linkages can be a decisive source of competi-
> tive advantage. . . . Gaining competitive advantage requires that a firm's
> value chain is managed as a system rather than a collection of sepa-
> rate parts. . . . Linkages not only connect activities inside a company
> but also create interdependencies between a firm and its suppliers and
> channels.[3]

Competitive advantage is based on a clear understanding and proactive management of the series of interdependencies that define the
organization and its interactions with the external environment.

The FMIS and Competitive Advantage

One of the major stumbling blocks in plotting a competitive strategy is lack of information about either external issues or internal
functions and costs. It is close to impossible for a firm to know if
it can attain a cost- or differentiation-based[4] competitive advantage

---

[2]Ibid., pp. 40–41.

[3]Ibid., pp. 42–43.

[4]Porter defines a differentiation-based strategy as one where the firm seeks to provide
unique and superior value to the buyer in terms of product quality, special features, or after-
sale service. A cost strategy, therefore, is one based on the firm's ability to design, produce,
and market a comparable product more efficiently than its competitors. See Porter, *Competitive
Advantage*, p. 37.

FIGURE 9–1
A Generic Value Chain

Organizational boundaries

Marketing and order acquisition activities
Order entry, scheduling, and materials acquisition

Release order	Setup	Production	Move	Inspect	Pack	Ship

Billing and collection activities
Post-purchase service and marketing support

---

unless it has detailed knowledge about its own structure and costs, feasible competitive scope, market segmentation approaches, and the expectations of the external customers (who purchase goods and services from the *value system*). The *value system*, or the larger stream of activities that spans the entire process flow from the acquisition of raw materials through the final use of the goods or services by the customer, can also be managed to attain competitive advantage, but doing so requires even more in-depth knowledge than that needed to understand the firm's existing cost and activity matrix.

The strategy literature appears to assume that information is available in the FMIS, and other areas of the organization, in the right form and in sufficient quantity and detail to do a complete analysis of internal and external activities, costs, and opportunities for competitive advantage. Yet this information, until recently, was not even defined, let alone obtainable, within most companies. It is an interesting gap, but also a troubling one. If long-run survival depends on competitive advantage, which depends on the ongoing knowledge of activities and their linkages, costs, and the overall effectiveness and efficiency of the value chain within the value system, are most companies doomed from the start?

COSTING THE VALUE CHAIN

Some values are ... like sugar on the doughnut, legitimate, desirable, but insufficient, apart from the doughnut itself. We need substance as well as frosting.

Ralph T. Flewelling (2)

In response to the implications of this gap between the strategic demand for information and its availability, an entirely new subdiscipline of the FMIS is being created: strategic cost management. Building from Porter's insights, the work in this area attempts to develop reliable numbers that coincide with the strategic perspective. As noted by Shank and Govindarajan:

> The value chain framework is a method for breaking down the chain—from basic raw materials to end-use customers—into strategically relevant activities to understand the behavior of costs and the sources of differentiation.... End-use customers ultimately pay for all the profit margins throughout the value chain.[5]

Shank and Govindarajan, two of the most noted proponents of strategic cost management, move outside of the organization in defining the value chain. Their term *value chain* is, it seems, the same as Porter's *value system*. To avoid confusion, this discussion will retain Porter's approach.

Basics of Strategic Cost Management

Strategic cost management builds from a value-chain framework by detailing how a company's products and services fit into the overall value system. By explicitly recognizing interdependence and the impact of industry structure and competitive scope on the firm's value

---

[5]John K. Shank and Vijay Govindarajan, "Strategic Cost Management and the Value Chain," in *Handbook of Cost Mangement*, ed. Barry Brinker (New York: Warren, Gorham and Lamont, 1991) pp. D1–4. This article, plus the book *Strategic Cost Analysis: The Evolution from Managerial to Strategic Costing* (Homewood, Ill.: Richard D. Irwin, 1989) written by these authors, form the core of the existing literature on strategic cost management. Others are pursuing topics in this area, but these two academics founded the techniques and concepts. If further information about how to implement or use these techniques is desired, it is suggested that these two references be obtained. The article provides detailed examples of how to utilize the concept.

chain, the technique shifts the focus to the total cost of a delivery system rather than the costs of individual subsystems, or components, within that system. In line with the "theory of constraints" promoted by Eli Goldratt and others, the objective is to look at the system's functioning with an eye toward identifying the constraints that inhibit the entire organization from operating at its peak level of performance. The underlying assumption is that while the product/service bundle is delivered through a linked series of interdependent activities, the organization can only be understood and managed by focusing on the constraints of the system, not its entire set of interrelationships.

The core of this approach to the FMIS is the fact that the boundaries around the costing process are pushed beyond the level of individual products, services, or functions to capture the activities and value-creating processes that comprise the entire value system. As these boundaries are pushed out, traditional concerns and definitions of direct cost, variable and fixed costs, and related topics fall by the wayside. Larger cost pools accommodate a more varied, and larger, set of resources and uses. The use of these cost pools in strategic analysis proceeds in the following way:

1. Identify the industry's value chain and then assign costs, revenues, and assets to value activities.

2. Diagnose the cost drivers regulating each value activity.

3. Develop sustainable competitive advantage, either through controlling cost drivers better than the competitors or by reconfiguring the value chain.[6]

The cost pools used incorporate the *industry* value chain as their starting point, rather than the firm's.

How can this be done? Undertaking a strategic cost analysis can often prove to be a simpler than redesigning the internal FMIS. Why? Because many of the details needed to conduct this type of study are already available in the company's published financial statements. That's the key to understanding this area of study: It builds from the traditional financial accounting model and existing required disclosures. Because it takes place at the firm level, is focused on analyzing existing industry characteristics in order to identify potential area where competitive advantage can be established, and covers an

---

[6]Shank and Govindarajan, in *Handbook of Cost Management*, pp. D1–10.

extended time frame, strategic cost analysis is supported by the FMIS as it is currently structured. It's an interesting paradox, but not an illogical one; the traditional FMIS is geared toward supporting exactly these types of analyses by external parties, such as stockholders.

In defining activities at the strategic level, the focus is on the activities that comprise the **industry** value chain. Strategic activities should be isolated and separated, according to Shank and Govindarajan, if they meet any or all of the following conditions:

- They represent a significant percentage of operating costs.
- The cost behavior of the activities (or the cost drivers) is different.
- They are performed by competitors in different ways.
- They are likely to create differentiation opportunities.[7]

At the industry level the activities become more global in nature. Once defined, though, the process of assigning costs, revenues, and assets takes place in the same manner as within an activity-based FMIS. When external transactions don't take place, some form of **transfer price** is established (preferably based on market considerations), so that the value-added element, relative productivity, and potential sources of competitive advantage can be clearly identified.

A sample value chain analysis, as suggested by Shank and Govindarajan, is presented in Figure 9.2.[8] As can be seen, the information, for the most part, can be obtained from existing company documents, such as the published financial statements and the SEC 10-K filings. Applying it to the hypothetical case detailed by the authors, the relative costs for key value-creating activities for this airline are noted. In other exhibits in the text, comparative analysis is completed, showing the relative focus of activities and resources between competitive firms in the airline industry.

Simply obtaining this level of data allows a company to undertake an analysis of current **return on assets** for itself and its competitors, which indicates the relative productivity of each firm's investment per major activity or segment. Since competitive advantage, whether achieved through differentiation or cost-based

---

[7]Ibid., pp. D1–11.

[8]Ibid., pp. D1–20.

FIGURE 9–2
Strategic Cost Analysis

Ajax Airlines: A Value Chain Analysis

	1988	1987
Sales	$8,800	$7,200
Ticketing and reservations	320	300
Aircraft operations	4,980	3,900
Customer service	2,600	2,400
Total expenses	$7,900	$6,600
Identifiable property, plant, and equipment (PPE) assets		
Ticketing and reservations	$2,000	$1,000
Aircraft operations	5,000	5,300
Customer service	0	0
Total	$7,000	$6,300

	Per seat mile flown		Per available mile	
	1988	1987	1988	1987
Costs				
Ticketing and reservations	$0.005	$0.005	$0.003	$0.003
Aircraft operations	0.077	0.069	0.049	0.044
Customer service	0.040	0.042	0.025	0.027
Total	$0.122	$0.116	$0.077	$0.074
Assets				
Ticketing and reservations	$0.031	$0.018	$0.020	$0.011
Aircraft operations	0.077	0.093	0.049	0.060
Customer service	0	0	0	0
Total	$0.108	$0.111	$0.069	$0.071

This figure is reproduced with permission from the article "Strategic Cost Management and the Value Chain" by J. Shank and V. Govindarajan, in *Handbook of Cost Management,* ed. Barry Brinker (New York: Warren, Gorham and Lamont, 1991), pp. D1–4.

strategies, stems from superior productivity levels, this information is important.

Drivers: A Unique Approach

While the next stage in employing cost management is the identification of drivers, this is not a comparable event to developing drivers in an activity-based FMIS. Here, the focus is on structural and executional elements of the company and the industry. For instance, structural drivers can come from any one of the following categories: (1) *scale*, or size of the investment in manufacturing, R&D, or marketing (this includes horizontal integration); (2) *scope*, or the degree of vertical integration; (3) *experience*, or how often the firm has successfully completed the activity; (4) *technology*, or the process used to support the activities in the value chain; and (5) *complexity*, or the range of products and services offered.[9] Structural drivers deal with the actual organization of the value-creation process.

Executional cost drivers, on the other hand, deal with the *capability* of these resources and the factors that augment or constrain this capability. This category of drivers includes work force involvement, total quality management, capacity utilization, plant layout efficiency, product configuration (the manufacturability of products), and the tightness of customer/supplier linkages.[10] The executional drivers are interesting, as they mirror many of the emphasized areas of operation within the Japanese management system. This tie is not accidental, it seems. Porter, in fact, suggests this when he notes:

> Careful management of linkages can be decisive source of competitive advantage. . . . Japanese firms have been particularly adept at managing linkages.[11]

Strategic advantage is derived from active management of the system, is focused on either cost reduction (decreasing costs while holding revenues constant) or value enhancement (increasing revenues while holding costs constant), and places significant emphasis on the interrelationships between activities rather than solely on the work itself. It is a **dynamic** concept of management.

It is also a concept of management closely reflecting the efforts proceeding on many fronts as companies attempt to reach World Class status in operations and performance. Executional cost drivers reflect the way that work is structured inside an organization and how effectively and efficiently it is managed. This is where the informa-

---

[9]Ibid., pp. D1-12.

[10]Ibid. pp. D1–13.

[11]Porter, Competitive Advantage, p. 42.

tion for internal decision making reenters the equation (see Chapter 8). If the right activities are tracked, measured, and costed internally, the financial results detailed in the FMIS's external reports will adequately support value chain analysis. On the other hand, if the FMIS is poorly matched to the company, these external status reports may end up being poor reflections of current and future performance.

When the FMIS is designed to reflect the strategy and structure of the organization, the information it provides for all its customers is of more value. Changing the internal reporting system to an ACMS structure does not change the way external reports are structured, but the information in them (especially in sections like "segment profitabilities" in the footnotes) become more reliable because it more accurately reflects the effectiveness of management. There is even downstream potential for enhancing external reporting once more adequate internal information is available.

World-Class performance begins with knowing what game is being played and what the score is. Whether the information used to gain this knowledge comes from internal sources or a review of external data is less important than having the ability to use it once the knowledge is gained. If companies use poor practices, or employ mismatched financial systems that reduce the effectiveness of the management process, they can lose the vital strategic edge that ensures long-term success.

THE MISSING LINK IN STRATEGY DEPLOYMENT

> Future: *That period of time in which our affairs prosper, our friends are true and our happiness is assured.*
>
> Ambrose Bierce, *The Devil's Dictionary* (3)

Interestingly, there appears to be a missing link between the short-term management focus and strategic concerns. How do they connect? Is the detailing of activities and drivers within the FMIS enough to support the transition between short-term actions and long-term profitability? The redefinition of the FMIS does not seem, in itself, enough to support these varied perspectives. It is, in scientific terms, a *necessary but not sufficient* condition.

In defining strategic cost management, the same concepts and approaches detailed in chapter 8 reemerge. The difference between the ACMS and strategic cost management is one of perspective rather than substance. In other words, the tools needed to perform the entire range of long-term analysis are the same as those required to build internal costing models for pricing and decision analysis. The difference is the period of time covered by the analysis and the underlying system of numbers and activities. In short-term decision making, almost everything is taken as a given; there is an inherent assumption that only minor modifications can be made in the strategy, structure, technology, resources, and processes utilized by the company at that point in time.

On the other hand, strategic cost management assumes that everything, including the company's positioning within its industry and the scope of its product and customer segment offerings, can be changed. In this setting, the key focus of the FMIS is not on causality, or how the resources are being used, but on the existing and potential *capability* of the firm, its attainable resources, structures, and processes. The two approaches are at opposite ends of the cost-time spectrum. As suggested in Figure 9–3, as a company expands its planning time frame, more and more constraints fall away. In the future, it would seem, everything is possible.

The gap between the short term and long term is the intermediate run, or the period of time over which some (but not all) of the key elements of the structural and executional drivers can be affected. The intermediate term is where the action really is, a fact that can be easily forgotten when strategic advantage begins to be discussed. In this period of time management is able to put in motion, and complete, action plans that provide the source of downstream competitive advantage.

For instance, Shank and Govindarajan suggest that employee involvement and total quality management are key executional drivers of value creation in a company. These two elements of the organization, though, are not static concepts; if they were, they would be unlikely to yield a sustainable competitive advantage. At their core, each of the executional drivers is a means for implementing continuous improvement within some area of the company.

Strategic advantage is gained through organizational learning, or the continuous, incremental improvement of existing methods. That means that, although the strategic cost management approach does not require activity-based FMIS information to do the initial analysis, it is totally dependent on its existence to actually change the status quo. Strategic cost management sets a vision, or set of action priorities, for the firm. It cannot actually change existing performance. The

FIGURE 9–3
Constraints and the Decision Process

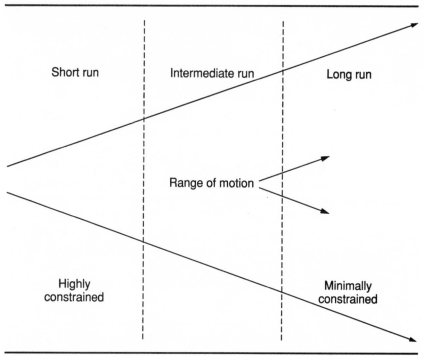

implementation tools, the true key to competitive advantage, are the methods and approaches that have been detailed in this text, and which form the core of the modern operating manager's vocabulary.

When a company implements just-in-time manufacturing, total quality management or any of the other emerging tools for eliminating waste within the internal value chain, it is providing the means for obtaining competitive advantage. A traditional FMIS, to the extent that it creates a roadblock to effective implementation of the continuous improvement philosophy and techniques, prevents or inhibits the attainment of competitive advantage. Long-term success is built from effective management of today's problems, opportunities, and resources. Tomorrow's hopes are built on today's decisions. This is the missing link between short-term and long-term analysis: The long term is the accumulation of short-term events.

Matching the needs of the short term and long term is based on identifying, understanding, and managing existing constraints on the value chain and the value system. The intermediate term is, therefore, that period of time over which constraints can be removed from the system. Each time a constraint is removed, the gap between short- and long-term goals and performance is narrowed. Gaining strategic advantage is an ongoing process of organizational learning; the strategy defines the courses to be taken, strategic cost management details the grades that have to be earned, and continuous improvement, or ongoing learning, is the path to their attainment.

This excursion into the strategic management literature, the strategic cost management techniques that have evolved from Porter's work, and the underlying assumptions made by them, provides only the most basic concepts in these areas. Since one strategic error can actually destroy a company, it is wise to do a careful reading of this material in depth before attempting to put any part of it into action. In addition, as the material is read, it is important to remember that although having a map is a good idea, you can't reach your destination by looking in the rear-view mirror (i.e., by using traditional, historical cost-based financial information).

TARGET COSTING: MANAGING COSTS FOR PROFIT

Aim at the sun, and you may not reach it; but your arrow will fly far higher than if aimed at an object on a level with yourself.

Joel Hawes (2)

Target costing is one of the tools the Japanese use to attain their long-term strategic goals. It is an *a priori* cost reduction tool that establishes, during the planning stages of a new product, the **allowable cost**, or total cost the item can bear and still generate desired profit levels. The technique focuses on active management of the profitability of a product over the entire length of its life cycle, attempting to keep profitability at or above a desired level throughout this period. This is in contrast to more traditional approaches that suggest that companies should attempt to reap excess profits early in the life of a product (during introduction and growth) to offset lower profitability levels as maturity is reached in the life cycle (the point at which cost competition is suggested to play a major role in generating sales). The basic approach used is shown in the following diagram:[12]

---

[12]Takao Makido, "Recent Trends in Japan's Cost Management Practices," in *Japanese Management Accounting: A World Class Approach to Profit Management*, eds. Y. Monden and M. Sakurai (Cambridge, Mass.: Productivity Press, 1989), p. 5.

Long-range profit plan

⇓

Profitability index

↓

Sales price − Profit needed = Allowable cost

↑

Target cost

The driving force behind this technique is the pursuit of **market share** as the key factor in reaping long-term economies of scale and profitability for a company. The Japanese recognize that they are price takers in the market; they attempt to project the expected selling prices for a product or product family over its complete life cycle, and manage their design and manufacturing activities to ensure adequate profits on a continual basis over this period. As noted by Takao Makido:

> The essence of cost reduction is to cut the present cost standards themselves. The essence of cost control is to maintain the reduced cost standards. . . . Cost reduction has little effect once production starts . . . consequently, it is common to plan a large cost reduction at the product planning stage.[13]

Target costing is a vital part of the production plan; it starts by recognizing that most costs are set in stone once the product and process have been designed. Costs can be maintained or minimally reduced once production begins, but the major savings occur earlier in the process.

Target costing begins with the identification of four items, as suggested by R. John Aalbregtse:

- *Customer requirements:* Understanding market requirements and the performance levels of competitors' products
- *Future cost structures:* Making target cost development an aspect of the ongoing design process
- *Product design:* Considering the impact of various cost drivers during product design

---

[13]Ibid., p. 4.

- *Continuous improvement:* Fostering continuous improvement of cost drivers during all stages of the product's life cycle, production, and distribution[14]

Therefore, target costing builds from a sound market analysis of existing and future demand for the product, the likely impact of competitive products, and the means available to the firm to attain, and maintain, desired cost levels.

Target costing is an intermediate-range planning and control tool that utilizes continuous improvement concepts to support the attainment of long-term strategic objectives. To put the technique to use, a company has to have performed at least the beginning stages of design and implementation of an activity-based FMIS. Because a new product affects the entire organization, it is crucial that these interdependencies and interrelationships be built into the target costing analysis. If the sales of the product are going to affect either existing revenues (by affecting sales of existing products) or costs (by increasing the demand for shared resources), a systematic analysis of this impact is the starting point for determining a suitable marketing plan. The analysis also needs to incorporate the key elements of the value system, the competitive structure of the environment, and the potential threats that may undercut future sales.

Target costing is the basis for developing a long-term marketing plan, but its focus is not on the marketplace per se, but on how the company can ensure the attainment of desired market share levels by actively managing its cost structure. This is in direct contrast to traditional plans, which take costs as a given, plan for cost reduction through economies of scale with no true analysis of whether these goals can or should be met, and ignore the fact that over 90 percent of the cost of a product is set once the design stage is completed.[15]

---

[14]R. John Aalbregtse, "Target Costing," in *The Handbook of Cost Management,* ed. Barry Brinker (New York: Warren, Gorham and Lamont, 1991) pp. D2–3.

[15]The CAM-I conceptual framework, which has been noted several times already in this discussion (Berliner and Brimson, op.cit.), argues and illustrates quite convincingly how important the design stage of the product development process is in establishing the costs of production and establishing the unchangeable constraints that can radically impair the firm's ability to make the product, or to make it profitably.

A Focus on the Customer

Customer requirements play a pivotal role in target-costing analysis. Since future market potential is based on the product's ability to meet or exceed customer expectations (including the value, and hence revenue, it can command in the marketplace), it seems clear that this knowledge is important. Gaining customer sales information from a traditional market study, though, is not the same as doing a detailed analysis of potential product features and the customer's response to them. If a product is overdesigned, providing far more "value" than the customer is willing to pay for, it will not reach its profit goals. Conversely, if the customer expected more quality or durability than was delivered, the product will not command the price, or have the same duration of sales, as was originally projected.

In today's demanding global marketplace, responsiveness to changing customer needs is often the prerequisite to success. **Design for manufacturability**, the tool used to ensure that a product can be made in a cost-effective manner, can also be used to increase the perceived flexibility, or variety-providing nature, of the product. If the true impact of variety can be kept at a fairly cosmetic level, and pushed back late in the production process, the company can easily respond to changing customer tastes. For example, Benetton, a European clothing manufacturer, purchases all of its cloth undyed. These undyed bolts can be used to make any type of garment, in any color currently in vogue. If colors or fashions change, Benetton is able to be one of the first chain stores to have the goods available. Variety is being actively managed by changing the normal operating procedures of the industry. That's the essence of a competitive advantage.

Putting Target Costing into Operation

Target costing provides the details on what improvements have to be gained over the life of a product if a competitive edge is to be gained and maintained. The action plan for achieving these goals, or eliminating the excess resources from the product's value chain, come from operations. The ideas embodied in the continuous improvement philosophy, and the tools that have been developed to implement it within organizations, are the means to obtain the goals established through target costing.

Returning to Figure 9–2, Ajax Airlines has identified several areas of its company that are linked to its competitive position in the industry. Specifically, it has noted that it currently costs 12 cents per seat mile flown to meet customer expectations, an increase of roughly 3.4 percent for 1987. This increase appears to be due to two only partially compensating forces: increased costs in aircraft operations (.077 in 1988 versus .069 in 1987) offset by decreased costs in customer service (.040 in 1988 versus .042 in 1987).

The information may be interesting, but it's quite likely management would rather know how it shapes up compared to its competitors and what its optimal level of performance could be. If it looked at this information today, it would be called *benchmarking*. Doing a benchmarking study would establish the current score and at least let management know if it is anywhere in the ball park in its cost structure.

Ajax finds out, in fact, that it is fairly competitive today, but that the trends in its aircraft operations and customer service costs appear to be moving in exactly the opposite direction of its rival, industry leader Best Airlines. Discovering that it has parity is not important; the trends make management nervous. More than that, recent press releases suggest that Best will be targeting its ticketing and reservations area for major cost reductions in the next five years, as it deploys new technologies and management procedures.

Ajax's management could seek ways to become as good as Best in these key areas (at least on a cost per mile flown basis), but trying to become *as good as* the competition is a losing strategy. Ajax's managers decide, instead, to expand their analysis to discover what level of service quality and cost they would need to have to improve their relative market share and increase customer loyalty for the long term.

Management needs more information. Customers are contacted, a market research firm is enlisted, and employees across the organization are pulled together into a project task force to determine what level of quality and cost is needed to meet its strategic goals for market share and profitability. The results of this extended market study are startling: Ajax will have to shave five cents off its cost per seat mile flown and improve the responsiveness and quality of its service in ticketing, reservations, in-flight operations, and all other areas if it is to overtake Best Airlines. Five cents per mile flown is Ajax's assessed *target cost*.

Figure 9–2 suggests that the cost savings could be achieved if Ajax simply flew more miles, perhaps getting closer to 100 percent of its available miles. But reaching and sustaining this level of performance assumes that more customers want to fly Ajax. Management believes that this theoretical savings will never come to pass unless it addresses internal problems first.

The action plan that Ajax decides to use to attack its target objectives starts with TQM and application of JIT (and other process improvement techniques) to its ongoing operations. In the area of quality, management asks for a rough cost-of-quality report to determine whether its customer service dollars are being spent on value-adding activities or are the result of nonconformance problems. The study reveals that over 50 percent of its customer service dollars are being spent fixing problems generated elsewhere in the system.

To get a handle on how to address this disturbing information, management asks for a list of the top five offenders in generating customer service requests. They are:

1. Baggage claims/lost or damaged—30 percent of all nonconformance costs; 250,000 claims per year.

2. Equipment problems—15 percent of all costs; requires rerouting, often at a higher fare, overnight accommodations, and related items; 25,000 customers per year are so inconvenienced.

3. Crew shortages—10 percent of all nonconformance costs; rerouting is the usual outcome, delaying customers significantly.

4. Ticketing or reservation errors—5 percent of all nonconformance costs; lost revenues and rerouting required.

5. "Short window" schedule changes—5 percent of all costs.

In looking at this list, mangement sees that improvements in its baggage claim area are first on the list. A process analysis is performed, as part of an internal benchmarking project, to determine what is currently being done within the company, and what the best-practice internal sites do differently. Management finds that its own best practices are also industry best practice; they're just not applied consistently across its many sites.

Under the guidance of the TQM project leader, the key elements of good practice in baggage handling are detailed, training programs are developed for individuals at every site, and TQM teams are created to help improve performance in this critical area of cost and customer satisfaction. TQM and the core features of the continuous improvement philosophy are used to drive home the changes needed to drive "defects" down below 10,000 claims per year. The cost reductions are immediately noticeable; costs in customer service areas are decreased and service levels are improved.

Ajax Airlines finds that the lessons embodied in JIT and TQM can help it improve service levels and reduce costs. Over a five-year span,

Ajax is able to wrest passengers away from Best Airlines through service enhancements and lower fares. Using target costing objectives, developed through sound strategic analysis, Ajax is able to successfully gain a sustainable advantage in customer service, at the same time eliminating waste (and customer dissatisfaction) from its operations.

This is an example of how the elements of target costing, as a strategic tool, interact with the continuous improvement approach to management to generate a sustainable competitive advantage. Knowledge without the tools to apply it in the global marketplace is not enough, nor is a good tool of value without the wisdom to apply it. World Class performance comes from understanding the root cause of performance shortfalls and the implementation of the right programs and policies to address them.

Notice that either tool alone would probably have been inadequate to the job. If Ajax had decided to cut costs to meet its cost objectives without factoring in the ideals of defect-free performance, it quite likely would have suffered from reductions in its customer base. It would have slowly lost ground as customer-valued services were cut. TQM alone also might have fallen short. Increasing service quality irrespective of cost is simply not an option in the cutthroat airline industry. Combining cost-based knowledge with effective management is the only way to gain long-term success.

Target Costing and the FMIS

Estimated costs from the backbone of the target cost analysis. Where do these costs come from? In a traditional FMIS, these numbers are difficult to obtain; making the projections often requires conducting an engineering cost analysis. The numbers that are generated, though, do not include the organizational costs of supporting the new product; the focus remains on production costs. That seems to be a far cry from the assumptions the model is built on. Can a target cost analysis be adequately completed without a clear recognition of how the product fits into, and affects, the rest of the organization? If Porter's logic is followed, the answer is no.

Many of the cost estimates used to develop a target-costing analysis come from prior experience with similar products and marketing plans. To the extent that the FMIS has actually tracked these costs, history can be quite useful. An activity-based FMIS is even better than history, though; it provides a set of current estimates for each of the major activities that will need to be completed to design, produce, and market the product. Each new product brings with it a demand for support services as well as manufacturing. These can be estimated, but if the FMIS doesn't track support areas on an ongoing basis, the numbers used in the marketing analysis will never be able to be verified.

This shortfall occurs because the market plan and the target-costing process are often be built from a different set of cost and resource estimates and assumptions than are present in the traditional FMIS. The planning stage tries to attach the costs *caused by* the new product; the traditional FMIS allocates all the indirect costs indiscriminately to the old and new products. This may prove advantageous to the new product, or it may prove deadly. If the overhead is attached based on direct labor hours, the new product will probably be designed to be made on machines, even if this requires a large capital outlay for new equipment when excess capacity is already in place.

The role for the FMIS in target costing depends on whether or not activity-based concepts have been developed. If they have, the FMIS can be used to develop a detailed bill of activities for the product that can highlight those activities that are already operating at capacity (leading to the need to acquire new or incremental resources) and those that are currently underutilized and will, therefore, not be radically affected by the new product. This approach implicitly builds in the interrelationships between products within a single facility or single company. Each product competes for the limited resources available: The resources consumed have to be minimized if profit goals are going to be reached.

Target costing is a key element of Japanese competitive analysis. They are actively using the technique to secure market share, eliminate competition, and secure long-term profitability for their products. Since the Japanese management accounting system is focused on estimates, it by definition provides the information needed by this model. Given the fact that the Japanese continue to outperform their rivals, it's quite likely that this and related techniques may become a critical element of every World-Class company's strategic arsenal. The accurate identification of value-added and non-value-added activities, costs, and resources early in the life cycle of a product is the vital element in putting this tool to work; relevant financial information has to support strategic, as well as operational, decision making.

A CUSTOMER'S VIEW OF LIFE CYCLE COSTING

He who chooses the beginning of a road chooses the place it leads to. It is the means that determine the end.

Harry Emerson Fosdick (2)

Life cycle costing is an area that has not been as clearly defined as many of the other emerging FMIS tools discussed in this chapter. It reflects an ongoing concern with the costs incurred over the full life of a product, but whose costs are of concern? Does the concept merely reflect the changing cost patterns for a product over its lifetime, as experienced by the firm that makes it, or does it include post-purchase costs by individuals and organizations throughout the value system? Shank and Govindarajan, in discussing this concept, take the following position:

> *Life cycle costing* is a costing concept that argues for including all the costs incurred for a product—from the time when a product is conceived until it is abandoned—as part of the product cost. Life cycle costing thus deals explicitly with the relationship between what a customer pays for a product and the total cost the customer incurs over the life of the product.[16]

They go on to note that the reason a company should be interested in life cycle costing concepts is that "explicit attention to postpurchase costs by the customer can lead to more effective market segmentation and product positioning."

The strategic perspective, focused on the customer's view of the total costs of a product, is a far cry from the more traditional view of this topic, captured in the following comments by Gerald Susman:

> [Life cycle] estimates should be used to help a company maximize revenue during the start-up and growth stages, maximize profits during the maturity stage, and maximize cash flow during the decline stage.[17]

This approach to life cycle concepts mirrors the internal focus of a traditional organization. The focus on the changing profitabilities of a product never addresses the costs of that product, or how the company

---

[16]Shank and Govindarajan, in *Handbook of Cost Management*, pp. D1–8.

[17]G. Susman, "Product Life Cycle Management," in *The Handbook of Cost Management*, ed. Barry Brinker (New York: Warren, Gorham and Lamont, 1991), pp. D3–21.

should take a long-run perspective in managing product life cycles. Target costing, as discussed earlier in this chapter, presents an alternative approach to the traditional life cycle management technique.

In a company striving for competitive advantage, reactive management of any resource, whether it be a physical asset, people, or products, is tantamount to giving up the game before the starting whistle is blown. To maximize the value of the firm, the company has to proactively manage its resources from a customer perspective. That means it has to aggressively look for ways to enhance value without increasing cost, or cut costs without impairing value, *as defined by the customer*—not the FMIS or the marketing department. Strategic advantage comes from looking outward, assessing competitors and the structure of the value system itself in the search for innovative ways to deliver products and services to customers.

Life cycle costing has to be addressed from an external viewpoint. The Japanese have followed this model; instead of focusing solely on minimizing purchase costs, they ensure that postpurchase costs remain at some minimal level. The low purchase price might attract a customer once, but reliability and low *customer-defined* life cycle costs will keep them. Japanese automobiles aren't the lowest priced commodity on the market at the point of purchase, but they are when the total costs over the useful life of the car are considered. Low life cycle costs are one of the primary elements of their competitive strategy. This is especially true as product life cycles continue to shorten; there is less and less time available for a company to recoup its investment in a product. Products need to be aggressively managed from inception to death.

The Consumption Side of the Life Cycle

Many writers in this area segment the life cycle into production and consumption stages, incorporating both the firm's and the customer's costs in their analysis.[18] Within this framework, the production life cycle consists of product conception, design, development, production, logistic support, and marketing support. Consumption costs include operating costs, support costs, repairs, and disposal costs. The latter grouping is what the customer sees and evaluates the company

---

[18]Susman does end up taking this tack in his article, but remains focused on the responses the firm can make to varying consumption patterns rather than attempting to define a strategic advantage by maximizing the value to the customer (in other words, by minimizing consumption costs.)

and its products on; it affects long-term profitability and repeat sale potential. The former is the area where the firm can increase its profitability per unit sold, a more short-term orientation.

Most discussions of total quality management and design for manufacturability focus on the benefits these techniques will provide, in terms of enhanced profits through increased sales and reduced costs. Yet these techniques are actually more accurately portrayed as internal methods for decreasing the costs incurred by the customer after the product is purchased (external costs). That sheds light on discussions about whether zero defect quality levels really make sense.

Many quality experts argue that there is a declining benefit received from each dollar spent on quality beyond some optimal point. That may be so, but this optimum cannot be defined from the production perspective; it must be defined from the consumption perspective. If strategic advantage is based on meeting or exceeding customer expectations, the optimal level of quality may well be one that reduces post-purchase costs to zero (if possible). TQM is important because it minimizes life cycle costs, not solely because it improves the effectiveness of ongoing operations. Unless the customer's post-purchase costs, monetary and psychological, are factored into the analysis to determine the optimum level of expenditures to prevent errors, the solution will dramatically understate this amount.

The ongoing success of the Japanese suggests that zero defect levels, which minimize consumption-based life cycle costs, may be a comprehensive and strategically viable competitive weapon. Only when a long-term perspective is taken—one that factors in the customer not as a blank entity but as the primary stakeholder—can the life cycle concept truly reap benefits for a company.

> *A great man is one who seizes the vital issue in a complex question, what we might call the "jugular vein" of the whole organism—and spends his energies upon that.*
>
> Joseph Rickaby, *An Old Man's Jottings* (4)

PRODUCT, CUSTOMER, AND SEGMENT PROFITABILITIES

> *True, you can't take it with you, but then that's not the place where it comes in so handy.*
>
> Brendan Francis (4)

In taking a long- or intermediate-term view of the organization and its profitability, the underlying issue is one of *relationships*. A single customer order, or product run, or even a segment of the business is not the proper focus; the focus should be the trends in these areas over time. This is especially true when companies attempt to identify the customer-caused costs in designing an activity-based FMIS. Customer-level costs, which encompass all of the costs associated with maintaining a customer, include the costs of making sales calls, evaluating a customer's credit, and sending samples, catalogues, and other mailings.

Each time a customer makes a request, places an order, requires pre- or post-sale support, or in any other way interacts with the company, costs are created. Service is not free. If the service leads to increased long-term sales, then it pays its way, but pretending that going the extra mile has no financial impact on the profitability of a customer or an order is unrealistic and could be quite damaging over the long run.

An example of how an activity-based FMIS supports the identification and valuation of customer-caused costs may help here. Eastern Soap Company[19] is a $25 million manufacturer of private label soap, with its major emphasis on bar soap of various sizes, colors, formulations, and packaging. Its traditional attitude had been that every customer, and every sale, could be profitable for the company if the internal systems were working properly. That philosophy had led the company to take every order received, even if it wasn't sure the product could be made to customer expectations. This practice provided the firm with a strong market reputation for quality and manufacturing capability.

As the company grew, though, demand began to outpace its available capacity. Three shifts were working, six days a week, and the back orders continued to grow. This may sound like a "high-class" problem, but at the same time that sales were growing, profits were declining. In fact, in one period the company had its highest sales level ever—and experienced its first operating loss. It was clear to company management that they needed to reassess their policies and manufacturing practices. TQM was one of the tools they decided to adopt to improve operations; an activity-based FMIS was chosen to enhance the profit picture.

---

[19]The name of the company is disguised here, but the events and discussion are based on an actual ACMS implementation.

Once the system was designed, it became clear that some customers and "divisions" (the firm's term for market segments) were not generating profits when laden with all of their costs. In addition, some orders and customers were so complex and time consuming that they were disrupting the entire production process for small orders of a high variety of differently colored and shaped soaps (the novelty soap division). Armed with this information, management decided to increase the prices for many of its products, and to drop two customers that were ongoing sources of problems, both in the back office and on the plant floor.

How did the company fare with this new approach? First, not a single piece of ongoing business was lost because of the price increases, even though some of these increases practically doubled the per bar cost to the customer. That meant, without a doubt, the company had been drastically underpricing these products. Second, profitability immediately improved, and is continuing to do so.

The activity-based FMIS has been used to redesign the pricing system for the jobs entering the company, passing along key customer-caused costs for special services and difficult production characteristics. The end result is that the company is now finding itself able to expand to the European market and is in the process of negotiating to set up a plant in Great Britain. The FMIS is a value-adding tool in this company, helping management identify profitable and unprofitable *customer relationships*, focus the TQM efforts on the plant floor, and change the "any order is profitable" attitude that was threatening its long-term survival.[20]

Segment and Channel Costs and the FMIS

Another way a company can strategically use the FMIS is to conduct market segment, and channel, profitability analyses. Costs included in these categories are:

- Costs of managing the channel.
- Costs of maintaining the channel.

---

[20]Some might say that Eastern Soap's management wasn't paying attention to the marketplace. This argument has merit; a cost system is not normally the best place to turn for setting prices. On the other hand, in a job shop environment populated by small competitors, there is often very little market information available. Nevertheless, prices are market-driven; not knowing the competition is a recipe for disaster in any setting.

- Costs for advertising, promoting, and marketing the channel.
- Advertising, promoting, and marketing costs to the general marketplace.
- Product liability costs.
- Trade shows costs.
- Marketing staff costs.

Attaching these costs to the channel or segment that causes them allows a company to make intermediate-term decisions that include adding or dropping a product line, changing its distribution channel strategy, varying its promotional efforts to reflect a newly gained strategic advantage, isolating highly profitable segments, and increasing efforts to gain market share. At this level of analysis, management is looking across its existing markets and attempting to isolate those product and customer segments that are currently performing well and those that aren't reaching profitability goals. With this information it can define an action plan that will, based on a competitive assessment of the relevant value chain and value system, improve overall performance in the segment.

Keeping an Eye on Unavoidable Costs

One of the most dangerous aspects of doing an analysis at this level is the fact that the activity-based FMIS can promote the misconception that unavoidable costs can be avoided when these decisions are made. In reality, although the costs caused by the products, customers, and segments bearing their cost can be identified, many of the cost items are unavoidable, at least in the short term. This means that a decision to drop a product, product line, customer, or segment will not improve overall profitability unless the costs entered into the analysis go away once the decision is implemented.

Unfortunately, many of the costs at this level are "sticky"; they are difficult to eliminate, there is a tremendous amount of interdependence bundled within them (e.g., the marketing group usually handles more than one product), and the resources can usually be bought only in fairly large chunks (they are stepped fixed, or fixed, costs). Eliminating a customer or a product line simply shifts more cost onto those that remain. The only way this strategy can be effectively used is if costs are decreased in total by the decision, or the idled resources are redeployed to support a new product, new market, or some other revenue-generating activity. Getting rid of activities, or work, without getting rid of the resources that support them simply increases cost and decreases profits overall.

A STRATEGIC PERSPECTIVE

Thinking always ahead, thinking always of trying to do more, brings a state of mind in which nothing seems impossible.

Henry Ford

Competitive advantage stems from the careful analysis and exploitation of structural and executional characteristics of the value chain and value system. It is, at its essence, innovation. Gaining a strategic perspective requires a clear understanding of the needs of the customer, the competition, and the productivity of the resources of the firm. As has been seen in this chapter, there are a variety of tools that can be employed in gaining a strategic perspective, including:

- Strategic cost analysis.
- Target costing.
- Life cycle costing.
- Customer, segment, and divisional profitability analysis.

Each of these tools provides a different view of the strategic position of the firm. Strategic analysis, looking outward to identify the primary *executional* and *structural* drivers for an industry and a firm's relative cost for them, is an excellent tool for isolating areas of opportunity for improvement inside an organization.

Target costing asks a more critical question: What level of performance is needed to gain a long-term advantage in the marketplace? It calibrates the strategic analysis, but it can also identify future challenges or opportunities that might be missed if only strategic cost analyses were performed by a company. In addition, target costing provides more actionable information, as it focuses on single products or product families. Target costing opens up avenues for using World-Class management techniques in areas where the company can benefit most.

Life cycle costing begins to expand the strategic lens to include the customer's total costs of owning a product or using a service provided by a company. It is the only management tool discussed in this chapter that explicitly factors in the customer's needs and expectations for a specific product. It is an area of burgeoning interest, as shrinking product life cycles drives companies to more effectively manage their products.

Finally, an effective FMIS has to provide ongoing, relevant, and accurate information about the profitabilities of various customer, product, segment, and divisional profitabilities. This is baseline information needed to feed the other strategic models described in this chapter. Sustainable competitive advantage starts with sound knowledge about current operations, competitor performance, and future customer requirements.

The FMIS plays a pivotal role in gaining and exploiting this knowledge. At the industry level, traditional approaches to the FMIS are sufficient to garner attention and set priorities, but achieving these long-term goals requires a series of action plans that require information not readily available in a financially oriented FMIS. These intermediate-run tools focus on relaxing or removing the systemic constraints that prevent the organization from reaching its long-term goals. Long-run profits build from ongoing learning and continuous improvement, approaches that require an activity-based approach to the FMIS to succeed.

The FMIS and Operations

Strategic advantage cannot be obtained through financial transactions. That fact ties the material in this chapter directly to the operating managers who provide the information for building strategic cost analysis, and who use the information to help guide ongoing strategic decision making. Traditional cost accounting and the financial accounting system can operate without input from the rest of the organization; strategic cost analysis cannot.

The topics covered in this chapter are targeted at the operating manager. It may seem unlikely that anyone but top management could put the concepts detailed here to work, but the knowledge necessary to build and implement strategies comes from an empowered and engaged workforce. If a strategy is devised that fails to incorporate the core competencies of the firm, or gives it away to a low-cost supplier, the whole organization fails. If internal strengths are not understood and factored into strategic analysis, or if weaknesses are overlooked, the best plan may fail.

The FMIS should always look toward the internal customer first. Value is created every day, in incremental changes to the activity matrix, the management of interdependence and interrelationships within the value chain and value system, and through the active pursuit of productivity improvements. Only if a company sets its sights high enough, utilizes tools that continually remind it what the current score is and where improvements are needed, and accepts the fact that change, rather than the status quo, is the essence of long-term success, will the competitive battle be won. Competitive advantage and strategic cost management are not static concepts—they are the basis for daily efforts to improve the quality of a company's products, processes, and service.

We choose our joys and sorrows long before we experience them.

Kahlil Gibran, *Sand and Foam* (4)

SUGGESTED READINGS

Aalbregtse, R. John. "Target Costing." *In Handbook of Cost Management,* ed. Barry Brinker. New York: Warren, Gorham, and Lamont, 1991, D2-1–26.

Berliner, C., and J. Brimson. *Cost Management for Today's Advanced Manufacturing.* Cambridge, Mass.: Harvard Business School Press, 1988.

Hergert, M., and D. Morris. "Accounting Data for Value Chain Analysis." *Strategic Management Journal,* June 1989, pp. 175–188.

Monden, Y., and M. Sakurai, eds. *Japanese Management Accounting: A World Class Approach to Profit Management.* Cambridge, Mass.: Productivity Press, 1989.

Porter, Michael. *The Competitive Advantage of Nations.* New York: The Free Press, 1990.

———. *Competitive Advantage: Creating and Sustaining Superior Performance.* New York: The Free Press, 1985.

Shank, J., and V. Govindarajan, "Strategic Cost Management and the Value Chain," In *Handbook of Cost Management,* ed. Barry Binker, New York: Warren, Gorham, and Lamont, 1991, pp. D1–37.

———. *Strategic Cost Analysis: The Evolution from Managerial to Strategic Accounting.* Homewood, Ill.: Richard D. Irwin, 1989.

Susman, Gerald. "Product Life Cycle Management." In *Handbook of Cost Management.* ed. Barry Brinker. New York: Warren, Gorham and Lamont, 1991, pp. D3: 1–29.

CHAPTER 10

NUMBERS FOR ASSET MANAGEMENT

The fox that waited for the chickens to fall off their perch died of hunger.

Greek Proverb

Asset performance refers to the effective utilization of a company's asset base to produce profit. These assets can be used to increase revenues or decrease costs, over both the short and long run. Every asset the company employs should be value adding, whether it is a short-term item (such as cash, accounts receivable, or inventory), or a long-term investment (property, plant and equipment; investments in other firms), a tangible asset (inventory), or an intangible one (patents and warranties). Hoping that the assets will increase in value isn't the game plan—making sure that they do is.

Profits result from the effective management of a firm's asset base—a fact that is often lost in a world focused on the bottom line. In the rush to meet income projections, asset management often falls by the wayside. Whenever inventory is built in order to absorb overhead costs and improve short-term financial performance, an income statement mentality is driving decision making. In this setting, carrying inventory appears to be "free"; no one is directly charged for the cost of tying up excessive amounts of working capital in inventory, or for the warehouse costs, increased obsolescence, and damage that occur as inventory levels grow.

It appears, though, that the stock market is aware of the role of asset management in generating profits, even if management sometimes appears to forget it. Repeated studies of stock prices as compared to various measures of the effectiveness of asset utilization reveal that investors place a high value on those firms that generate the most value with their assets.

Assets Are Everywhere

Many of the most important assets for the long-term success of a company are often immediately expensed by the FMIS, never really making their way onto the balance sheet of the firm. Some of these "costs" that immediately come to mind include employees, or the human capital, of the firm. Other expensed but long-term value-creating assets include research and development, advertising, all marketing expenses, promotions, and training and development. Finally, some assets are never entered into the FMIS at all, yet are critical to long-term competitiveness—a firm's reputation in the marketplace places high on this list of unrecorded intangibles, as does the effective management of its value chain and value system.

Each class of asset brings with it unique issues and unique opportunities for creating value and generating profits. Careful management of these unique characteristics, exploitation of them in light of existing or potential demand, and the ongoing quest to do more with less are the basis for long-term growth. In other words, there is an implicit *capabilities balance sheet* that represents a company's potential to create value. Whether recorded in the financial records or not, all assets are income one step removed.

Wherever assets are found, value creation can occur. In some cases the assets, and the value they create, can be easily measured and tracked. In others, the benefits of effective management may be difficult to pin down, but may well form the core of the firm's strategic advantage. Customers buy value, and the *perception* of value. Active management of this perception often spells the difference between competitive advantage and "also ran" performance. Managers who maximize the value-creating potential of "hard" assets, as well as less tangible ones, are able to bring more force to bear to combat competition; all are assets the firm can barter in the marketplace to generate ongoing profits for their stakeholders.

REVISITING THE BALANCE SHEET

Anyone who thinks there's safety in numbers hasn't looked at the stock market pages.

Irene Peter (1)

The set of financial statements that has been used throughout this text are presented again in Figure 10–1. Focusing on the balance sheet, its division into current and long-term assets captures the useful life of the various types of resources the firm holds for future use. At the top is cash, which was extensively examined in Chapter 4 through the statement of cash flows. It serves as the beginning of the value chain and is the signal that all its tasks have been successfully completed.

Cash, the Asset

Managing cash as an asset is a different concept than simply ensuring that there is enough of it to meet current needs. The latter is obviously a major concern, but the firm that recognizes that cash can be used to generate profits is ahead of the game. Profits are generated every time a dollar is placed in an interest-bearing account, whether it is left there for one day or one year. Effective management of the asset cash includes speeding up its receipt, slowing down its use for various payments, and minimizing the total outflow required to obtain other resources (e.g., by taking advantage of trade discounts on accounts payable). The objective is, as with all forms of asset management, to increase the *velocity* of the asset's turnover, or decrease the time required to complete the value-creation cycle.

Cash management includes putting money to work when it is in the hands of the company, as well as when it is not in the firm's possession. The latter, or transit time management, can be the source of significant incremental profits in a year. Transit time is made up of "mail float," "at-firm float," and "clearing float"[1] (see Figure 10.2). A float is a delay, or non-value-adding time period, during which the cash voucher (or check) is transmitted, received, recorded, deposited, and finally converted into cash. It is a period in which cash is placed in "limbo," unavailable to the firm and of little use to anyone else.

Mail float, or the time that elapses from when the check is prepared and placed in the mail at its source (the debtor) until it is received by the firm, is an uncontrollable factor in the cash cycle. This type of float can take anywhere from one to five days. Hearing that "the check is in the mail" is of little comfort to most financial

---

[1]Frederick C. Scherr, *Modern Working Capital Management: Text and Cases* (Englewood Cliffs, N.J.: Prentice Hall, Inc., 1989) p. 34.

FIGURE 10–1
Lawnmasters, Incorporated Financial Statements

LAWNMASTERS, INCORPORATED
Balance Sheets
December 31, 1990 and 1991

	December 31, 1991		December 31, 1990	
Assets				
Current assets:				
Cash.....................	$41,300		$31,000	
Accounts receivable (net of allowance for bad debts)..............	35,000		30,000	
Inventory.................	25,000	$101,300	29,000	$ 90,000
Long-term investments:				
Common stock in Quick-seed Corporation.......		10,000		15,000
Long-term assests:				
Property, plant and equipment..............	90,500		85,800	
Less: Accumulated depreciation.............	31,500	59,000	23,600	62,200
Total assets.................		$170,300		$167,200
Liabilities				
Current liabilities:				
Accounts payable..........	$35,000		$32,000	
Income tax payable.......	1,500		2,000	
Short-term notes payable..	15,000	$ 51,500	18,000	$ 52,000
Long-term liabilities:				
Long-term notes payable ..		15,000		10,000
Bonds payable............		35,000		40,000
Stockholders' equity				
Common stock, par $10...	50,000		50,000	
Contributed capital in excess of par...........	5,000		5,000	
Retained earnings (net of $7,000 in dividends paid out each year)..............	13,800	68,800	10,200	$ 65,200
Total liabilities and stock-holders' equity..........		$170,300		$167,200

FIGURE 10–1 (continued)

LAWNMASTERS, INCORPORATED
Income Statement
For the Years Ending December 31, 1990 and 1991

		December 31, 1991		December 31, 1990
Sales revenue		$160,000		$125,000
Cost of goods sold		100,000		75,000
Gross margin		$ 60,000		$ 50,000
Less expenses:				
Salaries	$25,000		$24,100	
Depreciation expense . . .	7,900		4,300	
Advertising	6,500		5,000	
Interest	3,000	42,400	2,400	35,800
Net income before taxes . .		17,600		14,200
Income taxes		7,000		5,600
Net income		$ 10,600		$ 8,600

LAWNMASTERS, INCORPORATED
Statement of Retained Earnings
For the Years Ending December 31, 1990 and 1991

	December 31, 1991	December 31, 1990
Retained earnings balance, January 1	$10,200	$ 8,600
Plus net income for the year	10,600	8,600
Total retained earnings available to stockholders . . .	$20,800	$17,200
Less dividends paid	7,000	7,000
Retained earnings balance, December 31	$13,800	$10,200

FIGURE 10–1 *(continued)*

LAWNMASTERS, INCORPORATED
Statement of Cash Flows
For the Year Ending December 31, 1991

Cash flows from operating activities:
Net income, per income statement.......		$10,600

Add:
Depreciation...........................	$7,900	
Decrease in inventories................	4,000	
Increase in accounts payable..........	3,000	14,900
		$25,500

Deduct:
Increases in accounts receivable	$5,000	
Decrease in taxes payable.............	500	
Decrease in short-term note payable ..	3,000	8,500
Net cash flow from operating activities.			$17,000

Cash flows from investing activities:
Cash received from sale of investments..		$ 5,000
Less cash paid for equipment...........		4,700
Net cash flow from investing activities....		300

Cash flows from financing activities:
Cash received from long-term note payable		$ 5,000

Less:
Retirement of bonds payable..........	$5,000	
Cash paid for dividends...............	7,000	(12,000)
Net cash flow provided by financing activities.............................			(7,000)

Increase in cash.........................	$10,300
Cash at the beginning of the year.........	31,000
Cash at the end of the year...............	$41,300

FIGURE 10–2
The Cash Cycle

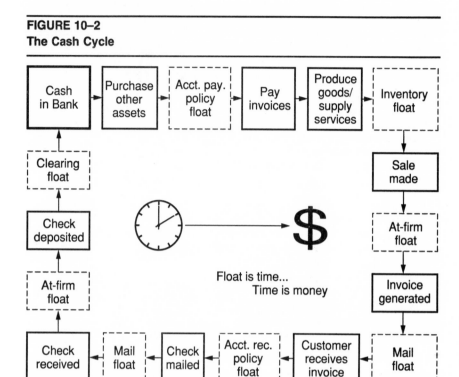

managers. It may or may not be true—but either way, the cash is unavailable to the firm.

Just getting the check in hand, though, does not mean it is available. The payment has to be recorded and the check processed for deposit. It may seem that getting the check in the bank would be the highest priority item on a company's daily agenda, but bureaucracy can get in the way. If check processing is not given high priority by management, it may end up being delayed for a day or longer. In this situation, every day lost is taking profits from the bottom line, a loss that management can easily curtail by simply changing procedures. The faster a check hits the bank the faster the cash becomes available for other uses. Any in-house delay is waste—waste that can be controlled through effective management.

The final aspect of the "float" is the actual time it takes the bank to clear the check. Clearing float, which can take anywhere from zero to ten working days for international accounts, is often addressed specifically by a bank as part of its search for strategic advantage. A bank may be reluctant to release funds when it is still at risk for the principle, but there are ways for them to hedge the payment cycle, especially as information system advances continue to revolutionize these transactions.

Effective cash management starts by actively seeking ways to reduce this "out of firm" float, as well as any excessive delays occurring in the credit management process: It is the *efficient and productive use of cash to create value and increase profits*. It starts by recognizing that any delay in the cash–to asset–to revenue–to cash cycle reduces profits. The opportunity cost of float, or foregone interest, may intuitively seem like a minor issue; how much interest can be earned in a day on a dollar? But in reality, more effective management here can yield significant annual profits, as interest is earned on reducing the outstanding dollars tied up in the float, on average, not on just a single dollar at one point in time.

Companies can improve their cash management procedures by selecting banks with accelerated check-clearing capabilities or by accelerating the check processing procedures at their own firm by using electronic collection procedures or utilizing lock boxes (post office box numbers distributed throughout the country that are directly serviced by a bank that collects the checks and processes them for the firm). As cash is freed up by reducing the total float period, it should be aggressively invested in short-term securities and money market accounts. If the cash is not needed in the near term, even more interest revenue can be generated by moving to longer term securities. In either case, cash itself is being used to generate incremental revenues for the firm.

The key element in cash management is to remember that *using it effectively is the goal*. That may not always mean holding on to as much as possible, but rather balancing off the available cash (and interest it can earn) with other factors surrounding the management of the business. For instance, a large company that recently adopted just-in-time inventory policies decided to make the transition more comfortable for its vendors by paying all invoices within 24 hours, or even upon receipt of the goods if requested. In other words, this company felt that JIT materials called for JIT cash. JIT intricately links the vendor to a company; if it faces cash flow problems, it may be in the customer's best interest to help out. The result is loyalty: The vendor loyalty that JIT supply channels depend on.

The Asset Management Process

The discussion of the issues in managing the asset *cash* provides a framework for understanding the concept of asset management in general. Cash is the most liquid of a company's resources and the source of all future value creation. It is not to be treated as a stagnant pool waiting to be put to use acquiring other resources—it can be effectively managed for profits the same way as any other resource. The velocity of cash flow through a company, consisting of the production–sales–credit cycle and the payment cycle, has the potential to generate profitability if aggressively pursued. To let cash lie idle is tantamount to throwing away scrap—both waste resources and reduce long-term profitability.

Each asset on the balance sheet can be dissected in the same way, looking for ways to increase its velocity, or turnover rate. Resources that sit idle do not earn profits. They waste them. A dollar of inventory is a dollar that can't be invested in other income-generating resources. If inventory is held long enough, it can totally lose value (become obsolete). That is a waste that can be seen. What is often ignored, though, is the fact that idle inventory consumes value-creating potential, preventing the company from exercising other options. The cumulative opportunity cost of holding inventory can, over time, wipe out any "profits" it generates downstream.

This fact is the basis for an emerging set of practices: *time-based management*. Time-based management suggests that *time* is the critical element within an organization; each asset and activity has to be aggressively used to create more value than the competition. The recognition that companies are swapping one asset (the capability to pursue opportunities) for another (inventory) is one revelation coming from this area. In other cases, it is leading companies to actively manage and reduce their *time to market* for a new product in order to gain a competitive edge. Time-based management focuses everyone's attention on the *process*, or flow of resources, as the key to sustainable competitive advantage. Idle assets, wherever they're found, are waste.

Asset management is a focused study of the resources at a company's disposal to look for ways to keep them generating value. For physical assets, this means holding them for as short a period as possible before turning them into profits (e.g., part or all of the asset may still be physically in the firm's custody, yet have already generated its equivalent value in sales or income). Human capital, R&D, and other "expensed" items, though, are most valuable if retained; the investment may not show up on the balance sheet, but its long-term value-creating potential does—in asset growth and increases in retained earnings.

Higher asset utilization leads to increases in stock price (from increased rate of value creation), return on equity, available cash, and revenue per asset employed. Improvements in asset utilization can also improve customer satisfaction with price, delivery, billing, and quality of service, as the company more aggressively and effectively manages the value-creation cycle. Finally, effective asset management is a people-based improvement process for the company; employees, not machines, make the decisions, analyze the value-creation process, and implement plans to improve them. This active involvement can lead to improved customer satisfaction as employees are empowered to use their skill and knowledge to improve company performance against customer expectations.

RETURN ON ASSETS: THE GENERATOR

If the shoe fits, you're not allowing for growth.

Robert N. Coons (1)

A company's return on assets (ROA) is a primary indicator of the effectiveness of its asset management process. It captures the relationship between income and the firm's investment of the financial resources committed to it. Whether those financial resources have been provided by bonds, other liabilities, or stock is of little matter; the key factor is how well each dollar has been employed to generate current and future profits. The basic ratio, or calculation, used to calculate a company's ROA is

$$\frac{\text{Net income} + \text{After-tax interest}^2}{\text{Average total assets}^3}$$

Using the numbers from Lawnmaster's financial statements, we find its ROA for 1991 is

---

[2]After-tax interest is added because it represents the funds that are available for the "owners"; the residual, of course, goes to the various taxing agencies. To get this number, reported interest expense is multiplied by (1 − tax rate percentage).

[3]Average total assets can be calculated by adding last year's total ending assets to this year's ending balance and dividing by 2. This is equivalent to taking beginning of year plus end of year balances and dividing by two to get the amount of net assets held, on average, by the firm.

$$ROA = \frac{\$10,600 + [\{1 - (7,000/17,600)\} \times \$3,000]}{[(170,300 + 167,200)/2]}$$
$$= \$12,407/\$168,750$$
$$= 7.4 \text{ percent}$$

Interest is added back to the net income because the funds provided by creditors are included in the ROA calculation. Since interest is part of the profits earned, in general, by the organization, it is added back in to reflect profits available to all providers of funds. Averaging the net assets in the calculation helps to match the characteristics of the flow-based income statement with the changing pool of assets that were used to create it.

Return on assets is the outcome of two different underlying processes in the business, as suggested by the following equation:

Return on assets = Assets turnover × Profit margin

where: Asset turnover = (Sales + After tax interest)/Average assets
Profit margin = Income/Sales

For Lawnmasters, these calculations now become:

Asset turnover = $160,000/$168,750
= .95 times
Profit margin = $12,407/$160,000
= .078
So

ROA = .95 × .078 or 7.4 percent

The **asset turnover ratio** reflects the fact that companies invest in assets to generate sales. The profit margin provides the information on how profitable each dollar of sales is for the company. Both are critical elements of the puzzle; when two companies or two industries are compared, both ratios provide information about the nature, as well as effectiveness, of the asset management process.

The **asset turnover** ratio can be subdivided into several basic asset classes: receivables (days sales outstanding), inventory (inventory turns) and long-term assets (property, plant, and equipment [PPE] turns). Conversely, a company's profit margin can be analyzed from several different perspectives: cost of goods as a percentage of sales, R&D as a percentage of sales, and selling and administrative expenses as a percentage of sales. In other words, the asset turnover ratio

---

FIGURE 10–3
Basic Measures of Asset Management Effectiveness

Overall performance measures:

Return on assets:
$$\frac{\text{Net income} + \text{Interest} (1 - \text{Tax rate})}{\text{Total assets}}$$

Return on invested capital:
$$\frac{\text{Net income} + \text{Interest} (1 - \text{Tax rate})}{\text{Long-term liabilities} + \text{Owner's equity}}$$

Return on equity:
$$\frac{\text{Net income}}{\text{Owner's equity}}$$

Profit margin:
$$\frac{\text{Net income}}{\text{Sales}}$$

Tests of asset utilization:

Asset turnover:
$$\frac{\text{Sales revenues}}{\text{Total assets}}$$

Working capital turnover:
$$\frac{\text{Sales revenues}}{\text{Current assets} - \text{Current liabilities}}$$

Fixed asset turnover:
$$\frac{\text{Sales revenues}}{\text{Property, plant, and equipment}}$$

Days sales outstanding:
$$\frac{\text{Average accounts receivable}}{\text{Average daily sales}}$$

Inventory turnover:
$$\frac{\text{Cost of sales}}{\text{Average inventory}}$$

Equity turnover:
$$\frac{\text{Sales revenues}}{\text{Owner's equity}}$$

---

incorporates all of the sub-elements of profitability the firm has at its disposal; it captures how effectively resources are utilized throughout the organization. A summary of these ratios, and how they are calculated is detailed in Figure 10–3.

These ratios allow a company to benchmark its performance against competitors, identify areas of opportunity, and develop programs and processes for improving long-term performance.

Managing Inventories and Receivables Before They Manage You

Accounts receivable is a key area where companies can increase their profitability. Each day that a receivable is outstanding, the customer is receiving a discount on their purchases equal to the total interest that would have been earned if the money had been collected by the company and placed in an interest-bearing account. In the same vein, when excess inventory is held, working capital that could be turned to more productive uses is tied up, making it impossible for the company to undertake other opportunities that may come along. Returning to the concept of time-based management, inventory replaces the asset *capacity* in the company's *capabilities balance sheet.*

There are two ratios that can be used to evaluate whether a company is effectively managing these current assets: days sales outstanding for accounts receivable, and inventory. Returning to Lawnmasters these ratios are

Days sales
outstanding = Average accounts receivable / Average daily sales

Where: Average accounts
receivable = (Beginning A/R + Ending A/R)/2
= [($30,000 + 35,000)/2]
= $32,500

and

Average daily sales = Current year's sales/360
= $160,000/360
= $444

So for Lawnmasters, the days sales outstanding for 1991 is

$32,500/$444 or 73 days

Another way to look at this is to say that Lawnmasters *turns* their accounts receivables 4.93 times per year (360 days / 73 days = 4.93). On average, it is taking 73 days to collect from customers on account; if credit terms are 2/10, net 30, which is a common industry standard, Lawnmasters' customers are taking an additional 43 days to pay, on average, tying up $19,092 in excess working capital to fund them (43 days × $444 average sales per day = $19,092). If Lawnmasters was able to invest this at eight percent interest, it could add $1,527 to its annual net income before taxes [$19,092 × .08 = $1,527]. That is an almost 10 percent increase on current year earnings ($1,527/$17,600). Obviously Lawnmasters' management could easily increase its available capital by simply handling its receivables more effectively.

What does the inventory analysis suggest about the effectiveness of the asset management process at Lawnmasters? Look at this ratio:

Inventory turnover = (Current year cost of sales/Average inventory)
= $100,000/[($25,000 + $29,000)/2]
= 3.7 turns per year

Let's look what would happen if Lawnmasters could increase its turn to 12 times per year, or once per month. The working capital that would be freed up would be

Current average inventory: $27,000

Required inventory at 12 turns = $100,000/12 = $8,400 (rounded)

Decrease in average inventory: $27,000 − $8,400 = $18,600

If this increased level of working capital could be freed up for investment at 8 percent, it would increase net income before taxes by $1,488 ($18,600 × .08). This understates the impact of decreased inventory levels, though, as it overlooks the non-interest related carrying costs that naturally accompany inventory. Warehouse space, insurance, additional record-keeping, increased obsolescence, and damage all add to the cost of inventory. These dollars of waste are one cost of keeping inventory; lost capability is another. Effective asset management requires aggressively attacking opportunity costs as well as more traditional expense items.

Simply stated, Lawnmasters could add at least $3,015 (1,488 + 1,527) to its net income before taxes by changing its policies for managing these assets. That is equivalent to the profits from an additional $8,040 in sales ($3,015/.375, the gross margin percentage). That may not seem like a major difference, but the numbers in Lawnmasters are very small. For a company of any size, a 17-percent increase in net income before taxes [$3.015/$17,600] is impressive. For larger companies this number grows rapidly. Also, the interest applied here understates the increased value these funds could provide if invested in other activities. Using conservative numbers, there's ample room for gaining profits by better asset management.

Before moving into other ratios that can be used to understand the overall return on asset performance of a company, it's important to remember that these analyses are most effective when **relative performance** is the focus. Is Lawnmasters doing better or worse than other companies of roughly the same size in its industry? What are industry norms for accounts receivable policies? Since these numbers are part of publicly available financial statements, it is useful to compare one company against its peers. If only one category is being analyzed, it may be possible to look at the company's performance relative to a firm that is *best-in-class* during a benchmarking study. In either case, the numbers in isolation can identify the magnitude of the opportunity cost of tying excess resources up in non-value-creating assets, but it can't give a definite answer on what policies should be pursued.

LONG-TERM ASSETS AND PROFITABILITY

Real generosity toward the future consists in giving all to what is present.

Albert Camus (1)

The effective use of long-term assets can make the difference between sustainable profits and mounting losses from idle capacity. In looking at capital asset management, the issues that need to be considered include the following.

1. Is there a bottleneck machine or area that is leading to excessive idle capacity in the rest of the facility?
2. Are there major assets that are not being used, and probably never will be?
3. As process improvements are made, are the excess resources being redeployed?
4. Are there ways to use *process* improvements to increase the effectiveness of capital asset utilization?
5. What is the true capacity of each major subsystem of assets? Will this level ever be reached?
6. How should idle capacity be accounted for and managed?
7. What is the replacement cost of our existing asset base? Are these costs, and the timing of replacement, being taken into account in our cash planning, long-term pricing strategies, and facilities planning?
8. What are the long-term issues in the industry? Does *economy of scale* still provide the best basis for competitive advantage,

or is increasing variety in customer demand suggesting that flexibility and *economies of scope* are more critical?

Ratios can be applied to begin the assessment of capital asset management. This is not as informative an approach as looking at current assets, however, because of the impact of obsolescence, capacity issues, depreciation charges that probably don't reflect the reduction in the asset's productive value, and related issues hidden from view in the one-line item "Property, plant, and equipment" on the balance sheet.

Traditional accounting records, it would seem, provide little insight into answering these questions. That is because each of these questions is concerned with effective *capacity utilization,* not revenue generation. Every asset can be managed with an eye on ROA, or asset turnover. Employing the *bottleneck* concepts detailed by Eli Goldratt in his *Theory of Constraints* is everyone's job; process analysis is the basis for understanding, and effectively using, a company's capability for creating value.

Asset management, though, does not necessarily mean using every asset to 100 percent of its potential capacity. Instead, it requires the active trade-off of the costs of idle resources in one part of the company against alternative solutions to the resource balancing problem. Since resources cannot be bought in "kits" that will provide just the right amount of value-creation potential for current needs, there is always going to be a need to actively recognize and manage the **trade-offs** being made. Sound asset management practice is the effective management of trade-offs.

Fixed Asset Ratio: A Starting Point

What ratios can be used to understand the importance of fixed assets in a company's profitability picture? Two that are of value to understand the relative impact of fixed assets to total asset profitability are

Asset turnover = Sales revenue/Average total assets

Fixed asset turnover = Sales revenue/Average fixed assets

Comparing these two ratios gives an indication of the **capital intensity** of the company. If a company has a high capital intensity, its profitability will be highly vulnerable to swings, or cyclical fluctuations, in its business activity level. This is because high levels of fixed assets bring with them high levels of fixed costs; these costs will not go away when volumes drop. In other words, when a large percentage of a company's asset base is made up of fixed assets, the impact of economies of scale is a very real concern.[4] Often, increasing the volume flowing through the system is the only way to remain competitive.

How does Lawnmasters fare against these measures? Returning to the financial statements (Figure 10–1) one more time, we see

$$\text{Asset turnover}_{1991} = \$160,000/[(170,300 + 167,200)/2]$$
$$= .95$$
$$\text{Fixed asset turnover}_{1991} = \$160,000/[(59,000 + 62,200)/2]$$
$$= 2.64$$

Fixed assets (net of depreciation) are approximately 35 percent ($59,000/$170,300) of Lawnmasters' total asset base. What that translates to in terms of the above ratios is that each dollar invested in general assets leads to $0.95 in sales, and each dollar invested in fixed assets generates $2.64 in sales revenue. The fixed assets are, on average, far more productive than any of the other assets maintained by the firm. This fits with the earlier discussion of their problems in managing receivables and inventories.

The benefit of this situation for Lawnmasters is that they can, in a fairly short time period, improve the return on assets by simply addressing their credit collection and inventory policies. These assets are much more responsive to changes in policies, leading to marked improvements in overall profitability in a very short period of time. For now, it appears that Lawnmasters' management should focus on short-term assets; when they perform up to the level of the fixed assets, another round of decision making and planning can occur.

When Fixed Assets Lie Idle

For Lawnmasters, the major idle resource is accounts receivable. For many other companies, though, fixed assets are the major source of concern. When fixed assets aren't performing, solutions that can return them to a reasonable level of productivity can be difficult to identify

---

[4]The effect being described here reflects the fact that the spreading of fixed costs over more units reduces the impact of these costs per unit made or sold. Since the costs are fixed, the only way a company can affect its costs is by increasing the utilization of its fixed assets.

and implement. And fixing problems in one area can actually generate more idle capacity in these areas.

That may not necessarily be undesirable; it may be cheaper overall to keep idle resources on hand to respond to market demand than to store excessive levels of inventory. Both approaches may make the company appear more responsive to the customer, but whereas the former holds capability as the asset, the latter holds an expensive physical asset. Capability wears out slowly; its *obsolescence ticker* moves quite slowly. Inventory, though, has a very fast meter; its value is decreased by a multitude of factors, all operating at once to drive its stored "value" to zero.

For instance, when the process flow inside of a factory is converted to a cellular design (JIT manufacturing), throughout improvements are gained. This, in turn, usually generates idle capacity, both for the plant in general (reduced inventories and improved process flows decrease the space needed to house the manufacturing process) and the manufacturing cells. Improving the velocity of materials through the plant actually creates idle resources in the fixed asset area. This is the reason why, although improvements are seen in inventory levels and turns, the fixed costs don't budge in many instances.

Unless the idle resources are put back to work making other products, or are eliminated from the asset pool, their costs don't change. It is a fact that needs to be recognized, but used in a practical way. Conscious recognition and acceptance of idle capacity costs as the price paid for increased material velocities is one thing; blind pursuit of JIT manufacturing (or any other management tool) is another. Each decision is, in reality, the management of a trade-off, the swapping of one asset or capability for another. Asset management simply means that this trade-off is made consciously, not by default.

Another way that fixed assets can be idled is when they are constrained by process bottlenecks. Bottlenecks impair the entire value-creating chain, reducing the potential return the various assets can generate for the company. This can be hard to see when inventory is lying everywhere, machines are run as islands of activity, and rush orders clog the system. When the process is straightened out, though, the impact of these flow-constricting areas becomes apparent. It may be necessary in this situation to spend money in order to make it; improving the throughout in the bottleneck area is a prerequisite to improving the performance of other assets.

Idle capacity is one of the most challenging areas of asset management. Because this "idleness" is bundled into the manufacturing system, it is expensive; part of each *nonbottleneck* machine's value-creating potential is being wasted. This fact led many of the early writers in management accounting to suggest that an **idle capacity account** should be maintained as an expense assignable to (and controllable by) upper management. Several income statements from the 1910–1925 period actually listed this expense for investors to use in their evaluations. This is unlikely to happen today, but it seems inappropriate to ignore these cost in internal reporting. Only if the actual cost of non-performing assets is clearly reported can the firm's asset management policies be improved. When numbers aren't reported, they're ignored.

How to put a "ticker" on idle capacity is a more difficult question. Should fixed assets be evaluated on their theoretical ability or normal usage? What cost should be assigned to each idle hour of a machine? Of a cell? As the capacity measure is increased, the cost per hour, whether productive or idle, goes down, but the number of hours to account for obviously goes up.

What capacity makes sense, then? Since the bottleneck resource is key to the system's performance, it should be rated at theoretical capacity, or as close to that level as deemed possible by the engineering group. The key is to get this number out in front of management in order to encourage them to search for ways to improve the system or increase the activity in the plant. Doing so will drop dollars directly to the bottom line, increase the asset turn ratios, and increase the return on assets figure—all desirable events.

On the other hand, managing every asset to its stated capacity is nonsensical. The outcome of this approach is huge mounds of work-in-process, as unbalanced production generates another form of idle resource: inventory. Managing assets means managing the **system** that creates value, not pushing every worker and machine to the limit every hour of the day. A smooth production flow is one of the primary paths to maximum profitability.

Other Fixed Asset Issues

One of the major shortcomings of using ratios to understand fixed asset performance is the fact that the value of these assets is often understated by the FMIS. Unless an asset is really going to be obsolete or retired once it is fully depreciated, the fixed asset should continue to be actively managed for profits. Idle capacity charges can provide one way to counteract the myth that fully depreciated assets are "free." Depreciation expense may have stopped, but there are still many other costs caused by the machine or asset. More importantly, the company incurs a substantial *opportunity cost* for not using the asset to create value. Effective asset management doesn't stop until the asset is sold or retired totally.

Recognizing that the value of capital-intensive companies was being understated by the FMIS, the FASB attempted to mandate the disclosure of **replacement costs** for the various fixed assets owned by the firm. This information was provided in order to direct attention to the very real need to replace the company's productive assets at some stage if its long-term survival was to be ensured. The belief was that many of these companies were overvalued because their assets were fully depreciated, making their apparent return on assets higher than it should be. Unfortunately, this disclosure met with enough resistance to overturn it in the late 1980s. Today, industry expertise is needed to garner an accurate picture of this aspect of a company's current and future potential.

Finding the Hidden Opportunities

Asset management is an art, conducted with a specific purpose in mind: to increase the velocity of the value-creation cycle. Traditional views of assets as the structure or heart of the organization are challenged when this *process-oriented* view is taken. Dollars that lie idle, whether in a bank account, in transit between the customer and the company, in uncollected bills, in excess inventory, or in underutilized fixed assets, represent a permanent but invisible loss of profits. Each dollar can generate profits, even if that profit is only interest on a deposit, but only if it is expected to do so. Anytime it becomes acceptable to let assets build up needlessly available profits drop.

Effective asset management starts with the understanding that assets aren't where the value of the company is, but where it is lost. Assets are only value-creating if they're being fully utilized to generate sales and profits. In mastering this area, the balance sheet has to take priority in the management process. What assets does the company have on the books? Which ones look free but are really capable of creating value on an ongoing basis? Where are the hidden opportunities for generating more activity with the same set of assets? Finding answers to these questions can lead to a competitive edge; ignoring them can lead to deteriorating profits.

The way to start employing asset management is to calculate the velocity of value creation, or turnover, of the various assets the company has invested in. Merging the information in the strategic cost analysis area, benchmarking concepts, and the basic ratios that have been suggested here, the relative performance of your company against its primary competitors can be more fully understood. Armed with this information, priorities for improving the way key assets are managed can be established.

By shifting focus away from the income statement to the balance sheet, asset management techniques trigger fact-finding missions focused on issues that can provide long-term benefits for the company, its customers, and other stakeholders. Rather than seeking a scapegoat when profit projections are missed due to the "mysterious" forces of the market, everyone's eyes can be clearly focused on improving the process to increase value-creating potential. Getting more done with less is the objective.

Effective asset management can be a central focus of the continuous improvement efforts within a company, a way to prioritize these efforts, and to pinpoint those assets that are creating blockages in the process. Profits aren't created in a static environment; they are the result of the dynamic utilization of every asset available to the company to increase the velocity of the value-creation cycle. A second key objective of asset management is not only to get more done with less, but to get it done faster. The shorter the cash–to asset–to cash cycle is, the more flexibility the company has to respond to changing conditions, and, not surprisingly, the more likely the company is to have satisfied customers.

Putting asset management concepts to work means implementing the **time-based management** approaches suggested by writers such as Stalk and Blackburn.[5] As suggested by Stalk:

> The opportunity presented by time is changing the paradigm for achieving corporate success. Historically, corporations have been successful by providing the most value for the least cost. The new paradigm for corporate success is providing the most value for the lowest cost in the least amount of time. . . . Time-based competitors direct the benefits of their value-delivery systems toward the most attractive customers,

---

[5]Two good sources of material in this area are *Time-Based Competition: The Next Battleground in American Manufacturing*, ed. Joseph D. Blackburn (Homewood, Ill.: Business One Irwin/APICS Series, 1991) and *Competing Against Time* by G. Stalk and T. Hout (New York: The Free Press, 1990).

the ones that are willing to pay for responsiveness, fast delivery, and choice.[6]

Putting these concepts to work means understanding the business environment, customer needs, the assumptions your company and your competitors are using to artificially *constrain* the value-creation cycle, and mastering the process-based techniques that have been suggested here.

Time is what a company really has to offer to the marketplace, whether the value of that time is stored in an asset (and, therefore, recorded by the FMIS as an asset), or quickly passes through the system (resulting in an expense). Removing bottlenecks, whether on the plant floor or in the back office, increases the velocity of asset turnover, and actually generates additional value-creation potential for the firm. Time-based competition puts asset management into high gear. It turns everyone's eyes to the critical role played by process analysis and material velocity in generating competitive advantage and improving profitability.

Asset management is intricately linked to time-based competition, the theory of constraints, and the goals of World-Class performance. It can also open a lot of eyes to the need to change. Awareness is the first step to making needed changes work in an organization; the analytic tools that have been examined above suggest one way this wake-up call can be made. It is a more productive approach than waiting for the FMIS to signal disaster with red ink, blown budgets, and cost reduction mandates. Proactive management doesn't start with the bottom line; it molds it.

PEOPLE, PLACES, AND FINAL POINTS

Our destiny changes with our thought; we shall become what we wish to become, do what we wish to do, when our habitual thought corresponds with our desire.

Orison S. Marden (2)

Achieving any goal in life is as much an attitude as a process. This fact is as true in the asset management area as any other. While analytics and numbers can focus attention, create awareness, communicate

---

[6]G. Stalk, "The Strategic Value of Time," in Blackburn, p. 69.

urgency, and generate movement, they cannot make the changes needed. That requires people. Not an earth-shattering statement, but sometimes the obvious gets lost in the process. In fact, the most valuable assets in the value-creation cycle are the people who keep the process going, who intervene when the machinery breaks down, and who see, learn about, and communicate better ways of doing things to those around them.

Productivity measures have been the traditional way to focus attention to how well people are performing within an organization. Unfortunately, these measures put a premium on physical output over the mental efforts required to generate organizational learning and innovation. Employing the whole person means more than pushing for more output with the same number of hours and materials:

> Under the whole person approach, idle time becomes "brain time"—a resource to be cultivated![7]

Fixed assets that remain idle generate no value, but idle people can. "Idle" people can be redeployed to value-enhancing projects, to find ways to improve the process, or to identify key areas of waste that present opportunities for improvement. People are the primary asset in the capabilities balance sheet.

In fact, the only way organizations can employ continuous improvement is through people. Machines can't learn the same way a person can (at least, not yet). And if they could, there would still be a need for a person to direct attention and set the system in motion. Effective management of the human resources in a company does not mean pushing for every last ounce of physical output; it means empowering individuals to work with others to get the job done better, faster, and cheaper.

Unfortunately, the FMIS is of little or no help in driving this message home. Of all the shortcomings that have been charged against these systems, this may be the most damaging. This fact has been debated by a group focused on **human resource accounting**.[8] The FMIS, which treats all labor as an unstorable expense of doing business, misses the mark in this area. If management follows the lead set in these statements, people become interchangeable with machines.

---

[7]R. Dixon, F. Nanni, and T. Vollmann, *The New Performance Challenge*, pp. 18–19.

[8]The primary proponent of the latest push in this area was Eric Flamholz. His writings were convincing, but he was unable to secure an ongoing place in the accounting literature.

There are plenty of horror stories in the trade press to underscore where this philosophy leads.

Is there any way to put a value on the people in the organizations? If this value can't be put in numbers, does it make their value-creating potential any less real? Obviously, the answer is that without people, value creation is impossible. If, instead, individuals are actively employed (both brain and brawn) in problem-solving as well as production, the value-creation cycle can be accelerated. The key to gaining these improvements is to remember that measures that focus attention on squeezing one more unit of output out of an individual are counterproductive. Effective human resource management is not equivalent to physical asset management; idle time is not idle unless management chooses to treat that individual as simply another tool of production. If the worker is involved, empowered, and encouraged to experiment, quantum leaps in performance can be achieved.

Putting "Expenses" to Work

Effective asset management means looking beyond the numbers and accounts that appear on the balance sheet to include the assets that are disposed of quickly by the FMIS (expensed as incurred), and those that may never generate a financial transaction at all. Making progress on the first front can lead to significant profit improvement, but without the latter, it cannot be sustained.

People are not the only assets that have only a momentary presence in the FMIS, yet are critical to the long-run profitability of the firm. Research and development, which determines the future of the company, is also expensed. This was not always so, but since the late 1970s companies have been required to treat R&D as a period expense, one that is not assigned any long-term value in the FMIS. Treating R&D as a "discretionary" expense is a troubling practice. Could this treatment account for the growing shortfall in this critical area in the United States? In a management arena heavily influenced by profits and stock prices, it is quite possible that expensing R&D could be one of the causes of this apparent decline.

If a company buys a new machine or upgrades an old one, the cost can be capitalized. On the other hand, when it invests in developing new markets, new products, and new applications for existing expertise, no asset is recorded. That makes it quite difficult to justify sustained spending in this area when financial performance is less than glowing. Yet the Japanese, who compete on their **core competency**, actually put these activities first on their list. No matter how the FMIS treats these costs, they are hardly discretionary, unless the company isn't planning to be around in the long run. That would seem to violate the **going concern assumption** in accounting, though—an interesting paradox.

Recording these costs as assets can provide industry with the facts needed to push for tax relief for innovation as well as capital investment. Reinstituting the investment tax credit may help the economy; providing incentives to innovate and create new processes, products, and markets will accelerate and solidify these improvements. As long as the FMIS disposes of these resources in the short term, though, it will be difficult for industry to engage this battle with the government.

R&D costs have to be treated as period expenses in most cases, but the oil and gas industry is allowed to capitalize the cost of exploration to find new wells, within certain parameters. This quirk in the rules and regulations suggests that a clear argument (or enough political pressure) was brought to bear on the rule-making process (FASB), to lead to change in this area. It was a change that allowed an industry to capitalize on its major value-creating activity. Even more encouraging is the fact that the FASB's decision to allow both *full cost* and *successful efforts*[9] in the oil and gas industry overturned a decision to disallow the capitalization of these expenses. Within the structure of this industry, that decision threatened the survival of the small wildcatter, who might go several years before drilling a sustainable well.

The small biotechnology companies are facing many of the same problems. Start-ups often fail because they can't get additional funding from the market. If they were able to capitalize their research and development costs, amortizing them against successful products, would they look less risky to investors? Quite possibly. And what about large

---

[9]More detail on what these terms mean can be garnered from a number of sources, such as the *GAAP Guide*, Delany, et.al., Englewood Cliffs, N.J. Prentice-Hall, 1992. The essential difference is that "full cost" approaches treat exploration as an operating expense; "successful efforts" approaches allow small producers to capitalize the exploration costs for a field, charging them off (amortizing) against the wells that are developed at some point in the process.

companies? If they were able to capitalize their development dollars, would these efforts receive more attention both internally and external to the firm? Would more active management of these resources take place? Once again, it can be argued that this would be the case.

The Who, What, and Why of Asset Management

This chapter has detailed the basic issues in asset management, starting with the recognition that the FMIS is only one tool needed to gain a competitive advantage in this area. Asset management, defined as *the effective utilization of a company's asset base to produce profit*, refers to the company's *capability*, or ability to create value, not its historical record in this regard. It shifts attention away from the income statement to the balance sheet, from profits to potential.

In looking at asset management concepts, the role of the cash–to asset–to revenue–to cash cycle was presented as a unifying theme. Cash represents potential; fixed assets reflect history. Several tools for improving cash management techniques were suggested. The discussion then turned to other assets recorded on a traditional balance sheet, analyzing the issues surrounding inventory mangement and its hidden counter-part, material velocity. Fixed assets were also analyzed, using financial ratios such as the *return on assets, inventory turnover ratio, and fixed asset turnover ratio*. Turnover ratios point out the velocity, or throughput, the company has attained over the prior period.

Asset management ties directly to time-based management concepts, bottleneck management, and throughout-enhancing tools such as just-in-time manufacturing and inventory management, the "quick changeover" movement, design for manufacturability, and approaches that reduce time-to-market. In the area of asset management, the key concepts required to achieve World-Class performance are brought together: It is an area that intergrates the diverse interests of individuals across the organization.

In fact, effective asset management starts with recognizing that people are the key resource in a company. The information needed to understand existing practice comes from the people who do the job. Suggestions for improving these practices, and hence accelerating the profit-creation cycle, come from the human resource asset. Implementation of these ideas takes place through people. It is not a financial tool for top management use; everyone in the company can participate in the quest to improve profits and create a sustainable competitive advantage through effective asset management.

Assets are everywhere. Some are recorded in the FMIS as assets, others as expenses, and some are not recognized at all by the general ledger. That does not diminish the importance of intangible assets. Instead, it suggests the need to create an enhanced financial report (the *capabilities balance sheet*) that will attempt to put a value on every resource. It will quite likely be a time-based system, reflecting the fact that the company's potential to create value deteriorates over time. It will also have to provide the means to actively understand and manage the trade-offs between one type of idle resource and another; idle capacity may prove to be the cheapest way to achieve flexible, real-time manufacturing.

Asset management drives home the very real fact that the FMIS is not a perfect tool. It can prevent action, focus it in the wrong areas, and derail change. Yet it is only a tool. If management understands it, is not unduly influenced by transitory "blips" in profitability, and keeps its eyes on performance measures that promote continuous improvement and innovation, the negative impact of the FMIS will fade away. The tool should not drive the management process; the fact that it does suggests that the "numbers" are not the only area needing change. Attitudes—the minds directing the use of the tools—are the key elements in any social system. The tool can help or hinder—the choice remains to be made.

> *Two essential qualities in a good organizer are a thorough and constant perception of the end in view, and a power of dealing with masses of details, never forgetting that they are details, and not becoming their slave.*
>
> Sir Arthur Helps, *Organization in Daily Life (4)*

> *No values are effective, in a person or a society, except as there exists in the person the prior capacity to do the valuing, that is, the capacity actively to choose and affirm the values by which he lives.*
>
> Rollo May, *Man's Search for Himself (4)*

SUGGESTED READINGS

Blackburn, J., ed. *Time-Based Competition: The Next Battleground in American Manufacturing*. Homewood, Ill.: Business One Irwin/APICS Series, 1991.

Dixon, J. R., A. Nanni, and T. Vollmann. *The New Performance Challenge: Measuring Operations for World-Class Competition.* Homewood, Ill,: Business One Irwin/APICS Series, 1990.

Howell, R., and W. Schwartz. "Asset Deployment and Investment Justification." In *Handbook of Cost Management*, ed. Barry Brinker. New York: Warren, Gorham and Lamont, 1991.

Scherr, F. *Modern Working Capital Management: Text and Cases.* Englewood Cliffs, N.J.: Prentice Hall, 1989.

Stalk, G., and T. Hout. *Competing Against Time.* New York: Free Press, 1990.

CHAPTER 11

NUMBERS FOR BUDGETING

Nothing is more terrible than activity without insight.

Thomas Carlyle (2)

Budgets are the backbone of the planning process in most organizations. Starting from forecasted sales, these "crystal ball" gazings are only by accident correct, yet continue to be a critical management tool. The reason for this lies in the budget process itself, where communication and negotiation are emphasized, and the boundaries for future results and evaluations are detailed. The social dynamics of budgeting are by far their greatest contribution; the plan that results is a symbol of the compromises that have been reached and the limits everyone has agreed to abide by. Budgets are one of the primary tools for ongoing communication and coordination.

The power of the budget stems from several characteristics. First, because it is stated in financial terms, it appears to be objective. The numbers tend to mask much of the underlying politics and negotiations of the budget process from view. Second, the financial manager ensures that the game can be played by completing a cash flow analysis of the plan, which serves as the stop or go light in the process; at its core, the process is grounded in hard economics. Third, the budget helps the organization rationalize the planning process, assign responsibilities, and create common goals. It is a tool that can generate the insights needed to guide activity.

Yet the politics of budgeting is never far from anyone's mind. The harsh realities of organizational life are that the total demand on resources is greater than their supply. The budget shapes the allocation of the firm's scarce resources, focusing them in areas that are believed to be best for the long-term success of the organization. The budget, though, cannot ensure that sound strategic planning occurs. It is a mechanism to support the development of the long-term perspective that can lead to competitive advantage, but it does not guarantee that it will occur. Without budgets, management is in a reactive mode, constantly renegotiating the future. With them, this renegotiation is directed toward a specific goal.

An organizational view of budgeting stresses the politics, communication process, and the creation of goal congruence (e.g., everyone playing from the same game plan). Individuals within this process, though, often lose sight of the "common good" as they attempt to secure resources to support the goals of their area and the expansion of operations under their control. When this happens, the budgeting process becomes less effective as a tool for generating goal congruence.

The type of budget process that evolves in an organization is almost totally a function of its underlying culture. A highly political organization will have a very political budgeting process; a nonpolitical organization will probably use the budget to query facts and assumptions, not people. Additionally, the way that the budget is factored into the evaluation process can have a major impact on the way the game is played. If individual incentives are heavily dependent on reaching stated budget goals, people will build in enough slack to make sure they have a reasonable chance of making them.

The incentive issues surrounding budgets are one of the major ways they shape the organization and the actions of individuals within them. It's hard to be aggressively proactive if your future is going to be jeopardized by a budget "blow." In approaching the budget process, the guiding maxim, "You get what you measure and reward" has to be kept uppermost in everyone's mind; if it is forgotten, the actions that are generated may not be in anyone's best interest.

World-Class management techniques can take some of the mystery out of the budget process. For instance, the central position played by a sales forecast in the development of a manufacturing budget and production plan is well known. Yet if the manufacturing process can become highly *responsive*, able to make goods in less time than the customer allows or expects it to take, then this linkage between sales forecasts and production begins to loosen. More resources can be kept in their *capability stage*, awaiting commitment to a firm order, freeing up cash and management time for other opportunities.

Gaining this flexibility, and removing the slavish tie of resource commitment to the forecasting process, is not an option. Most companies are facing increasingly turbulent environments, shifting customer expectations, and heightened competition. All of this translates to a need to constantly analyze, position, and budget for future events. Planning is not a once a year event, but rather part of the ongoing process of effective, World-Class management.

These issues interact to make budgeting one of the most interesting and controversial areas of FMIS-based management practice. This chapter will open with the technical side of the budget process and the issues that have been raised about them, such as the role of variance analysis in these systems. Traditional budgeting will then be reshaped to reflect activity-based accounting concepts. The politics and common sense of budgeting will be examined, focusing on the double bind created when people are asked to honestly report their expectations when they know those statements can come back to haunt them downstream.

A CLASSICAL VIEW OF BUDGETING

Men commonly think according to their inclinations, speak according to their learning and imbibed opinions, and generally act according to custom.

Francis Bacon (2)

Most traditional discussions of budgeting describe it as a tool for planning and control in the organization. The assumption is that, prior to the beginning of a new year, a sales forecast is prepared, the resource implications of making these sales projections are determined, and the game is set in motion. Once the plan is established and the productive process has begun, a *control loop* is triggered; results are compared to budget, with any differences between the two (the variances) analyzed for their cause (see Figure 11–1). In creating the budget package, activities and expenditures are split into two major groups, operating and programmed, in order to more accurately identify the responsibility framework for the coming year.

The Budget Sequence

Within this traditional control framework, the budget process occurs in a fairly predictable manner in most companies. First (see Figure 11–2), marketing is asked to develop detailed sales forecasts by product for the upcoming fiscal year. Normally summarized on a monthly basis, these sales estimates are based on prior years' results, the sales group's best guess on buying patterns for existing and potential customers, and the relative performance of the various products offered

FIGURE 11–1
The FMIS-Based Control Loop

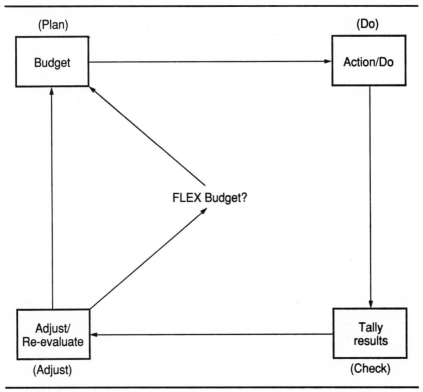

(the sales mix). The sales forecast is the basic schedule for the planning process; it is built from intuition and experience.

The sales forecast is seldom completed in one pass. Top management has a set of revenue numbers in mind based on its plans for the coming year, and marketing has another based on the complex mix of experience, expectations, and accountability. Since sales bonuses are often a major part of the total compensation for salespeople, they are constantly aware of the need to state numbers they can reach, so that bonuses are assured. Marketing is playing a "minimax" strategic game (minimize the maximum risk of missing their goals); management is playing a "maximax" game (maximize profits).

The negotiation of final sales goals can often take three to six iterations between marketing, which slowly moves its sales estimates up, and management, which slowly moves its expectations down. In

FIGURE 11–2
The Budget Cycle

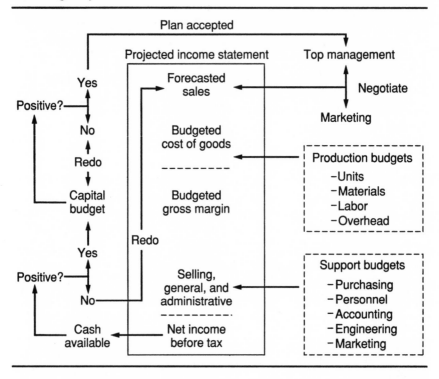

the end, the sales forecast represents a negotiated game plan that is seldom what either group initially wanted.

It is important to keep in mind that this is the *traditional* approach to budgeting. There is no question that in this setting, the entire organization is forecast driven. That is a major problem in a world where little is certain, and precise foreknowledge of events is difficult to come by. As long as the rest of the organization remains locked into time-consuming processes that require more time to complete than the customer is willing to tolerate (e.g., long lead times), the forecast remains a critical element of the planning process. As the time required to complete tasks, and the entire value-creation cycle, is driven down below the customer's expected, or allowable, lead time, the forecast becomes a much less critical tool. In making this leap, much of the built-in tension between marketing and the rest of the organization dissipates.

Generating Production Plans

Once the sales forecast has been established, the next stage of the budget process entails determining the operating impact of the forecast on the production area.[1] As can be seen in Figure 11.2, manufacturing translates the forecast into a production budget that reflects the projected demand and compensating inventory balances. Once the number of units needed to meet the budgeted sales volume has been determined, materials, labor, and overhead budgets are created. These are usually based on standard cost models of the projected amount of resources needed to complete a unit of output.[2]

The standards are normally applied to the materials and labor components of the production budget; overhead budgets are developed from prior experience. Manufacturing overhead costs, which include the cost of the building, supervision, utilities, and a range of other indirect expenses, are computed as gross dollar amounts in the budget process; once the budget is completed these estimates are transformed into per unit burden rates.

As we have seen in earlier chapters, these costs are sometimes charged out (allocated) on the basis of direct labor hours or dollars, material dollars, or a related activity measure. That means that for each hour of labor used, a product will also be charged a portion of the overhead cost. The burden rate can then be applied to estimate the total cost for the various products offered by the company and the projected profitabilities of the product lines (projected sales price less estimated total cost); summing these profitabilities provides a usable estimate of the gross margin for the coming period.

Once again, traditional approach to budgeting reflects traditional management practices. Each of the steps in this process is constrained by the underlying assumptions and methods for managing the organization. As each of the underlying constraints is removed, new options become available for budgeting, costing products, projecting profitabilities, and controlling and evaluating performance. In fact,

---

[1] A manufacturing budget is used here as a starting point; in service companies the key analysis at this stage becomes a labor and overhead budget.

[2] Standard costs are usually developed by industrial engineers, and reflect the basic materials plus "normal" scrap, labor plus "normal" down time, and related efficiency and effectiveness factors. These estimates are built from detailed analysis of the actual operating characteristics of each task performed to complete the product.

improving operations often simplifies and improves the planning (budgeting) process. Enhancing the responsiveness of the firm benefits internal and external customers alike.

Moving Below Gross Margin

Once the manufacturing budget has been put together, the budgeting process begins to address cost items and activities that appear below the gross margin line on a traditional income statement. The gross margin sets the spending limits for all of the other areas of the organization. Once this point is passed, the "discretionary" budget items begin to be developed, such as sales, marketing, advertising, all general and administrative functions, and research and development. Each functional area puts together its expense and capital equipment budget.

These budgets are usually limited to the percentage of total sales that management feels comfortable assigning to the various support functions. Areas like advertising and R&D are often set aside as the total resource implications of the plan are calculated. Since the expenditures in these two areas can be easily cut with no definable short-term impact on customers or profits, they are often the balancing tool in the budget process. This is unfortunate, because the company is playing with its long-term competitiveness when these "discretionary" cost items are reduced. The completion of the operating budget occurs when the estimated net income (all revenues less all costs) is at an acceptable level. Getting there may require ongoing negotiation as the realities of scarce resources in a world of infinite demands are dealt with.

This orientation changes as effective asset management techniques, the lessons of the continuous improvement philosophy, and the impact of World-Class technologies are added to the mixture. The goal is to minimize resources consumed in meeting today's demands in order to generate the ability to provide enhanced value to the customer in the future. Each dollar saved in making a product can be redeployed to creating long-term value; innovation is the key to sustainable competitive advantage.

Capital Assets: Factoring in the Big Ticket Items

Up to this point, the budgets have been constructed on a piecemeal basis, moving through the organization like a floating income statement, picking up passengers as they go. The capital budget, on the other hand, is done jointly across the organization. All requests for capital assets for the coming year are pulled together and analyzed to determine which ones represent the best use of the company's scarce funds.

The backbone for this analysis is one of several capital budgeting techniques, such as *net present value analysis, internal rate of return,* or *payback.* The first two of these techniques factor in the time value of money, as detailed in Figure 7–1 (restated here for your convenience). The difference between the two is that net present value techniques assume a desired rate of return, and accept proposals which show a positive net present value at the stated rate (see Figure 11–3). Internal rate of return approaches, on the other hand, identify the actual rate of return the project will yield by finding the present value factor that will drive the present value of the project to zero. If this interest rate is above the desired return for the company, the project is passed on; otherwise, it is turned down.

Payback methods for evaluating capital projects are a bit simpler, and are not recommended by most experts in this area. The objective is simple: Determine how many years it will take to get the investment back. Projected cash inflows are simply tallied until the invested capital is returned. The faster the invested capital is returned, the better the project is seen to be.

As noted, payback methods are not usually suggested as the method of choice in capital assets models, yet they continue to be widely used by management. One reason given for this is the fact that they are simple to perform and understand. The arguments made against them is that they fail to level the cash flows to comparable dollars across multiple periods. The fact that the method continues to be relied on raises the question, "Why?" Is management unaware of more sophisticated approaches? That's not likely, given the fact that MBAs populate the corporate landscape. The answer may lie simply in the fact that the farther away a cash flow is, the less *certain* management can be that it will materialize. The cash flow projections become far less reliable as they are extended out in time: They are riskier.

Payback methods implicitly factor in the risk of an investment. When used in tandem with one of the other discounted cash flow techniques, they can provide a read on the total projected profitability of the asset assessed against the riskiness of the projected cash streams. The benefit of factoring both views of the asset acquisition puzzle

---

FIGURE 11–3[†]
Present Value and Project Analysis

Western Soap Company is continually receiving inquiries about available capacity. Since it recently rented out one of its soap lines on an ongoing basis, it has had to turn a lot of this business down. Faced with a high-class problem, the CFO, Fran Gammell, has decided to explore the possibility of adding adding another line. Two companies have quoted on systems, each having different start-up costs and run capabilities (e.g., speed and capacity). Fran feels a good return, or cost of capital percentage, is 15% for this type of investment. The breakdown of the two alternatives is:

Year	Cash flow line A	PV_f	PV_A	Cash flow line B	PV_f	PV_B
0	($350,000)	1.00	($350,000)	($450,000)	1.00	($450,000)
1	75,000	.870	65,250	100,000	.870	87,000
2	125,000	.756	94,500	150,000	.756	113,400
3	150,000	.658	98,700	200,000	.658	131,600
4	150,000	.567	85,050	200,000	.567	113,400
5	200,000*	.507	101,400	250,000*	.507	126,750
Totals	$350,000		$ 94,900	$450,000		$122,150

Based on these calculations, Fran decides to purchase the second line. Although it has a higher initial cost, it will yield an additional $27,250 in incremental cash flows over its lifetime than its less expensive competitor.

[†]This is Figure 7.1 restated for convenience.

NPV_f = the net present value factor, or discounting rate, that will make a dollar in the future equivalent to a dollar today.

NPV_A = the net present value of the projected stream of cash inflows. It is derived by multiplying the net cash flows by the present value factor.

*The final year's cash flows include the projected salvage value of the assets.

**In making a decision in a present value framework, the project with the highest *net present value* (total of the present value column) is the one chosen, given everything else is equal.

---

into the analysis are obvious; both a long-term and short-term view of the impact of the various projects can be established. This allows management to build a portfolio of investments that can balance off cash demands and future profitability.

One other factor has to be mentioned before moving on to the cash budget and the conclusion of the budgeting process. The cash flows that are entered into the capital budgeting process are estimates. It is difficult to isolate the cash inflows that a particular investment will generate because it creates value throughout the organization.

The fact that these estimates are difficult to make, let alone verify, makes the capital budgeting process something of a game. The participants want a certain set of assets to improve the effectiveness of their area, but there are only so many dollars to go around. Each group develops asset proposals that are likely to be rejected in order to ensure that those that are really needed get through. This is not a bad practice; managers are communicating the fact that they are willing and able to compromise on their needs for the best of all. It's important to remember that the underlying cash flows that serve as the basis for the game are "magical" numbers that are difficult to track after the fact.

This is a cursory view of the capital budgeting process. In reality, generating the projected cash flows, determining current and future costs and benefits from the asset, and factoring in the qualitative issues that need to be considered make capital budgeting a complex process. Constrained by available resources and strategic plans, capital budgeting represents the firm's commitment to fixed assets as the basis of competitive advantage. Once purchased, these assets affect the organization for a long period of time, constrain future options, and structure the processes that the firm can employ.

Capital Budgeting—Another View

The realities of the capital budgeting game have led some companies to remove some of the magic from the process, asking managers to classify their capital projects as *survival*, *growth*, or *replacement* in nature. The rules applied to make each class of decisions are different; assets required for the survival of the firm (pollution-abatement devices) are not negotiable. They have to be acquired. The only relevant question surrounding them is, "Can we get it any cheaper than this?"

Capital assets designed to support strategic initiatives are a second class of projects. Items like computer-integrated manufacturing are difficult to justify when the underlying reason for their acquisition is strategic. Strategic investments are not easily tied to specific cash inflows; they are projected to be necessary to remain viable in the long term. Just as survival-based asset decisions are not negotiable, once a strategy has been chosen, growth items are equally nonnegotiable. The key question here is, "Can it wait a while, or does it need to be done now?"

In each of these cases, the capital asset models are really inappropriate. The functionality of the asset, and the company's reason for acquiring it, are not based on specific cash flows or benefits. Both reflect deeper issues in the organization. The final class of assets, though, does lend itself readily to the various capital asset evaluation techniques. Replacement assets are being acquired for a known process, a known function, a fairly stable flow of products, and a recognized period of time. The information necessary to create a reliable cash flow analysis of the asset and its benefit to the company are available. Replacement assets should always pay for themselves.

When the three categories of assets are used during the capital acquisition process, effective *ex post audits* of their effectiveness can be used. Survival assets can be audited to make sure they are providing the required services. Growth assets can be evaluated against their stated functionality; is the CIM line really improving quality and responsiveness? Finally, the replacement assets can be readily audited against the projected cash flows in the investment analysis.

A logical approach to capital budgeting incorporates the role the asset will play in the short-term and long-term survival of the company, its strain on current resources versus the benefits it should provide, and a negotiation of the timing of various acquisitions based on the projected profits for upcoming periods. Capital assets are the basis for long-term competitiveness; they cannot be overlooked in the budget process.

Taking a Tally: The Cash Budget

Once everyone has spoken for their piece of the available resources, the game turns from fiction to fact. Preparing the cash budget is the critical step in the budget process, and it is the only one centered in the financial group. Here the estimated sales patterns, expenses, and capital requests are tallied for their cash implications. Revenues are detailed based on existing payment patterns—sales become cash when the customer pays the invoice. Expenses are recast in terms of the company's payment policies—when will the bills have to be paid? Finally, major cash outflows for dividends, interest payments, and capital assets are added to the cash budget.

The cash budget is the final screen on the budgeting process. If the cash balance, given the estimated receipt and expenditure patterns, is positive, the budget is done. If it shows a negative balance, the game starts all over again. The hard rule is simply that, like an individual, a company cannot overspend its cash balances. When more cash is needed than ongoing operations will provide, the company is driven to the financial markets for an infusion of cash. When this happens too often, the pool of eager investors begins to dry up.

Investors are probably willing to fund growth (and to a lesser extent survival) assets and activities, but are likely to believe that the company should be able to cover its ongoing operations on its own. The statement of cash flows was designed to help an investor make an assessment about whether the funds the company is requesting are going to ongoing operations or long-term growth. Reviewing the cash flow statement of a company is a good starting point for understanding how well management is attending to cash flow issues and assessing the long-term success of the organization. If a company is having to dip into outside funds to cover ongoing operations, the future of the firm is suspect. On the other hand, if most of the funds needed for long-term asset acquisitions are being internally generated, the company is quite healthy and should continue to be competitive.

The cash budget serves as the internal meter on the reality of a budget, while the cash flow statement provides an ex post tally of how the game was really played. The former is a management tool, the latter a scoreboard for external use. Both are useful; they are parts of the FMIS that serve different customers at different points in time.

KEY ISSUES IN BUDGETING

Financial sense is knowing that certain men will promise to do certain things, and fail.

Ed Howe (1)

The budget process itself appears quite mechanical, setting spending limits and creating the game plan for the coming year. Yet it is a game of uncertainty and guesses, one that can be unraveled by reality on a moment's notice. There are several issues surrounding the budget process that have to be recognized:

1. They are subject to change at any moment.
2. They are the primary tools for assigning responsibility for the successes and failures during the game.

3. Their presence does not ensure that dollars are directed toward value-creating activities.

4. They can inhibit action as well as motivate it.

The first of these factors is the basis for a modification to the budget process that recognizes the impact of varying volumes of activity on the projected results of the year. **Flexible budgeting** is the term used for these types of budgets. In completing the budget, contingency plans for several ranges of activity are developed. These are used to modify the spending plans of the company, to adjust the product costing formulas, and to ensure that falling revenues are accompanied by equally falling costs (i.e., profitability is maintained where possible).

Focusing in on the variable and discretionary parts of the budget puzzle, these contingent budgets attempt to provide a game plan for the range of outcomes management believes may occur. They also provide a way for management to control the organization more effectively when volumes are shifting. Most companies incorporate some form of flexible budgeting into their annual plan, making it possible to react more quickly to changes in the market.

In addition to flexible budgets, management often has to deal with extensive changes in their markets or customer demand within the time frame of a budget. That has led many companies to institute **rolling budgets,** where a new quarter of activity is projected each time another is completed. In other words, as the first quarter of 1991 is completed, managers forecast the expected activities for the first quarter of 1992. In this manner, there is always a one-year plan in place, and revisions to plans are constantly being made as new information arrives. This constant budgeting may seem to be a waste of time, but if the environment is highly volatile, it is a necessity. Also, rolling budgets keeps everyone's mind on the long run; competitive games are not artificially set on a one-year cycle.

Responsibility Accounting: The Control Side of Budgeting

The second major issue in the budgeting arena is the assignment of responsibility for various outcomes and activities. As part of the ongoing management control process, the objective is to identify those individuals who can control outcomes, and to assign accountability for them. The FMIS term for this is **responsibility accounting.**

At the core of responsibility accounting is the belief that individuals should not be held accountable for outcomes or events they cannot control. This basic tenet of fair management suggests that cost allocations are undesirable; managers cannot control the service function that is generating the cost. Yet companies continue to allocate in the belief that operating managers will pressure their service-providing counterparts to keep costs down if, and only if, they directly bear the consequences of costs in these areas.

Assigning responsibility does have a down side. It promotes parochialism, or the splintering of efforts in the organization: an "us versus them" attitude. Many of the new management approaches are designed to counteract the functional silos that have been reinforced by the responsibility accounting framework. While it is based on hard-to-dispute logic, the playing out of its assumptions and techniques can often impair coordinated efforts within the organization.

Some of this can be addressed by thinking of budgeting in nonfinancial, as well as financial, terms. Given that financial results are the outcome of the management process, it is important to remember that they are designed to generate action, not inhibit it. To the extent that budgets reflect the existing accounting representation of the firm, it is important to balance their message with more strategically oriented views of current and future performance. Continuous improvement approaches provide a way to "budget" operational performance outside of the FMIS loop. Improvement goals lead to profit enhancement and attainment of strategic objectives. Budgets are simply one tool to be used in guiding an organization toward World-Class status.

Variance Analysis: A Brief Review

A vital part of the responsibility accounting system in most companies is **variance analysis.** Here actual costs are compared against budgeted allotments for the various activities and outcomes of the company. The objective—to understand the reason for the "misses"—should be used to help the organization learn about its processes and business. Yet variance analysis is usually a *blame-attaching* event in which budget shortfalls are directly assigned to individual managers. When variances lead to the question, "Who screwed up?" they are counterproductive tools of control. The right question, "What went wrong?" often never gets asked.

Variance analysis, one of the primary control tools maintained by the FMIS, is not a favorite topic among operating managers for several reasons. First and foremost is the way that the accountability question is played out; a scapegoat is often a necessary outcome of the process. Second, variances are a late arrival to the control scene. By the time the traditional FMIS creates a variance report, two to six weeks may have passed since the triggering event. In fact, the report encompasses all of the events, positive and negative, that occurred during the measured period of time (usually a month). Pinning the variance on one or several of these is a pointless game. Third, the information is seldom used to make improvements in the system; once an explanation is attached to the variance report, the process is considered complete. The variances are entered into the general ledger to balance the accounts, and the reports are sent along to management.

Variances are a natural outcome of a budget process that is built on countless estimates in an environment that is constantly changing. The key fact to keep in mind is that variances should be used to motivate and learn, not to assign blame. As with many of the FMIS-based control tools, it is not the tool that is critical in shaping individual responses; it is the *use* made of those tools. Control, or the efforts made to influence the behavior of others, is not necessarily negative. Yet when blame and accountability are the core concern, FMIS control tools can generate counterproductive finger-pointing exercises that blur the company's focus on long-term competitive issues. When blame is the basis for responsibility accounting, it is little wonder that the technique is viewed with distaste.

Overhead Creep—Costs that Grow Unabated

The overhead rate that is developed as part of the budget process is already one step removed from the underlying expenses that the company will incur to support production. The actual dollar amounts projected for each overhead category, usually based as much on history as the forecast, are not created from scratch, but instead arise from adjustments to prior year figures. This *incremental* approach to budgeting is the most common method for developing these financial tools. Unfortunately, it is also a technique that has led to an upward "creep" in these dollar amounts from year to year.

Since the dollars requested for overhead are seldom tied to any definable outcome or product, they tend to grow unattended. Spreading them out over the products through a burden rate hides this fact from view. It often appears that overhead becomes a given number that can't be changed, only distributed. This is unfortunate, because high overhead rates can often cause outsourcing or discontinuing of various product lines. The allocation of the "glob" of overhead that is accumulated based on prior experience, whether that experience was economically favorable or not, creates a snowball effect, with profits being rolled into the overhead as the snowball makes its way downhill.

Asset management techniques can help inhibit and control overhead creep. If every resource, every asset, every process is continuously managed to optimize the value-creating potential of the entire organization, wasted resources and excessive spending can be spotted and stopped before they get out of hand. Also, asset management techniques remind us that each asset, not the glob of overhead, is what generates value. Waste in any area cannot be accepted or tolerated.

As will be seen, an activity-based FMIS requires management to associate some metric of value-adding work with each dollar, or cluster of dollars, in the overhead budget. A similar attempt to understand overhead and reduce its creep was instituted by the federal government under McNamara in the 1960s. Called **zero-based budgeting**, the objective was to make everyone start from zero in every category of the budget, and to add cost to the overhead budget only when the item could be justified. The program did not catch on as well as might have been hoped, but the exercise of querying the numbers in the budget proved valuable.

The underlying lesson of budgeting for any item other than direct costs is to recognize that dollars spent on overhead items are the same as the dollars spent in production; both should generate profits through value creation. When this fact is overlooked, the soft side of the budget grows, taking profits away from the future of the business, increasing prices to the customer, and decreasing the dollars available for internal stakeholders and owners. To assume that the dollars need to be spent is tantamount to giving up on their ability to generate value.

Companies attempt to control overhead creep by instituting across the board cost reduction mandates. The familiar "everyone is to cut five percent from their budgets" refrain can send chills down the backs of managers already struggling to make do with inadequate resources. The incremental budgeting–cost reduction cycle, suggested in Figure 11–4, is one of the most common business cycles taking place in modern organizations. It is a reactive management approach; the costs are allowed to get out of hand before actions are taken to cut them. When the cuts do take place, value-adding and non-value-adding costs are cut an equal amount. This isn't logical, but since value-adding capabilities weren't part of the initial budget, they can't be used later to remove waste.

Incremental budgeting is the normal state of affairs in most companies. Overhead is not given the same type of attention as more easily indentifiable and traceable costs, such as direct labor. Because it is treated as a glob, with little or no understanding of the linkage between activities in an overhead area and the organization's value-creation cycle, good and bad practices proliferate. In addition, history becomes the primary driver of the future, as new methods and procedures are added on top of old. Seldom does anyone stop to ask,"Why are we doing this?"

This state of affairs is rapidly changing today. Activity-based FMIS approaches start with "Why?" questions, and move beyond them to assess the value-creating potential of various activities and groups. When objective information is needed, the external environment is queried through benchmarking and industry analysis. As companies become more centered on the product-service bundle approach to managing their operations, the systemic view of value creation will spread.

The entire organization, above some minimal level of operations, should add value to the customer. Everyone within the company needs to be aware of, and concerned about, their role in meeting customer expectations. The basic analysis that underlies activity-based FMIS installations leads to a clear understanding of the firm's value chain, the value system, and the potential for improvements across the organization. The goal? To reduce or eliminate non-value-adding work, wherever it may occur, whether on the plant floor or in the back office.

Inhibiting Action—A Constant Concern

The final issue of ongoing concern for financial managers is the recognition that the plans cannot take precedence over reality. When opportunities arise that are not in the budget plan, management has to

FIGURE 11-4
The Incremental Budgeting Cycle

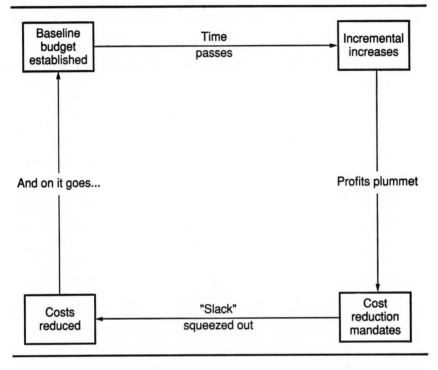

take advantage of them. A recent article in *Business Week* describes how Johnson & Johnson keeps their managers' eyes on the competitive marketplace. The core of their plan—decentralization—is based on the belief that managers have to run their business without undue interference from corporate. As noted in the article:

> At Johnson & Johnson, the presidents of its 166 separately chartered companies are not just encouraged to act independently—they're expected to. Beyond traveling at will, they decide who will work for them, what products they will produce, and which customers they'll sell to. They prepare budgets and marketing plans, and many oversee their own research and development.[3]

---

[3]J. Weber, "A Big Company That Works," *Business Week*, May 4 1992, pp. 124–132.

In this situation, managers are given free rein to creatively utilize the resources at their command to generate value for the customer and the company. It works because the decentralization is accompanied by empowerment of the management of each division.

The budget in these settings is not the tool to coerce individuals to succeed; it is a means to make sure that the plans can be attained. When budgets are used to guide and to communicate expectations, they are value-adding tools. When they are used as a bludgeon to assess responsibility for performance shortfalls, and to mete out punishments, they are value-diminishing. Which event comes to pass has nothing to do with the physical structure of budgets, but rather the intent of management as the tool is put into motion.

Attaching budgets to incentive systems skews their impact, tilting them toward control and away from motivation. If an individual is held accountable for events outside his or her control, if the budget process is highly political, or if individual performance is overlooked in favor of budget-based evaluations, the budget game can create a host of undesirable side effects (such as slack-gaining behavior, data manipulation, parochialism, and negative attitudes). It is clear that an individual should be evaluated against clearly defined goals, but results should not be the sole factor in handing out rewards. If this is overlooked, a company is conveying a clear message: "The ends justify the means." The ethics of management would suggest otherwise.

If individuals freely participate in the budget process (as opposed to pseudoparticipation),[4] many of the negative side effects of budgeting can be nullified. Control-oriented uses of the budget can lead to gamesmanship as individuals seek to ensure that they will perform well against preset goals. Understating goals provides individuals with the slack necessary to make their goals. Is this bad? Within the setting it is rational behavior; it is the setting that has to be questioned, not the individual's morality.

The negative issues surrounding the budget process, and its ability to generate undesirable events, have led many to suggest that budgets have outlived their usefulness in organizations. Yet that seems to be throwing the baby out with the bathwater. Instead of eliminating

---

[4]Pseudoparticipation is often the reality. Here, individuals are asked for their input, but top management has already defined the game. The goal is merely to make it look like individuals had an input into the plan, not to really shape it. Pseudoparticipation has been found to have negative behavioral effects on the people caught up in it.

budgets, they need to be viewed more realistically as the games they really are. This spirit of playfulness, or autonomy, appears to be the critical factor in separating productive from counterproductive budget exercises, as suggested in the following comments by Hofstede:

> Both motivation and job satisfaction of a budgetee are positively affected when the atmosphere created around the fulfillment of standards is one of sportsmanship; of seeing budget control as a game. This game atmosphere is related to the control-autonomy balance, because a game presupposes a certain free area to play in, a certain margin or scope of "play" . . . Without this freedom, there can be no game spirit. Budgetees need free scope in budget fulfillment.[5]

It would appear that Johnson & Johnson is actively encouraging the gaming spirit, by supporting the empowerment of its management teams and the corresponding trust that they will work toward the best interests of the organization.

The control element of budgeting can actually countermand the motivational effects of framing the budget plan. When a gaming attitude is adopted, everyone understands and clearly communicates that no events are set in stone and that the objective is to fully utilize resources in the best alternative available at any one point in time, within a generally accepted field of action. Treating budgeting honestly as the game that it is can support its motivational effects and diminish many of its less desirable side effects. Autonomy, or *empowerment*, is the basis for productive budgeting and competitive advantage.

UPDATING BUDGETS: AN ACTIVITY-BASED PERSPECTIVE

Better a dish of illusion and a hearty appetite for life, than a feast of reality and indigestion therewith.

Harry A. Overstreet (2)

The discussion to this point has dealt with traditional budgets and the problems they have been identified with. The activity-based

---

[5]G. Hofstede, *The Game of Budget Control*, Assen: Van Gorcum and Company, 1970, pp. 17–18. This source may appear out of date, but it is the seminal work in this area. Being based on extensive field studies of companies using budgets, the study provides a refreshing, operational view of the budget process itself. It is highly suggested as a source of understanding the dynamics inherent in the budget process.

approach to developing budgets is another area where change is occurring, although the pace of this evolutionary process is slow. Why? Because in adopting activity-based budgeting, management is agreeing to strip away the illusion from the support activities by asking everyone to report the types of things they do, and why. In an activity-based budget, incremental increases in budget line items never go unquestioned; every increase, as well as every budget item, is queried for its value-creating potential. Should the item fail to pass this rigorous screen, it is added to the pile of costs to be eliminated.

Many companies are beginning the implementation of their activity-based FMIS at the time budgets are made. It is the most natural time to ask people what activities are going to be undertaken in the year to come, what the expected workload is, and what types of resources they feel will be needed. Extending the analysis, existing activities can be segmented into value-adding versus non-value-adding segments, supporting the development of cost control programs.

Cost control occurs *before* money is committed or budgets get out of hand; it is a proactive cousin of cost reduction. The objective in undertaking a cost control exercise is to reduce the total dollars being spent on non-value-adding work before it becomes necessary to mandate deep reductions in the face of falling profitability. Controlling costs means asking "why" before they creep beyond acceptable levels. Each time an increase in a budget item is asked for, it has to be accompanied by a justification that substantiates the fact that extra work will be done with the funds, and that the resources cannot be gleaned from improving the completion of other activities.

The Activity-Based Budget Packet

To understand the relationship between traditional budgeting and an activity-based approach, one of the departments (cost centers) that appeared in Figure 11–2 is reexamined in Figure 11–5. The initial costs requested by the materials acquisition group are noted at the top of the total budget. These dollars are spread across the natural expense accounts that are found in most general ledgers (e.g., salaries, supplies, space charges, and so on).

The objective in completing the activity-based budget is to match up these resources with the work they are going to support. In the first schedule, the various activities that are planned for the upcoming year are noted. They include such items as routine purchase order processing, special orders, vendor negotiations, vendor qualifications, expediting, paperwork, training, and meetings.

Each of these activities will consume a significant amount of the various resources dedicated to the materials group. To get the resources into the right activity pool, individuals in the materials group are asked to respond to a brief survey that asks for an estimate of the time spent completing each of the various activities, the travel costs that each activity generates, and any other key resource-affecting issues. These are only estimates, not fact, but there is no alternative. In fact, these "guesses" are usually as well-founded in reality as the budget itself.

Armed with this information, the financial manager now only needs to apply the resources based on the estimates provided, leading to the activity-based cost pools on schedule two of the exhibit. To ensure that every dollar is accounted for, Figure 11–5 includes a series of summary sheets that tally each natural account to its budgeted level. To complete the activity-based analysis, one final question needs to be asked at this point: "Approximately how often will this activity take place?"

Answering this last question is perhaps the hardest part of designing an activity-based budget. As individuals attempt to identify the drivers for each of the various activities, they are constantly trading off accuracy for practicality. A driver has to be a sound, *countable* proxy for the activity itself. The driver, often noted to be the cause of the cost, it is the trigger for the work to occur. If a countable trigger is

---

FIGURE 11–5
Original Purchasing Budget and the ACMS Budget Packet

Salaries	$300,000
Perquisites/benefits	75,000
Office supplies	100,000
Telephone	18,000
Postage	12,000
Travel	100,000
Miscellaneous	24,000
Total budget for FYE 1992	$629,000

FIGURE 11–5 (continued)
The ACMS Budget Packet

GROUP: _Purchasing_

STEP ONE: Activities List

Please list the major activities that you have identified for your area of responsibility:

Activity	% Time	Driver
Regular P.O.'s	20%	# P.O.'s–Class A
Special P.O.'s–New Materials	10%	# P.O's Class B
Special P.O.'s–Major Purchases	5%	# P.O's Class C
Vendor Negotiation	10%	Total Vendors
Vendor Certification	10%	# Qualified Vendors
Expedite	25%	Late Notices
Meetings, Misc.	20%	On Demand

STEP TWO: Assigning Costs

Activity: _Regular P.O.'s_

Resource	% of Cost	Estimated Cost
Salaries	20%	$60,000
Perks	20%	15,000
Office Supplies	40%	40,000
Telephone	30%	5,400
Postage	50%	6,000
Misc.	20%	4,800
Total Costs		$131,200

FIGURE 11–5 (continued)

Activity: *Special P.O.'s Materials*

Resource	% of Cost	Estimated Cost
Salaries	10%	$30,000
Perks	10%	7,500
Supplies	5%	5,000
Telephone	20%	3,600
Postage	15%	1,800
Travel	5%	5,000
Misc.	10%	2,400
	Total Costs	$55,300

Activity: *Special P.O.'s—Major Purchases*

Resource	% of Cost	Estimated Cost
Salaries	5%	$15,000
Perks	5%	3,750
Supplies	5%	5,000
Telephone	5%	900
Postage	10%	1,200
Misc.	20%	4,800
	Total Costs	$30,650

FIGURE 11–5 (continued)

Activity: *Vendor Negotiations*

Resource	% of Cost	Estimated Cost
Salaries	10%	$30,000
Perks	10%	7,500
Supplies	5%	5,000
Telephone	10%	1,800
Postage	5%	600
Travel	25%	25,000
Misc.	10%	2,400
Total Costs		$72,300

Activity: *Vendor Qualification*

Resource	% of Cost	Estimated Cost
Salaries	10%	$30,000
Perks	10%	7,500
Supplies	20%	20,000
Telephone	10%	1,800
Postage	20%	2,400
Travel	60%	60,000
Misc.	10%	2,400
Total Costs		$124,100

FIGURE 11–5 (concluded)

Activity: *Expedite*

Resource	% of Cost	Estimated Cost
Salaries	.25%	*$75,000*
Perks	.25%	*18,750*
Supplies	.20%	*20,000*
Telephone	.20%	*3,600*
Misc.	10%	*2,400*
Total costs		*$119,750*

Activity: *Meetings, etc.*

Resource	% of Cost	Estimated Cost
Salaries	.20%	*$60,000*
Perks	.20%	*15,000*
Supplies	5%	*5,000*
Telephone	5%	*900*
Postage	0%	*—*
Travel	10%	*10,000*
Misc.	.20%	*4,800*
Total costs		*$ 95,700*

identified, the design of the activity-based FMIS is facilitated. Often the paper trail that is created to control the process, such as move tickets, can be a useful way to proxy support activities. Also, MRP programs can be farmed to identify other usable drivers that are currently being collected as part of the operational control system.

Drivers are a critical element needed to complete schedule four in the sample budget packet. In attempting to develop an estimated cost per activity, the financial manager is transforming the sundry mix of variable, fixed, semivariable, and semifixed costs that comprise the overhead pool for each area into a *pseudovariable* cost. If major volume shifts lead to different cost patterns, the activity-based budget can be "flexed" in the same way that a traditional budget can be; the flexible budgeting simply takes place around different types of volume measures (e.g., activities) and for a smaller, fragmented set of costs.

Another interesting issue surrounding activity-based approaches to budgeting is whether dollars are necessary at all. It is clear that the activities part of the budget can be generated, and have value, without the financial estimates. Yet to be useful in changing behavior, the dollarized estimates are required. At planning time, they provide a way to control the level of resources committed to certain activities and generate an awareness of what existing policies and processes mean in terms of economic survival. During the year, these estimates provide a valuable decision-support database, as well as underscoring the very real fact that profits are made and lost every day. Placing price tags on internal goods and services can help generate an overall awareness of asset management issues and the importance of eliminating defects on the way to World-Class performance.

Revising the Activity-Based System

The first time the activity-based budget is completed, the estimates are fairly ambiguous. The activities identified, drivers chosen, and mapping of general ledger costs to the activity pools are based on estimates that build from other estimates. Luckily, once the budgets have been instituted, it is possible to start analyzing and revising the activity-based estimates. Either quarterly, semiannually, or annually the budget should be revised, not only from the expense side of the equation (traditional budgeting) but also from the workload side (activity-based budgeting). Significant changes in either element should be factored into revised estimates. How often the revision takes place depends on the natural cycles within the company. If a manufacturing plant shuts down twice a year, there are two natural half years in any fiscal year. This provides a natural break in business that can be used to revisit the activity-based estimates.

Since the activity-based analysis is founded on projected costs that are tied directly to workloads, these estimates can be updated by the actual costs incurred in an area. This is an improvement over traditional budgets and variance analysis; the linking of the operating and financial control systems supports learning. Variances are very much a part of an activity-based system. In fact, more variances are created than ever before. But the question a variance raises is radically changed. Instead of asking "Who screwed up?" the focus turns toward changes in activity levels, or to changing patterns of resource utilization. This information added to the FMIS allows the variance analysis process to actively identify areas of opportunity, spots where costs are moving up faster than activity levels justify, and places where continuous improvements efforts are paying off.

The People Side of Activity-Based Budgets

Better cost control is one benefit of an activity-based approach, but the approach also supports improvements in incentives. First, activity-based systems measure individuals against the same range of activities as the operational control system does. This eliminates confusion and prevents much of the data manipulation that characterizes traditional budgeting. Everyone can be evaluated based on improvements in their performance of key activities, and not just on the financial outcomes of those efforts.

It is also easier to identify and eliminate non-value-added activities than it is to determine which employee will have to go when a cost reduction program is put in motion. If activities are constantly managed to eliminate waste, the latter seldom has to occur. Controlled growth of support areas can prevent downstream cost reduction drives that can demoralize the organization and prevent future improvements.

Decoupling the evaluation process from the financial results has many positive effects on the organization and morale. As individuals respond to questions about what they do, they begin to feel that someone does care about their work. This may lead them to be more conscientious in the future. Second, individual improvements can be closely monitored; if individuals have signed up for improvements in certain parts of their jobs, an objective measurement of their progress can now be taken. Third, people are no longer being penalized for the vagaries of the costing process. They are evaluated based on the work they perform, not the accounting outcome associated with that work. This provides a greater feeling of autonomy in the control process, if it is supported by empowerment.

Finally, it is impossible to develop an activity-based budget without the active participation of the workforce at all levels of the organization: The source for the activity-based budget is the individual. Top management can't tie costs to activities; they can, at best, get them to cost centers. The individual can, on the other hand, approximate the activities and resources that will be needed to support them. They are a critical part of the budgeting process.

BUDGETING: PLANS WITH A PURPOSE

Imagination is a quality given a man to compensate him for what he is not, and a sense of humor was provided to console him for what he is.

Oscar Wilde (2)

Budgets, whether traditional or activity-based in nature, are built on history and imagination of a brighter tomorrow. The future, always one step away, is where everything will work out, success will be ensured, and everyone will meet their personal and professional goals. Or so we are told. Yet the budget is more than applied imagination; it is a tool for negotiating the murky waters between what is and what is desired to be. It establishes a common language, a common set of goals, and defines the path necessary to reach them.

Capacity and the Budget Process

Countless issues underlie the budgeting process. Most of these will not be eliminated if an activity-based approach is taken, because they are endemic to the estimating process. First and foremost are the assumptions made about *capacity*, whether in the plant or the back office. What is a reasonable level of activity? How much work should a pool of resources provide? When are more resources needed because a "step" in the costing model has been reached?

None of these questions has an answer. The definition of capacity, although critical to the way resources are managed, is an illusory item. Should efficiency be based on normal operating levels, budgeted levels, or actual levels of activity? What level of waste should be included, if any? Should the estimated standards be based solely on historical actual costs, trending toward theoretical perfection, or not? If waste is built into the process, it will quite likely never be removed.

That means that some form of theoretical capacity measure has to be kept at hand to provide a basis for continuous improvement efforts.

Capacity for the system is defined by the bottleneck resource. If that bottleneck is removed, the entire system can increase its output. Given this fact, should the resources that are constrained by the bottleneck be treated as "idle" or wasted assets? When a system is analyzed, the issue of constraints becomes the primary concern. Constraints reduce the potential capacity of the system; if they are removed, capacity increases. Yet if this increased capacity isn't needed, improvements will generate idle capacity. Idled resources are wasted resources; putting a meter on them may generate activity, but it cannot change the facts.

In setting capacity constraints, management is also initiating behavioral assumptions about the "best" a group of people can be expected to do. This constraint is often accepted with little or no querying of the underlying process, yet it is likely that process improvements can radically improve the effectiveness of resource utilization. In approaching the budget process and the constraints that define it, management has to question every assumption.

Customers and the Long-Term Perspective

Customers are often overlooked in the budget process; they are factored in as abstract sales dollars and little else. Yet the customer is the driver of enterprise well-being and success. Customer requirements and satisfaction have to be continually monitored and evaluated. At all times, management has to keep the customer perspective in mind as they look to maximize the long-term viability of the organization. Value is not created only in the short term; many of the "discretionary" budget items are the long-term basis for meeting changing customer needs. If they are cut needlessly, or are pared instead of other non-value-adding activities, the long-term survival of the organization can be placed at risk.

Budgets are not one-year plans of action; they are long-term views of where the company wants to go. If that journey fails to incorporate the needs of both internal and external customers, or neglects the value-creation criteria that form the basis for long-term competitiveness, desired destinations may not be reached. A budget is a game in which everyone involved in the organization speculates about the future, commits to those pieces of it they feel strongly about, and negotiates the resource issues that these plans create. None of it is fact; all of the process is critical.

Summing Up: Budgets and World-Class Performance

This chapter has presented a view of budgeting that started with the traditional tool familiar to most individuals in organizations, including the politics those techniques generate, and ended with suggesting an activity-based budgeting packet that can more effectively integrate ongoing activities. The theme has been the need to recognize that the constraints on budgeting derive from the inflexibility or unresponsiveness of the underlying value-creation process. Budgets are plans for future action; to the extent that those actions take more time than the customer would like them to, they can inhibit long-term value creation and growth.

In looking at traditional budgets, the discussion showed how marketing forecasts provide the impetus to the budgeting process, driving the development of production budgets, which leads to an estimated *gross margin* for the planning period. The gross margin represents the dollars left over for the rest of the organization to spend on its ongoing activities and long-range plans. In reviewing these issues, the cyclical nature of budgeting and its tie to the control cycle were detailed. Because budgets are used to plan and evaluate performance, they generate a significant amount of political activity and controversy.

Capital budgets and the concept of "discretionary" expenses were briefly reviewed. The underlying theme in this section was that improved asset management techniques and process improvements can be used to generate additional resources for these projects that generate future revenues. The future is made up of sound management today; short-changing the future because less effective management techniques are allowed to continue is myopic.

Activity-based budgeting concepts were suggested, with an example of what this tool might look like in practice. This is a new area of FMIS practice; there are few existing activity-based budgeting systems, yet those that do exist are providing ample proof that refocusing everyone's attention on the process generates major performance improvements over those possible in traditional settings.

Throughout, the people side of budgeting has been stressed. The objective in setting out a plan of action is to generate goal congruence and to encourage everyone to pursue strategic objectives. When budgets are developed without a clear recognition of the messages they'll send out to individuals in the organization, they can impair performance rather than improve it. Developing a clear understanding of customer requirements, and using this externally defined concept of value to guide the budget and management process, is the basis for generating goal congruence that is aimed at the right target: sustainable competitive advantage.

No matter what environment a company competes in, it has to keep a clear eye on the future. Reaching long-term goals is based on the completion of a number of intermediate-range action plans and the effective management of daily operations. The long term is not a nebulous concept that will be reached by wishes and dreams; it is a common destination arising from the ongoing efforts of the organization to meet or exceed customer expectations.

Few enterprises of great labor or hazard would be undertaken if we had not the power of magnifying the advantages we expect from them.

Samuel Johnson (2)

SUGGESTED READINGS

Clark, J., T. Hindeland, and R. Pritchard. *Capital Budgeting: Planning and Control of Capital Expenditures.* 3rd ed. Englewood Cliffs, N.J.: Prentice Hall, 1989.

Ferris, K., and J. L. Livingstone. *Management Planning and Control.* Columbus, Ohio: Publishing Horizons, 1975.

Hofstede, G. *The Game of Budget Control.* Amsterdam: Van Gorcum, 1970.

Hopwood, Anthony. *Accounting and Human Behavior.* Englewood Cliffs, N.J.: Prentice Hall, 1976.

Merchant, E. *Rewarding Results: Motivating Profit Center Managers.* Cambridge, Mass.: Harvard Business School Press, 1989.

CHAPTER 12

NUMBERS FOR EVALUATING PERFORMANCE

"Out of sight, out of mind," when translated into Russian [by computer], then back again into English became "invisible maniac."

Arthur Calder-Marshall (1)

Information systems are powerful because they record and play back vital details about prior performance: They are the basis for **management control.**[1] Control, or the attempts management makes to influence the behavior of individuals in the organization, is the most critical use made of the FMIS. It is the reason why the numbers need to point in the right direction. Why? Because of the basic law of management: *You get what you measure and reward.*

When the FMIS translates reality into a set of numbers and measures, it is providing a perspective on how well that organization is doing. That is the evaluative aspect of the FMIS. At the same time, the way in which that information is used sets the stage for future action. The numbers that are reported almost take on a life of their own: they are perceived to be snapshots of reality, a way to score the game. If reality has been translated and retranslated as accurately as the opening quote, future actions can be less than rewarding. There is always a danger that the measure used to motivate can generate a lot of action, but not necessarily in the right direction. People may be working at a furious rate at the wrong thing . . . chasing the invisible maniac.

These comments are not meant to put a cynical spin on the area of performance measurement. It is important to remember that each and every time a measurement is taken, it generates a signal to other people that spells out desirable or undesirable behavior and outcomes. The response to this challenge is *not* to quit measuring, but simply to do so with a clear view to the behavioral side of measurements.

---

[1]Throughout this chapter the terms "management control," "performance measurement system," and FMIS are used interchangeably to capture the measurement of performance and the use of these measures to change behavior within an organization.

Measures can encourage, and help a company achieve, World-Class performance.

That is why the field of performance measurement is one of the hottest management topics today. Many of the writers in this emerging field suggest useful measures and measurement concepts, but many neglect the basic issues surrounding the way that people respond to any type of number system. Developing a set of numbers can transform a vague argument or event into a key issue for everyone to see. It *objectifies* a certain part of the ongoing muddle of organizational life, making it seem more real and more important than those activities and processes that are not measured. Measurements are very powerful management tools, and as with all such tools, have tremendous ability to generate postive results.

Given that the ultimate objective of the control process is to encourage individuals to do those things that are in the best interest of the organization as a whole, the behavioral perspective will be used to frame the following discussion of integrated performance measurements. Integration of the measurement process, a key to clear communication of desired behavior and outcomes, is a critical first step in achieving competitive advantage. Without it, chaos and political manipulation and gamesmanship can dominate daily action, limiting the firm's potential.

The traditional view of the control process is presented first, not because it is right, but because it is so commonly used. While the "new stuff" might have been more enjoyable to see, it is important to know the basic assumptions guiding the control process in companies today before these measurement systems can be refocused effectively. If the early material sounds a bit harsh, outdated, and cynical, it is because it is. Traditional discussions of control place the worker at odds with the organization. Leaving this model behind will require more than good intentions; active understanding and change in the performance measurement area is the key to long-term success.

BASIC ISSUES IN PERFORMANCE MEASUREMENT

Action to be effective must be directed to clearly conceived ends.

Jawaharlal Nehru (2)

Performance measurement has, as its basic goal, the establishment of a common game plan for everyone in the organization to follow. Called **goal congruence** in the management literature, achieving this objective is a critical first step to achievement of any plan. If everyone is pursuing a different set of goals, they won't only be working at cross-purposes, they will quite likely destroy any forward momentum for the group as a whole. Goal congruence, or the establishment of common objectives and the necessary incentives to encourage people to strive for them, is the heart of the control process, and also the basic cause of most of the control problems that occur in organizations. Clear communication of goals by everyone involved in the organization is the precursor to effective action.

Many experts are querying the concept of goal congruence today, suggesting that it has outlived its usefulness. But World-Class organizations depend on a vital common interest: meeting or exceeding customer requirements. Having a common *mega-goal* does not mean that everyone has to be placed into lock-step positions, providing only the required inputs and little else. This would be a value-reducing action for the World-Class company.

Instead of abandoning goal congruence concepts because they appear to be tied to old ways of doing business, there is a need to recognize that the term "goal" has many different levels. In the horizontally-oriented, customer-driven company of today, the development of goal congruence means accepting that the next individual in line is a customer to be served. Meeting customer requirements can be done by establishing a chain of customers, as suggested by Richard Schonberger.[2] This approach provides the ultimate in goal congruence, tightly defined, easily measured, and clearly communicated by the next individual in the value creation chain.

Empowerment does not mean chaos. There is an increased need for clear communication of company goals when individuals are given a wider autonomy to make their own decisions. Companies that are effectively using empowerment have one thing in common: A clearly stated corporate vision that includes a list of characteristics, or behaviors, that should guide everyday actions. This form of control may be a bit "looser" than traditional models that attempt to tightly define goals, objectives, and allowable actions, but it is still based on the need for goal congruence.

---

[2]R. Schonberger, *Building a Chain of Customers: Linking Business Functions to Create the World-Class Company* (New York: The Free Press, 1990).

The lack of goal congruence is one of the key reasons why performance measurements are used in organizations. If everyone clearly understood their role in the overall performance of the firm, accepted this role, and worked vigorously for its achievement, there would truly be little need for measurements. Performance measurements are needed because of basic flaws in the control process in the organization. Whether these shortcomings stem from poor communication or self-interested behavior, the results are the same: Organizational performance and goal achievement are impaired.

In discussing the control problem in organizations, Ken Merchant notes:

> Control... involves influencing human behavior.... Controls are necessary to guard against the possibilities that people will do something the organization does not want them to do or fail to do something that they should do.[3]

As can be seen the basis of the *traditional* approach to control, and the need for ongoing measurements, is the underlying belief that the organization needs to guard against the actions of individuals. Expanding this argument, Merchant goes on to identify three basic control problems: lack of direction, motivational problems, and personal limitations. The first of these is a leadership, or management, problem. It reflects the fact that sometimes people don't do what is desired because they simply don't know what that is.

Inadequate or contradictory information can lead to lack of direction. If management fails to state clearly the objectives being pursued, or asks for one thing while measuring and rewarding something else, employees become confused. Not wanting to look like slackards, though, they'll do *something*... it's that something that an effective control system attempts to guard against. When this control problem exists, it is not the person who is at fault—it is the goal-setting and communication process. No matter how motivated someone is, if they aren't clear about why they're doing what they're doing, it is impossible for them to consistently add value to the firm. Most of the ongoing concern with the need to integrate the performance measurement process stems from the recognition that conflicting signals are the source of numerous errors and inconsistent results in organizations. In other words, there are a lot of good people who are

---

[3]K. Merchant, *Control in Business Organizations* (Boston: Pitman, 1985), p. 5.

being directed to do non-value-adding things by a poorly designed or communicated performance measurement system.

The second control problem stems from the fact that individuals may not want to pursue the goals of the organization. These motivational problems are often believed to be based in the fact that individuals will pursue self-interest at all times, regardless of the overall impact of their actions on the organization. It is an interesting argument, suggesting that pursuit of the common good is not so common after all. Yet there are numerous examples of people working above and beyond the call of duty to ensure that the organization's goals are met. What is the reality here? Motivation is not always self-directed, nor can it be assumed to be company-directed. It is a changeable part of the individual's relationship with the organization.

Measurement and performance evaluation play a critical role in the motivational process. But what measures lead to the best performance? Because measurement takes place in a social system, is applied to individuals with diverse interests and core characteristics and competencies, and is an imprecise science at best, the level of causal understanding of the role of measurement in influencing motivation and behavior is limited. That doesn't keep everyone from trying; it's simply not clear what works when, where, and why.

The final control problem identified by Merchant is personal limitations. It suggests that the Peter Principle really does exist: People can rise to their level of ineffectiveness, impairing organizational performance. Not every person is equally suited to do every job. Yet identifying and matching a person's core competencies with the demands of a job is difficult. Several models have been developed that attempt to make this a more objective process, but the reality of the matter is that it is very hard to know if someone is capable of doing a job until they try to do it. One of management's primary tasks is to help identify promising candidates for future advancement. If this game was played on a level playing field, with competency as its key criterion, there would probably be less of the "Peter" in this principle of management. Unfortunately, advancement is often a political game, which can impair long-run competitiveness.

It seems that traditional models of management control reflect a dim and unpleasant view of personal motivation. These models are as tightly tied to the scientific management view of the organization as are standard costing systems. They start from the assumption that workers are lazy and incompetent. Their end point—tight controls and punitive measures—is no surprise.

This type of management control process is being increasingly called into question. Unfortunately, not much change has occurred to date, but management in most leading edge firms recognizes that measurements need to be recast to match World-Class objectives. This process starts with trusting the employee to do the job and to provide insights into how existing procedures can be improved. It is likely that the concept of "control" will be radically changed as new methods of management continue to take hold in companies throughout the Western world.[4]

Control Types and Issues

Performance measurement systems traditionally have been targeted toward controlling individual behavior. This has led to the development of a series of control tools, which Merchant[5] has segmented into three basic categories based on their overriding focus: **results controls, action controls,** and **personnel controls**. Results-based controls revolve around the outcomes of the process, rather than the process itself. This class of controls "involves rewarding individuals or otherwise holding them accountable for accomplishing particular results" (p. 17). At the core of Western control practices, results controls leave the process to individuals, relying on their expertise to get the job done.

Results controls are the most common approach used in Western companies. Budgeting, management by objectives (MBO), and most other common control tools all focus on the outcomes of processes; the "how" and "why" are left out of the management equation. Unfortunately, the desired results can be accomplished using either acceptable or unacceptable methods. Management should not be directly involved in day-to-day operations, but leaving the means for achieving results unchecked can lead to downstream problems.

---

[4]The author has been participating in an international study of performance measurement systems used by leading edge companies for the past two years. The study did *not* uncover any major changes in this area, although many managers were worried about the ability of their measurement systems to generate and sustain desired levels of performance. Customers are being seen as the key force in shaping the redesign of measurement systems, but exactly what this is going to mean for the long haul is not clear.

[5]Ibid., pp. 17–45.

There are a series of *dysfunctional consequences* that have been directly attributed to the excessive reliance on results controls, including gamesmanship, negative attitudes, myopia, and displacement. **Gamesmanship** refers to the manipulation of the numbers to ensure that desired outcomes are achieved, without necessarily creating value in the process. Many writers include slack gaining in this category because it covers the ex ante manipulation of expected results and outcomes to make them more attainable.

When games are the means for ensuring success, **negative attitudes** are often part of the fallout. In addition, the excessive focus on outcomes from a short operating period (one year or less) tends to focus everyone's attention on short-term events to the detriment of long-term performance. **Management myopia**, one of the attitudinal impacts of excessive reliance on outcome controls, is one of the major concerns voiced by management writers today. When companies put a premium on short-term performance measurements, organizational life turns into fire-fighting brigades focused on putting out fires that threaten meeting goals, whether or not the underlying cause of the blaze is understood.

The final dysfunctional consequence—**displacement**—encompasses all the design errors that can be committed in putting together a control system. It is often described as "the folly of rewarding B while expecting A." Displacement is the result of control measures that do not focus on the key element of the process, or focus attention on the issues that matter. The cause of displacement can be poor communication or understanding of desired results, over quantification of performance outcomes, or unclear goals and objectives. In all these cases, the individual is encouraged to work hard at the wrong thing—hardly a value-adding event.

At their core, results controls look at the outcome of the value chain, assess performance based on this outcome, and pass judgment (including passing out incentive bonuses) on the effectiveness of individuals and units of the business over the prior period. This leads to a tremendous number of undesirable outcomes, many of which stem from the obsession with measurement and immediate results that frame Western management practice. Lost in the shuffle are the long-term objectives of the firm, the true needs of the customer, and the need to continuously improve the process to ensure competitive advantage. Peter Drucker makes this point in the following way:

> The more we can quantify the truly measurable areas, the greater the temptation to put all-out on those—the greater, therefore, the danger

that what looks like better "contol" will actually mean less "control" if not a business out of control altogether.[6]

When numbers are created, they command attention. That places responsibility on the shoulders of those individuals supplying this type of information to make sure their numbers are objective, accurate, and do not cause more harm than good. It is a responsibility that can be ignored only at the peril of long-term survival of the firm.

Control: An Alternative Perspective

Western management control systems usually focus on outcomes, but most managers know that "action" controls and "personnel" control can be options. An action control, which focuses in on how the job is done, is, in a traditional control setting, *individual-centered*: It is concerned with determining and enforcing efficient methods for performing certain jobs. Captured in standard operating procedures or detailed time-and-motion studies, action controls have traditionally been constrained to lower level jobs. Personnel controls—the recognition that a person's self-motivation, the pressure of peer groups, or the general culture of the organization can drive behavior—are shadowy concepts in Western control systems; most writers recognize their presence and power, but don't adequately factor them into the design process.

The emerging view of the management control process specifically factors in action and personnel controls as the dominant forces for learning and continuous improvement (see Figure 12–1). Underlying this shift is the reorientation of the control process from a concern with individual accountability to a focus on understanding and improving the process itself to better meet customer expectations.

This shift becomes noticeable in the area of action controls. In the past, action controls focused on regimentation of the procedures for doing one job. The issue was not "How can we do this better?" but "How can we ensure they do this job right?" The underlying belief of management was that the worker really didn't have the skill to design the job or improve the process—that was the bailiwick of the industrial engineer. The worker was to be controlled, right down to the last movement if necessary, to ensure efficient operations.

---

[6]Peter F. Drucker, "Controls, Control and Management," in *Management Controls: New Directions in Basic Research*, ed. C. Bonini, R. Jaedicke, and H. Wagern (New York: McGraw-Hill, 1964), p. 294.

FIGURE 12–1
Shifts in Control Focus

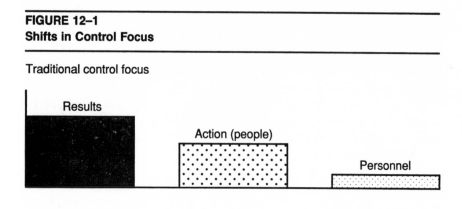

Traditional control focus

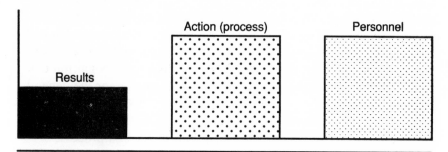

Emerging control patterns

In a continuous improvement environment, the worker is the source of learning and change, not the weak link in the chain. That means that "action" controls in this setting become focused on ensuring that the process is proceeding as planned. The Japanese are intent on developing strong process controls; they are focused on the actions being performed, with one key difference from the traditional setting. The question being asked and answered by the control process is "What went wrong?" and not "Who screwed up?" In line with the belief that people are trusted resources, the objective is to ensure that the process is understood and constantly improved.

Personnel-based controls are the primary means used to ensure goal congruence. In a modern control system, it is critical to develop a strong culture focused on improvement, to encourage the formation of well-functioning teams, and to build trust into the organization. Management has to trust the workforce to do the best job possible, and the workforce has to trust that management will deliver on its promises.

Tom Vollmann calls this the "whole person" concept.[7] It suggests that an organization needs to understand that it not only hires brawn, it hires brains. In fact, an idle brain is a more dangerous waste of resources than an idle hand—intellect leads to long-term improvement, hands to short-term output. As detailed in Chapter 10, the FMIS ignores the value of the people in the organization; they show up as period expenses that are accounted for, then disposed of. In this area, the FMIS is of little use in implementing long-term strategies for growth. It is also of little use in the control process; its focus is on financial results, not the means used to achieve them.

Contrary to the effciency concerns of traditional control systems, Vollmann and others suggest that improved efficiency, at the cost of learning, isn't the best path to tread. If individual workers can be freed from ongoing production, they can put their minds to work looking for ways to improve the product, process, or responsiveness to customer needs. This creates a far different world from one where workers are constantly monitored to make sure they keep busy—one far more likely to lead to competitive advantage.

A Horizontal View of Control

Modern control systems have to capture the horizontal flow that leads to results as their core dimension. Where handoffs occur, some form of customer-defined measurement systems needs to be used to ensure fumbles are minimized. Flow-based control systems are different creatures from traditional responsibility accounting systems (traditional management controls): They focus on the value chain, omit individual controls, minimize individual incentives, and reward improving the process rather than hitting some predefined target. In such a setting, someone who misses financial goals, but improves the performance of the product or process, is to be rewarded; meeting financial goals is not the driving concern.

These revamped control systems can be thought of as controllability networks. They include individuals in different parts of the organization, focus on the process instead of individual performance,

---

[7]J.R. Dixon, A. Nanni, and T. Vollmann. *The New Performance Challenge: Measuring Operations for World-Class Competition* (Homewood, Ill: Business One Irwin/APICS Series, 1990), p. 19.

and are concerned with meeting customer expectations. Customers, whether internal or external to the organization, are the basis for defining adequacy in the "outcomes" produced—outcomes that include the handoffs as well as the static product, activity, or paperwork that passes through the system. These networks intricately link individuals into value chains, reward the performance of the system, encourage improvement rather than specific results, and place customer interests above all else.

A controllability network is a customer-defined, customer-driven approach to generating action and defining accountability within an organization. It is designed around the process flow that creates value, rather than historical fact or the chart of accounts. Controllability networks are not FMIS tools; they utilize numbers from across the organization. Individuals throughout the value chain establish objectives for their suppliers and respond to the measures and requests made by their customers. Some of these measures may have a dollar sign attached, but it is likely that this will be more the exception than the rule. Effective performance generates profit; controlling activities, not costs, is the means to attain this goal.

INTEGRATING THE CONTROL PROCESS

Nodding the head does not row the boat.

Irish Proverb (2)

The essential message delivered by modern writers on control is the need to integrate the financial and nonfinancial measures of performance. For many, the best way to begin to do this is to deemphasize the financial numbers, perhaps even throw them away, and put everyone to work creating long-term process improvements. This may sound like a logical path to tread, but unfortunately, companies continue to be short-term profit-seeking entities. Failing to factor economic issues into ongoing decisions can lead to downstream disasters. Separation of the two systems has been the traditional path, but the more "objective" financials often win the day in these settings. If disagreement exists between the performance measures, the dollars usually dominate.

Another position surrounding the question of integrating the financial and nonfinancial systems is that, in the longrun, if you do the right things every day the numbers will bear you out. This is the application of trust to economics, which in itself appears to be an oxymoron. Yet the core objective is to gain competitive advantage through superior performance. Achieving this goal requires careful analysis of alternatives, careful selection of a strategic approach, and the ability to keep the system on track. Waiting for the long run may be a great idea, but it is not one that will be easy to sell to stakeholders.

Conflicting Signals—and When the Dollars Matter

At the core of most of the discussions about performance measurement systems is the recognition that conflicting signals confuse employees, create chaos throughout the organization, and hinder improvement efforts. Confusion about desired ends is one of the primary behavioral problems in organizations; acknowledging and yet failing to fix obvious flaws in the existing control process is tantamount to leaving the playing field in the middle of a game. Since no one knows the score anyway, the victor is the individual or group that argues longest and loudest that they are right. There is no other domain for alleviating conflict: The numbers don't work, so politics comes to the forefront. In fact, the degree of political maneuvering in a control system is one measure of its ineffectiveness; politics are used when objective measurements can't, or won't, do the job.

Several methods have been suggested for actively managing the integration of the financial and nonfinancial elements of the control system. One of the most detailed of these is presented by Lynch and Cross.[8] These authors create a balanced scorecard that actively plots the trade-offs between the primary performance dimensions for any process: quality, delivery, cycle time, and waste. Using an innovative measurement approach, Lynch and Cross actively trade off improvements across the multiple dimensions of performance in a World-Class organization.

---

[8]R. Lynch and K. Cross, *Measure Up! Yardsticks for Continuous Improvement* (Great Britain: Basil Blackwell, 1991).

The interesting aspect of this approach is that it actively supports the integration of the FMIS. In discussing when and where financial and nonfinancial performance measurements need to agree, McNair, Lynch, and Cross note that several issues underlie the integration process:

1. "Fit" of the measures to the key decision characteristics, including decision time span and reporting time span.
2. Timing differences between resource purchase and its use within the value chain.
3. Long-term, or strategic, operating effectiveness versus short-term profit goals.
4. Focus of the measurements.[9]

One of the key design variables in a control system is the desired linkage between the decision-impacting feedback loop and the evaluation or reporting feedback loop. In an effective control system, managers receive information in time to alter the final performance or outcome of their area. Information is needed to change the process *before* mistakes lead to downstream failures.

Most managers, in fact, would like to get multiple "signals" from their control systems before they have to report outcomes to top management. In the *vertical* control process, there are plan–do–act loops embedded at each level of the organization that provide the information necessary to achieve preset performance targets. This results-based view of control has been increasingly questioned, yet it serves as the dominant form of control in most organizations today. In designing a control system, the FMIS manager has to make sure that individuals get enough information, on an ongoing basis, to modify the process and improve final results. This underlying set of interconnected decision and reporting control loops is a critical and often overlooked element in the control process. It is not unusual for a manager to be held accountable for one set of numbers while knowing that another dimension of operations is critical.

A second major issue in designing a control system is to recognize that different measures really do apply to different parts of the organization or different classes of decisions. Down on the plant floor,

---

[9]McNair, C., R. Lynch, and K. Cross, "Do Financial and Nonfinancial Measures Have to Agree?" *Management Accounting*, November 1990, pp. 28–36.

there is little value to having financial control reporting in place. Why? Because by the time these numbers arrive, it is too late to affect the decision. At the lower levels of the organization, financial measures for *control* are of little value. On the other hand, financial *estimates* for the various alternatives open to operational management can prove to be quite useful. Estimates help prioritize and guide decision making; financial-based controls actually muddy the water ex post because they are too aggregate, too late, and focused on many of the wrong things.

Most of the criticism of the FMIS may stem from using it in the wrong way, and at the wrong level of the organization. The FMIS is a scorecard for a period of operations, not a real-time measure of current performance. A well-designed FMIS can provide good cost estimates to guide decision making at the operational level (e.g., an activity-based system), and should, in total, reflect the same profitability patterns as the other measurement systems that are better suited to short-cycle control loops. But compatability is not substitutability; the FMIS can never take the place of short-cycle controls on the plant floor.

The FMIS and the operational control system begin to merge as the decision time span extends. This usually happens at higher levels of the organization (see Figure 12–2). In fact, it appears that the FMIS begins to be relevant for decision support in a "control" mode at the middle management level. In this setting, managers focusing on quarterly results may find monthly results informative enough to guide their interventions lower in the organization.

The activity-based FMIS is designed to merge information at approximately this level of the organization. Here, the timing differences between the relevant financial and operational measurements are not quite as severe; operational measures begin to average out and financial information begins to be available. In fact, a good middle manager is usually one who can take the financial objectives of the organization and translate them into action plans for lower levels of the organization. Usually this translation is done based on intuition and experience. In a modern, activity-based FMIS, intuition is transformed into systematic estimates of the relationship between activities and costs.

The control implications of an activity-based FMIS are clear. If properly designed, these systems integrate the financial and operational perspective. Below the middle level of the organization, ex

FIGURE 12–2
Different Measures for Different Purposes

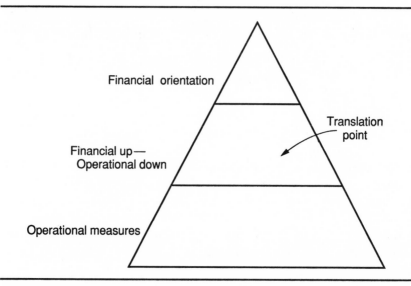

post financial measures may be meaningless, but ex ante cost estimates can be valuable. In the middle, management can actually begin to project how changes in activity should affect results. And because the activity-based cost estimates are the outcome of dividing a financial measure by an operational one, the two systems are measuring the same facets of the work process.

At the top level of the organization, the dominant focus continues to be on the financial results. The reason for this is clear: Top management is held accountable by the firm's owners (the stock market) for financial performance. That fact seems to justify their almost total disregard for operational details. Or does it? If the stock market really knew how operations were proceeding, would they change the tools they use to assess a company? What if the realm of insider information was pared down, as more and more operating details became common knowledge? To argue that the stock market demands short-term financial results is to give up the long-term game; it also suggests that investors cannot learn or understand long-term concepts of value. If that is the case, no amount of measurement will make a difference.

Using the Customer Perspective

The above discussion reflects a vertical view of the control process in the organization. Integration of the measurement process on this dimension is important because goal congruence depends on it. If everyone is following a different scorecard, the organization as a whole cannot operate effectively. Vertical integration can be achieved through the implementation of an activity-based FMIS that, due to its inherent characteristic, merges the operational and financial domains.

Yet the game can still be lost with a vertical control system because it fails to reflect the customer-driven value chain. To make "control" a usable concept, it has to focus on the process, or the velocity of materials or work through the value chain. Velocity, called by some *time-based management*, is a concern with asset utilization. Velocity means that value is being created; value creation is a dynamic concept that requires a different perspective in the control process.

The shift required is toward a "systems" view of the control process. In this situation, the key focus is on the handoffs, or inter-relationships, that constitute the value chain. Whereas a traditional, vertical control orientation measures the results, or static dimensions, of organization performance, horizontal measures highlight the flow through the system. Eli Goldratt's theory of constraints is a horizontal system that addresses bottlenecks; the system's velocity improves as bottlenecks are removed. In this model, the only key measurements are those that reflect the effectiveness and efficiency of the bottleneck resource. Effective management and control of the bottleneck areas ensures optimal performance of the system.

Other "horizontalists" focus on the customer perspective in designing measurement systems. Here, any fumble is equally undesirable—the objective is to identify them. When internal customers are asked what they need, when, and in what form, measurements can be developed to ensure that this level of performance occurs. This is the focus of the Lynch–Cross performance measurement model. They suggest that the entire value chain can be reflected in a series of horizontal measurements that ensure meeting customer expectations in total by meeting them at each stage in the value-creation process.

Within a horizontal control perspective, the dominant concern is with ensuring continuous improvement. That leads some authors to suggest that "control" itself is a questionable event. Yet the Japanese clearly factor control loops into their management processes. How else can learning occur? Control in an individual sense is not necessary; control in the process sense is. A domestic bicycle company is learning this lesson the hard way; having thrown away all of their measurements in response to a concern that they would inhibit learning, management now has to attend countless meetings to find out what is going on. Measurements are a form of organizational short-hand; they summarize, in terms everyone understands, key facets of ongoing operations. No measures means chaos; so does no control.

Reorienting the Control Process

To reorient the control process, management has to begin to understand that the desire to "control" is one of the core issues it has to resolve. Within a continuous improvement setting, "control" is a misnomer—the process is improved, and people are empowered. Empowerment suggests that traditional forms of control, which focus on coercing individuals to take desired actions, is no longer needed. Instead, leadership has to emerge through a process of letting go of the controls.

The needed measurements are focused on helping individuals throughout the organization resolve ongoing operational problems, enhance the velocity of materials and orders through the system, and ensure that customer expectations are met on a consistent basis. These measures are not individualistic; when evaluative information is needed, a different set of measures and approaches should be used. In the process of divorcing the control process from individual evaluation, companies will be finally reaching beyond the **control paradox**.

What is the control paradox? It is everything that is right and wrong about traditional control systems. The heart of the paradox is that individuals are expected to provide estimates of their future performance at the beginning of a process, knowing that future rewards will depend on how well they meet these self-defined goals. The individual is placed in a *double bind* in this situation. The process of goal-setting, if done honestly, creates the potential for downstream sanctions. Honesty is not necessarily rewarded.

The control paradox is quite likely the reason why, in a far-reaching study of the performance evaluation process in major corporations, Ken Merchant found that the budget goals for most profit center managers were relatively "loose" (could be easily attained 50–60 percent of the time).[10] This suggests that the control process in organizations functions as a game that attempts to reward individuals for moderate performance and reduce the risk faced by managers.

Taking this concept further, the separation of performance evaluation from the management control process may help eliminate many of the undesirable side effects of the control process. Some may wonder if this will lead to confusion and a lack of goal congruence, but hybrid control systems are already beginning to emerge in the field. Motorola, one of the United States' most promising companies, has turned around its performance by focusing its measurements on those elements of the process that matter. Recognizing the need to address individual performance issues, they have split their evaluation process to incorporate 50 percent of the team's process improvement gains and 50 percent of the individual's personal growth in the total evaluation for promotion and raises.

Gain-sharing programs are also providing a mechanism for ensuring that individuals remain motivated to search for process improvements, while eliminating the individualized focus in the FMIS. In most companies employing these programs, bonuses are based on improvements made across the organization (the gain in productivity is shared between the company and the employees), and individual raises and promotions are based on improvements in the individual's skill mix. The control system is allowed to focus on the process; the evaluation mechanism creates the incentives for continuous improvement.

Revamping the performance measurement process in companies will require the integration of financial and nonfinancial control systems around the process itself. The individualized control orientation is being dissipated in these situations, providing the means to finally break out of the control paradox. In the process of revamping these measurements, the issues are more far-reaching than a

---

[10]Kenneth Merchant, *Rewarding Results: Motivating Profit Center Managers* (Cambridge, Mass.: Harvard Business Press, 1989).

simple concern with the relationship between financial and nonfinancial measures; they encompass the core assumptions of the measurement process, the objectives being pursued, and the criterion of success that the measurements gauge. The only sure outcome at this stage is the fact that existing systems will have to change; the unknown factor is exactly how.

MEASURES THAT MATTER

Error of opinion may be tolerated where reason is left free to combat it.

Thomas Jefferson (2)

Organizations are undergoing a multitude of changes as they come to terms with a global marketplace focused on heightened service and the necessity of maximizing the value created by the resources at the company's command. Competitive advantage is no longer a one-dimensional issue or a guarantee of future success. One by one, competitors are rising up throughout the world, seeking to improve their quality of living by selling to the markets that were once the property of Western entrepreneurs.

In this state of change, management is seeking more effective ways to gauge the current status of their companies against the marketplace, to understand and deploy their resource potential in innovative ways, and to secure a place in 21st-century business. To gain this knowledge, they are turning to new forms of manufacturing, management, and measurement, looking for the Holy Grail or the next mousetrap. Where does a company start in revamping its measurements and putting the FMIS to work for the long-term survival of the firm?

Many tools are being suggested for getting a start on improving existing practice, but it seems that benchmarking is the vehicle of choice. Benchmarking, or the use of external information about the way other companies manage and control the various aspects of the value chain, provides an objective measure of a firm's performance in relation to similar companies or functions. A rapidly growing field, the interest in benchmarking is currently outstripping knowledge about how to do it, and how to maximize the benefit obtained for the sponsor firm and all participants. Yet the fact that management is looking for a better way to do things is a positive sign; when the score is tallied there is seldom any doubt that improvement is possible.

Benchmarking studies are being conducted in many areas of business. The management of financial services is no exception. Companies like AT&T, Lifeline Systems, and many others, both large and small, are beginning to look for better ways to manage the daily routines of FMIS maintenance, and to improve the value-adding nature of financial work. In the scaled-down organization of the 21st century, there is no room for free riders or slack. Scaling down an organization means looking hard and long at what is currently being done, and daring to ask "Why?" There are no sacred cows when survival is the issue.

The results from benchmarking studies provide measures of the effectiveness of various functions, as well as suggestions for improvement. Studies such as that completed by Keating and Jablonsky for the Financial Executives Institute[11] provide a starting point for this process of change, and the ample supply of trade books give examples of how different companies and different experts are pursuing the rebirth of financial management.

A Rebirth of Performance Measurement

One of the most important changes that is occurring is the revamping of the performance measurement process. There are a seemingly endless number of measures being created; each new book brings new measures and new ideas (see Figure 12–3). What each of these measures has in common is an increased focus on providing relevant numbers for decision making. Just as the types of decisions made vary as one moves across the organization, so does the information required to make sound decisions.

A second feature of these emerging measurement systems is an increased concern for operational measures and a deemphasis of the financial metrics. This is a much needed change; the financials have tremendous value, but are seldom available on time, or in the form needed, to meet the expectations of the internal customer. In fact,

---

[11]P. Keating and S. Jablonsky, *Changing Roles of Financial Management: Getting Close to the Business* (Montvale, N.J.: Financial Executives Foundation, 1990).

FIGURE 12–3
Sample Measurements

Measurement focus

Quantity and quality of engineering change	• Number of engineering changes
	• Severity of engineering change (i.e., class 1 (major))
Part standardization	• Number of products
	• Options per product
	• % common parts per product
Product complexity	• Number of components per finished product
	• Number of manufacturing operations per finished product
	• Number of tools required per finished product
	• Life/cost of tooling per finished product
Parts quality	• First pass reject rate versus test results
	• Yield of finished product per raw material batch
	• Scrap %
	• Rework %
	• Yield %
Quality control checkpoints	• Effectiveness—number of returned units
Supplier performance	• Number/frequency of deliveries
	• Lead time from order initiation to delivery
Velocity of units through facility	• Queue time between operations
	• Value-added time % = Production time/total time
Customer service levels	• Late deliveries
	• On-time deliveries
	• Back orders
	• Canceled orders
Complexity of flow	• Bills—number per product
	• Routings required per product
Resource limitations	• Bottleneck capacity level
	• Set-up time
	• Lot size constraints

---

the long-term implications of driving the customer orientation into the organization may be best tracked by watching the development of the FMIS. This area, which always saw its customer to be the external stakeholder, is increasingly being asked to radically change its perspective and to reorient itself to the needs of internal users.

Measurement: A Fluid, Ever-Changing Process

Change is the basis of organizational action and has to be reflected in the measures used to gauge the effectiveness of its activities. One of the most important issues in designing a performance measurement system is to recognize that it is a job that is never completed. Each time a new process is added to the company repertoire, new technologies are adopted, or the strategic objectives of the firm are changed, the measurement system has to be redefined and refocused to ensure that it supports the achievement of these goals.

There is no one set of measures, or measurement approaches, that will work in every company every day. In fact, a measure that does exactly what is needed today may generate chaos a year from now. Measurement is a fluid, ever-changing process that is constantly reevaluated and recalibrated as the strategies, activities, and realities of organizational life evolve.

In developing World-Class performance measures, it is important to keep in mind that it is a process that will be continually revisited. Continuous improvement means more than changing the way work is done; it affects the measurement process and the management structure of the organization. As the customer perspective is adopted and the value chain becomes the defining characteristic of a company's structure, change will be built into the measurement process by default. Why? Because changing customer expectations are a constant reminder that the value chain needs to be redefined on a continuous basis, looking for more effective ways to deliver value today and create a sustainable competitive advantage for tomorrow. Meeting and exceeding customer requirements starts with a sound measurement process that helps coordinate the diverse activities performed throughout the organization into a smoothly functioning machine.

Removing the Barriers of the Debit-Credit Machine

Where do these changes leave the traditional financial manager? Perhaps in a panic, perhaps at the back of the pack, but a prepared manager will learn and grow to meet these new challenges. Yet making these changes will require more than a simple change in report formats, or the adoption of activity-based costing methods. It requires a refocusing of the role of the financial manager and a movement away from the audit mentality that is the underpinning of the financial area.

In keeping with the broad mission of this book—to provide information of value to both the financial and nonfinancial manager—it is critical at this juncture to reopen the discussion of the accounting mentality and its adherence to the double-entry bookkeeping model. The double-entry system is the backbone of the FMIS and the underlying art that fascinates most of its adherents. Yet it can blind financial managers to asking or answering the important questions.

Common questions when this type of information is presented to an accounting audience include "Will it pass the audit?" and "If we don't do full costing, who's going to pay for the unallocated costs?" The underlying mechanics of the accounting process sneak in almost immediately, preventing an open discussion of the types of information needed and how it can be provided. Yet management accounting has never had to be concerned with these issues—there are no rules guiding internal reporting. Concerns for balancing the books and attaching all costs to some type of output are worries for the auditor, not the customer-oriented financial manager. The books have to be balanced, but is that the only game in town? Or the most important? If the books balance but the company goes down because of faulty internal information, who will care about the auditor?

The major challenge facing the financial area is not the revamping of its number systems or the integration of its numbers with those provided by the operational control systems, but rather the adoption of an internal perspective. Everyone else is being asked to look outward and to factor customer needs into their daily activities, but it is important for the financial function to finally look inside—to begin communicating with its internal customer and taking as much care for the responsible use of financial data in internal decision making as external stock market transactions.

Internal customers are a strange lot. They are savvy, intelligent managers of their area, open to the vast upheaval in the marketplace and capable of crafting workable responses to these challenges. But most remain naive about the rules of the road, and the perspectives that shape the financial function. Decisions are made based on the numbers, but few are capable of challenging the assumptions. The financial function has to undertake the challenge to educate internal users of financial information on the do's and don'ts of accounting, when the assumptions matter, and what the right numbers are in a variety of decision contexts.

To provide that insight, financial managers have to first accept the fact that full cost accounting may have a nice philosophical ring to it, but if a cost can't be changed by a decision, then full cost numbers may not be the right ones to use. Decision relevance means that the right numbers are available, and used, based on the characteristics of the decision itself, the time frame the action covers, and the degree to which total costs can be changed in the process. Financial managers know what numbers are the right ones to use, but do their customers? Is the financial function safeguarding the assets of the firm if they allow other managers to make decisions using the wrong numbers? Where does responsibility lie in forging an intelligent link between decisions and value creation?

For over 50 years, accountants have been fighting the full cost–direct cost battle. In the process, they appear to have lost sight of the key issue: the avoidability of various costs. If a cost is direct to a product line, but won't go away when the product is dropped, is it really relevant to a decision? Are full costs really the best way to incorporate the very real fact that revenues have to cover all of the firm's costs, in the long-run, if the company is to remain in business? Do the measures have to be based on objective fact, or can systematic guesses provide better information when it is needed? All good questions, with no answer to date. The only fact that remains unquestioned is that the financial function has to change—there is very little time left for the continued adherence to an external perspective when internal customers are in need of support.

The Proactive Accountant

The objective is to create the proactive accountant—one who is willing to work from estimates, ensure that financial measures do not undermine improvement efforts, and yet retain an objective stance, signaling when the system is out of control. This person will not emerge naturally from an organization's staff, although many financial managers have, or are beginning to, respond to the call for relevance. The ability to understand the types of methods that are being created, the mindset necessary to put them to work, and the curiosity to go beyond the obvious are traits seldom associated with financial managers. Can individuals who really enjoy the challenge of balancing a set of books find the same fulfillment in creating performance measurements that may never use a dollar sign at all?

This is the real challenge lying ahead as organizations begin to pursue, learn about, and master the tools for continuous improvement: Can existing employees make the leap? Interestingly, it appears that most lower level employees are rising to the challenge; utilizing this idle resource is leading to performance improvements in company after company. Managers in operations, marketing, and other value chain-based individuals are also keenly focused on implementing change and improving the effectiveness of their own activities and those of their subordinates. The trouble spots in this sea of change appear to be staff groups that have never had to think of the job they're performing from a customer perspective. It is an alien concept, just as justifying their existence in terms of value-added criteria is.

The financial function is one of these indirect value-creating areas of the company. The fact that it is coming to the table a bit late is of concern, when coupled with the fact that the information provided by this group is very influential in the ongoing decision process of the firm. Given this position of responsibility, it is critical that the financial manager pursue a proactive agenda, searching out his or her customers anywhere they may be, whether on the plant floor, in one of the backwater bays of overhead, or out in the field. The proactive accountant, constantly seeking ways to enhance the service provided to the rest of the organization, is the goal. The audit mentality is the roadblock that has to be overcome.

Starting the journey will be difficult, yet the "customer" knows that the job can't be done without a clear understanding of the economics of the decision process and the marketplace. Providing this information is the true goal of the financial manager; external responsibilities cannot be served if internal needs are overlooked. And since the customer seems a bit gun-shy, the proactive financial manager has to begin seeking out ways to serve, not wait for a request from the field. To free up this time, traditional, detail-intensive and time-consuming tasks have to be streamlined, using benchmarked information as the starting point. The destination? Value-added accounting and the attainment of a competitive advantage.

FINAL NOTES

The busier one is in a group of activities, the more acceptable an excuse one has for avoiding commitments on a deeper level elsewhere—commitments one feels less than adequate to handle.

Myron Brenton, *The American Male* (4)

The FMIS is in a state of transition, as it begins to reawaken to the needs of internal decision makers for relevant information. Changes that are beginning to be implemented in companies across the environment suggest that, although the final nature of the FMIS is unknown, it will no longer serve the same role in the organization of the future. In refocusing the financial area, the future is the question. Will the financial system continue to play a pivotal role, or will it remain focused on external reporting, thereby sliding into oblivion in the internal domain?

Whatever the outcome may be, the fact that the FMIS has far-reaching impact on the organization cannot be denied. What needs to occur is for the financial manager to assume responsibilty for internal information and the decisions that are being made with existing numbers. When a question is broached, will full costing really provide the best long-term perspective for the issue at hand, or will traditional methods bias the analysis and lead to plant closures, outsourcing, or competitive decline?

When numbers are used, they lead to a feeling of complacency and confidence in the ensuing decision. Yet these very rational-looking numbers are full of assumptions, bias, and subtleties that can be disastrous if not understood. If the future of Western business is to be ensured, both the users and creators of vital information have to learn, change, and improve. There is no standing still in a tidal wave; a strong swimmer may ride out the storm, but a weakened one will not.

What can a company do to strengthen its position and ensure long-term survival? If that answer were known, everyone could relax.

What is known is that every function, activity, and process that does not add value, that does not support continuous improvement, is a millstone around the organization's neck. As these nonperforming resources grow as a percentage of the total assets, the company goes down for the count.

Understanding and improving the FMIS is everyone's responsibility. The financial manager has to enact the changes, but has to listen to the customer before taking action. If properly focused, the FMIS can be a strategic weapon; if poorly aimed, it can do more harm than good. Which it becomes is a matter of choice, not chance.

It is a good answer which knows when to stop.

Italian Proverb (2)

SUGGESTED READINGS

Dixon, J. R., A. Nanni, and T. Vollmann. *The New Performance Challenge: Measuring Operations for World-Class Competition.* Homewood, Ill.: Business One Irwin/APICS, 1990.

Hall, R., H. T. Johnson, and P. Turney. *Measuring Up: Charting Pathways to Manufacturing Excellence.* Homewood, Ill.: Business One Irwin, 1991.

Lynch, R., and K. Cross. *Measure Up! Yardsticks for Continuous Improvement.* Cambridge, Mass.: Basil Blackwell, 1991.

Maskell, Brian H. *Perfomance Measurement for World-Class Manufacturing: A Model for American Companies.* Cambridge, Mass.: Productivity Press, 1991.

Merchant, Kenneth. *Rewarding Results: Motivating Profit Center Managers.* Cambridge, Mass.: Harvard Business School Press, 1989.

—————. *Control in Business Organizations.* Boston, Mass.: Pitman, 1985.

Sink, D.S., and Tuttle, T. *Planning and Measurement in Your Organization of the Future.* Norcross, Ga.: Industrial Engineering and Management Press, 1989.

GLOSSARY

absorption accounting   The accounting approach that requires that all the costs incurred in a period to directly manufacture or support the production of products be charged to the units completed.

accounts payable/payables   The recording of expenses owed but not yet paid by the company.

accounts receivable/receivables   The account where sales that have been made on credit are recorded until the cash is received from the customer. It is the result of an accrual accounting transaction.

accrual accounting   The basic accounting model that records revenues and expenses when they are *economically* incurred, rather than when the cash is paid for them. It consists of a system of accrual and deferral accounts that allow a company to recognize income when the primary revenue-generating activities have been performed, which leads to the *matching* recognition of the expenses incurred to generate those revenues.

accruals   Accounts used to record expenses that have been incurred but not yet paid and revenues that have been earned but not received.

accumulated depreciation   The accrual account in which the annual depreciation charge is recorded. It is called a contra-account because it offsets the value of the assets recorded in the "property, plant, and equipment" account.

action control   A control that focuses on how an activity is performed.

activity   A discrete unit of work with a definable output.

activity-based accounting   An accounting system that pools costs based on the activities those costs support, and charges out these costs whenever this type of activity occurs, whether the cause is a product, customer, or special request.

activity-based budgeting   The application of activity-based concepts to the planning process for a company.

activity-based costing   A subdiscipline of activity-based accounting that employs two-stage allocation procedures to develop the full cost of a product.

activity-based cost management   A comprehensive performance measurement system built around the horizontal activity structure of the organization; it merges operational and financial data. It is focused on decision support, employing relational data-base structures for flexibility.

A wide range of estimates can be included in this system, not all of which tie to the traditional accounting system.

allocation The arbitrary assignment of overhead to the units of product or service of a specific time period.

apportionment The use of operationally derived estimates to attach costs to specific cost objects.

articulation The term reflecting the fact that the three basic financial statements (balance sheet, income statement, and statement of cash flows) are linked; the two "flow" statements close into the balance sheet, and the balance sheet reflects the changes in accounts due to income and cash transactions.

asset Objects, claims, and other rights owned by, and having value to, a company.

asset management/asset performance The effective utilization of a company's assets to produce profits.

asset turnover ratio A ratio that looks at the relationship between the total dollars invested in a specific class of asset and the revenues generated by the firm.

assignable cost Those costs that can be reasonably attached to a specific cost object.

attributable costs The costs that will "go away," in the long term, if a specific course of action is followed. Costs that are caused by an activity over the long term.

audit The annual review of a company's books and financial statements to determine if they conform with generally accepted accounting principles. It is required of all publicly traded companies.

avoidable cost Costs that can be eliminated in a very short period of time if a specific course of action is undertaken or a decision is made.

backflushing An accounting procedure that assigns all the costs for converting raw materials to finished goods at the completion of the production process. At this time, raw material costs are also moved from this account to finished goods.

balance sheet A listing of the account balances of a company as of a specified date.

batch A group of output units made at the same time.

batch costs The costs incurred because of the decision to make a batch of product.

behavior of costs The relationship of a cost to changes in the output volume of an activity.

benchmarking   The study of a company's performance as compared to one or more similar firms. The benchmarking study can compare industry performance or look for best-in-class achievements for a specific function or area.

book value   Purchase price of an asset less its accumulated depreciation.

bottleneck resource   Within a system, the asset or activity that constrains the total output that can be produced.

breakeven volume/sales   The point at which all costs are covered by revenues; total fixed costs are equal to total contribution margin at this point.

budget   A financial plan for a future period of time.

budgeted capacity   The expected volume of production for the coming year.

burden rate   A colloquial term used for the ratio of overhead to direct labor cost.

capability   The future potential to create value.

capacity   The total amount of work, or value, that a resource can provide.

capacity utilization   The percentage of total available capacity that is dedicated to producing goods and services.

capital budgeting   The budgeting and planning for large ticket expenditures for fixed assets, processes, and projects for a company.

capital intensity   The ratio of fixed assets to the total assets owned by a firm.

capital lease   A lease that represents an installment purchase, and that must therefore be recorded as a liability and asset by the company.

capitalization   The recording of an expense on the balance sheet, creating a permanent asset.

cash basis   An alternative accounting process that only records revenues when cash has been received, and expenses when bills are paid. All transactions are based on the flow of cash, not economic value. Used in many small businesses.

causality   The cost accounting principle that attempts to assign costs to their causes.

classification   Categorizing accounting data into a logical and useful framework to support reporting and analysis.

competitive advantage   Superior performance in some aspect of the value chain, which gives a firm an edge over its competition in securing market share.

complexity The level of interdependence in a system; reflects the total number of products, parts, processes, activities, and shared resources that combine to support organizational action.

conservatism A key accounting principle that requires that expenses be recorded and reported as soon as it is likely they will have to be paid, and revenue recognition put off until it is likely payment will be received. Its outcome is the minimization of the reported net income of a firm.

control/control orientation The use of accounting measurements, or any performance measurements, to guide individuals in organizations to perform required tasks; it also covers the use of this information to evaluate performance, and make adjustments where necessary.

controllability The degree to which costs can be controlled, or removed, when a decision is made; often used to denote the degree to which a manager can influence the costs in his or her area of responsibility.

controllability network A loose control structure that factors in the multiple performance expectations and goals for any one aspect of the value chain. Incorporates the fact that interdependence is the basis for control in modern organizations.

contribution margin Selling price less variable cost, or the dollars remaining after paying variable costs to cover fixed costs.

core competency The primary technological or administrative expertise of a company.

cost An outflow of service potential or the creation of an obligation to relinquish serviceable items owned by the organization; the resources used up in making a product, performing a service, or to support operations over a defined period of time.

cost accounting The branch of the FMIS concerned with attaching costs to various cost objects to support product costing, decision making, planning, and control.

cost control The active, ongoing management of the costs for delivering a specific product, service, or product-service bundle to a customer.

cost drive/driver The activity that causes a cost (e.g., the consumption of resources). The underlying reason for cost consumption.

cost object The reason for the use of resources, or the question being analyzed.

cost reduction A program of mandated cuts in the costs of performing established activities or producing existing products and services. Usually part of a budget packet.

cost of capital   The cost, in terms of interest on invested funds, that has to be paid by a company. It is a combination of the dividend and interest percentages for each of their respective financing instruments. What it costs a company to borrow money.

cost of goods sold   The total amount of expense assigned to the units sold by a company in a period. It is required to include the full costs of production for the period.

cost of quality   An FMIS report that details the costs incurred for conformance (prevention and detection) and nonconformance (internal and external failures) quality efforts.

cost-volume-profit analysis   A short-term decision model that specifies the point at which fixed costs are recovered by a product or group of products, based on estimates of the total fixed and variable costs associated with the cost object.

cross-allocation   The charging of service costs from one part of the company to another, usually from nonproductive to productive departments, as part of the full cost accounting model.

current asset   Any asset acquired by a firm that is projected to have a useful life of one year or less. This includes cash, marketable securities, inventory, and accounts receivable in most firms.

current liabilities   Unpaid debts that are due within one year or less.

customer perspective   The basic philosophy for organizing a company that builds from the notion that every individual has a customer, and that the company is really a chain of customers, intergrated horizontally to provide final goods and services to the external customer.

debt-to-equity ratio   A financial ratio that details the leverage of the firm, or how much of its total capital comes from debt versus equity financing. Total debt divided by owner's equity.

deferrals   Accounts that record expenditures made before the expenses were incurred, and revenues that have been received before earned.

depreciation   The expensing of the acquisition cost of a fixed asset over an extended period of time, based on the useful life of the asset. The most commonly used methods include units of production, straight-line depreciation, double-declining balance, and sum-of-the-year digits. This area is tightly defined for *tax reporting* purposes. A company may use different depreciation methods for tax and financial reporting, and for different assets. This choice can be reversed at any point in the life of the asset.

differential analysis   Decision analysis that focuses on the different costs and benefits of a range of alternative actions.

direct cost   Costs that can be unambiguously assigned to a specific product, service, or cost object.

discounted cash flow   An analytic tool that factors in the present value of a stream of cash flows in order to compare alternatives with differing cash flow patterns.

dividends   The payment of a portion of a company's annual net income to the stockholders of record. Can take the form of cash payments or additional shares of stock.

double-entry accounting   The system of checks and balances based on the use of "debits" and "credits" that is the basis of financial recordkeeping.

economic order quantity   An inventory model sometimes used to determine the level, and timing, of inventory replenishment.

economic transaction   An accounting transaction recorded when the economic event is completed rather than when cash changes hands.

economies of scale   An economic theory that states that, as a company increases in size, it can generate more output with a less than proportional increase in the inputs used.

efficiency variance   The difference between the quantity of labor or materials used in a product and that allowed by the engineered standard or budget.

empowerment   The granting of decision-making authority to the individuals closest to the point of action in a firm. Goes hand in glove with the "whole person" approach to human resources.

equivalent units of production   The accounting estimate for the amount of work performed in a period in a process industry. Transforms in-process work to their "whole-unit" equivalent.

expected value   A decision model that factors in the riskiness of a projected stream of cash flows.

expense   Resources consumed by a company to generate the revenues of that period.

factoring   Turning over accounts receivable to an outside agent for collection. This can be done on an ongoing basis to generate cash immediately on sale of goods. A fee is charged for this service by the factoring firm.

flexible budget   A budget that is recalculated for a range of potential levels of activity.

financial accounting standards board (FASB)   The self-regulating body that oversees the practices of public accountants, audit procedures, and responds to disclosure shortcomings by creating and issuing GAAP pronouncements and rulings.

financial cycle The period of time between the closing of the books of record. Often denotes the preparation of a budget through the recording of actual events.

financial management information system (FMIS) The entire range of procedures and responsibilities performed within the financial function of a modern organization. It includes the detailed recording of transactions in the general ledger, financial statement preparation, and the creation of internal information to support decision making.

fixed cost A cost that does not change, in total, with changes in production volumes within the relevant range of activity.

flexible manufacturing systems (FMS) Any one of a number of advanced manufacturing methods that focuses on minimizing the set-up time required to change from one product to another. These systems can consist of one computer numerical control machine or an entire assembly line. The key feature is flexibility and responsiveness to changes in demand.

full costing Another term for absorption accounting; the process of attaching a product or service's direct cost plus a fair share of indirect costs in order to assign all costs incurred in a period to some output unit.

gamesmanship A dysfunctional consequence of control systems. Involves the manipulation of numbers, or the excessive reliance on them, to the detriment of performing the desired activities in an efficient and cost-effective way.

generally accepted accounting principles (GAAP) The body of formal regulations, pronouncements, rulings, and accepted practices that guide the compilation of a company's financial statements.

goal congruence The situation that occurs when everyone in an organization is pursuing the same, or complementary, objectives.

going concern assumption Approach that treats an accounting entity as though it has an infinite life, or period, of future operations.

gross margin Revenues less cost of goods sold. The dollars left after covering the cost of goods to use for other purposes.

gross margin percentage Gross margin divided by reported net revenues.

historical cost The accounting principle that requires that every transaction be recorded in terms of its cash value at the time the transaction occurred. It is the required method for recording accounting events.

holding costs The costs incurred to hold inventory, including carrying costs for the capital tied up, warehousing, record keeping, and related activities and expenses.

homogeneity The cost accounting principle that requires the grouping of like costs, either by output supported or input characteristics.

human resource accounting A branch of the FMIS that concerns itself with attempting to value the human resources in a company.

identification Selecting the accounting transactions and events that affect the financial status of the firm.

idle capacity Available capacity that is not used for production at any one point in time.

income statement The financial report that captures the effects of changes in the source or use of funds during a period; the matching of revenues for a period against related expenses to determine net income.

incremental budgeting Budgeting that is based on prior year expenditure patterns.

incremental cost The increase in cost that comes from accepting a specific offer for additional business, or pursuing an additional course of action.

indirect cost A cost that cannot be unambiguously assigned to a specific product, service, or cost object.

interpretation The accounting task that analyzes the financial statements to explain their meaning and limitations.

inventory Goods received and held for production (raw materials), work-in-process, or finished goods held for shipment. It is a current asset.

inventory costing methods The accounting policy choice that determines what dollar value is assigned to the inventories and cost of goods sold for a company. Includes first in–first out [FIFO], last in–first out [LIFO], weighted average, and specific identification methods. Company chooses which policy to follow, then must consistently apply it over time. Note: The GAAP requirement is simply for a *reasonable* method to be used in valuing inventory.

job order costing A cost accounting model that attaches costs to a specific job, or order, based on actual consumption, and then burdens output with overhead using a prescribed rate.

just-in-time accounting An accounting model that pools costs together around the cellular design of just-in-time manufacturing, and charges these costs out to goods units produced upon their completion. Direct labor is usually not kept as a separate cost item in these systems.

just-in-time manufacturing (JIT) A manufacturing approach that focuses on eliminating the move and queue elements of the production process by resequencing work stations to reflect the assembly, or process flow, path of a product, product family, or service.

liability Creditor's claims on a company's assets.

life cycle costing   A cost model that examines the total costs incurred and revenues generated, over the lifetime of a product, from either the customer's or company's perspective.

linearity   The degree to which the same number of units are produced, or same level of activities performed, on a day-to-day basis.

line of credit   A pre-established credit line for companies; can be used on demand without establishing need.

liquidity   A company's ability to generate enough cash from its daily operations to pay the bills those activities create.

management control   The process of keeping an organization on track.

management myopia   An excessive short-term focus in the management process.

manufacturing cycle efficiency   A ratio that compares processing time to the total cycle time for producing a good or service. It details the effectiveness of current capacity utilization.

matching principle   The accounting principle that requires that revenues recognized in a period be matched against the expenses incurred to generate them.

measurement   The analysis, and attaching of a value to, an economic transaction, operational event, or any other activity or asset within an organization.

net income   The residual amount of revenues remaining after all expenses for a period are paid.

nonconformance costs   Those costs incurred because a product or service does not meet customer expectations; also refers to internal "rework" in either the production or support groups due to *not doing the job right the first time*. The cost of work and rework that does not meet specifications.

normal capacity   The average amount of production within a facility.

off balance sheet financing   The use of leases and related financial instruments to avoid recognizing a liability for an asset that is committed to the company for an extended period of time. The company legally has the liability to pay the lease, but does not record this debt on the books.

operating cycle   The time that elapses from the time material is ordered until the receipt of payment for finished goods.

operating lease   A lease that does not qualify as a capital asset transaction, which means that the company will not retain control over the asset for most of its useful life. This allows a company to employ off balance sheet financing.

opportunity costs   The costs or benefits of a foregone opportunity. When one course of action is taken, resources are committed that are then no longer available for other uses. The "next best use" that could be made of resources is the opportunity cost of committing them to a specific course of action.

overhead   The term used for the indirect costs of doing business, or those costs not directly traceable to a specific unit of product or service.

overhead allocation   The use of some prescribed scheme for charging overhead out to units of product or services within a specified time period.

overleveraged   Term used to describe a company that carries an excessively high debt load (debt is *over* 50% of its total funding).

owner's equity   The funds provided by the company's owners, as well as the retention of earnings from prior periods.

period costs   Those costs that are deemed to provide value only in the current time period.

personnel control   The human side of the control process.

practical capacity   The "best" level of production, given existing constraints and traditional patterns of down time and output.

prepaid expense   An expense that is paid before it is due. This creates a short-term asset on the balance sheet that is "written off" as the economic event occurs.

present value   The value today of a dollar to be received some time in the future.

process/process orientation   The horizontal value chain used to deliver goods and services; a focus on how work is actually done (the sequence of activities).

process accounting   A cost accounting model designed for use in process industries that pools all cost spent in converting materials to finished goods and assigns it to the estimated volume of output for a period.

product cost   The expenses directly assigned to a product.

product-service bundle   The linkage of a product to a specified set of services, which are offered as a package to customers.

purchase price variance   The difference between the budgeted cost of material and the actual cost at time of purchase.

realization principle   The accounting principle that states that revenues are only earned with disposable funds are available. It guides the recognition of revenues and expenses based on the criteria that they are "very likely" to occur.

recording   Using a systematic method for keeping track of transactions.

registered securities The securities of a company that have been approved by the SEC for trading on public exchanges.

regularity The degree to which the same products are made, or same activities performed, within an organization over an extended period of time.

relevant cost A cost that is directly related to or affected by a decision.

relevant range The range of production over which the assumptions about the behavior of costs holds true.

repetitive manufacturing A manufacturing process that repeatedly makes the same goods in the course of a year, or production cycle. The goods are usually discrete, countable outputs.

reporting Periodically summarizing the collected and classified financial information into statements and reports.

responsibility accounting The branch of the FMIS that is concerned with assigning the responsibility for outcomes to individuals; accounting-based control that is normally vertical in nature, following the chain of command.

result control A control that is focused on the outcome of an activity.

retained earnings That portion of a company's annual net income that is retained for future use.

return on assets A financial ratio used to evaluate a company's performance. Net income divided by total assets.

return on investment A financial ratio used to evaluate the effectiveness of management in generating profits for investors; net income divided by total invested capital.

revenues Resources received by a company as a result of providing products or services to outsiders during a specified period of time.

revenue recognition An accounting policy choice that specifies the point at which the majority of the productive activities of a firm have been completed, and hence revenues can be recorded as earned. Can occur at the point of sale, at shipment, or during other key stages in the productive process.

sales discount A company policy that allows customers to deduct a specified percentage of an invoice for early payment.

sales mix The ratio of unit sales, or revenues, for a company's various products.

salvage value The projected residual value of an asset at the end of its useful life to the company.

securities exchange commission (SEC) The governmental body charged with overseeing the public reporting process for all publicly traded companies. Established under the auspices of the Security Exchange Acts of 1933 and 1934, this body has the final word in specifying required disclosures and accounting practices.

semifixed, or stepped fixed, costs Costs that are fixed over a smaller relevant range than the majority of the total pool of fixed costs.

semivariable, or stepped variable, costs Costs that do not change in direct proportion to changes in output volume, but which respond to small changes in these volumes.

spending variance The difference between what was actually spent for a unit of raw materials, labor or overhead, and what was allowed by the engineered standards, or budgeted, amount.

standard cost A costing model developed by the scientific management school that develops engineered cost and efficiency estimates for the amount of materials and labor a product should consume. Overhead is then applied based on one of the measured activities.

statement of cash flows A detailed disclosure of the sources and uses of cash broken out by operating activities, financing activities, and investing activities.

strategic cost analysis That branch of the FMIS concerned with identifying the strategic position of a company in its industry, and analyzing various strategic options for their long-term effect.

sustainable competitive advantage A competitive advantage that can be maintained over an extended period of time.

systems perspective A management approach that focuses on the activities within an entire value chain, looking for improvements by identifying bottlenecks and eliminating them.

sunk costs Dollars that have already been spent, and will not be changed by a new decision.

target cost The difference between the projected allowable cost, given desired market share and profitability figures, and that which currently exists. It is the excess cost targeted for elimination through continuous improvement. This is a primary Japanese tool for strategic cost analysis.

target profit The desired profitability level for a product, product family, segment, division, or time period.

theoretical capacity The "best" a system could do, if there were no down time or related inefficiencies.

time-based management A philosophy of management that focuses on time as the critical element within an organization; the objective is to maximize the velocity of materials through the system, or minimize the time required to respond to customer requests, using a variety of analytic and physical tools.

time period   External accounting records and transactions are bordered within specified periods of time.

time value of money   The recognition that interest changes the value of a dollar over time.

timing difference   Discrepancies between the flow of cash in or out of a business and the recording of the revenue or expense in the accrual accounting system.

total quality management (TQM)   A management technique that focuses on the elimination of waste through the process of continuous improvement. This objective is obtained through empowering the workforce to make process decisions, such as stopping the production line when an error is detected.

transfer price   The cost attached to units of goods or service that are traded within a company.

unavoidable cost   A cost that will not be eliminated if a decision is made, or course of action chosen, *even though* that cost appears to be linked to, or caused by, that activity.

unearned revenue   The account used to record the receipt of money from customers before the required economic revenue-generating event has been completed.

units of production depreciation   A depreciation method that charges off the cost of the fixed asset on a regular basis to the units produced by it.

value   The price a customer is willing to pay for a good or service.

value chain   The linked set of activities required to meet customer requirements.

variability   The relationship between a unit of output and the amount of a specific input it consumes.

variable costs   Costs that change, in total, based on the output volume. Costs that are incurred each and every time a unit of output is made.

variance   The difference between a standard and actual cost.

volume variance   The difference between the overhead actually applied to products and that which was estimated at the *budgeted* level of production.

weighted average contribution margin   The average contribution margin for a company's product portfolio.

zero-based budgeting   A budgeting approach that forces all expenses and programs to be reapproved on an annual basis.

INDEX

ABOUT APICS

APICS, the educational society for resource management, offers the resources professionals need to succeed in the manufacturing community. With more than 35 years of experience, 70,000 members, and 260 local chapters, APICS is recognized worldwide for setting the standards for professional education. The society offers a full range of courses, conferences, educational programs, certification processes, and materials developed under the direction of industry experts.

APICS offers everything members need to enhance their careers and increase their professional value. Benefits include the following:

- Two internationally recognized educational certification processes—Certified in Production and Inventory Management (CPIM) and Certified in Integrated Resource Management (CIRM), which provide immediate recognition in the field and enhance members' work-related knowledge and skills. The CPIM process focuses on depth of knowledge in the core areas of production and inventory management, and the CIRM process supplies a breadth of knowledge in 13 functional areas of the business enterprise.

- The APICS Educational Materials Catalog—a handy collection of courses, proceedings, reprints, training materials, videos, software, and books written by industry experts, many of which are available to members at substantial discounts.

- *APICS The Performance Advantage*—a monthly magazine that focuses on improving competitiveness, quality, and productivity.

- Specific Industry Groups (SIGs)—suborganizations that develop educational programs, offer accompanying materials, and provide valuable networking opportunities.

- A multitude of educational workshops, employment referral, insurance, a retirement plan, and more.

To join APICS, or for complete information on the many benefits and services of APICS membership, **call 1-800-444-2742** or **703-237-8344.** Use extension 297.

Other titles of interest to you from The Business One Irwin/APICS Library of Integrated Resource Management . . .

MANAGING HUMAN RESOURCES
Integrating People and Business Strategy
Lloyd S. Baird
By teaming examples of successful human resources experiments with his own practical tips on human resource objectives, employee recruitment, and appraisal, Baird examines and reveals the success potential for integrating people and business strategy. (268 pages)
ISBN: 1-55623-543-7

PURCHASING
Continued Improvement through Integration
Joseph R. Carter
A complete, integrative resource for purchasing goods and services in the United States and abroad! As free trading zones open up around the world, the possibilities for sourcing nationally and internationally expand with them. This guide will help you enrich the buyer-supplier relationship that can lead to higher-quality products from suppliers and more lucrative contracts from buyers. (200 pages)
ISBN: 1-55623-535-6

FIELD SERVICE MANAGEMENT
An Integrated Approach to Increasing Customer Satisfaction
Arthur V. Hill
How do companies like 3M and Whirlpool consistently rate high with customers in areas of field service repair? Hill, an established researcher and consultant in service operations management, examines their tactics and offers practical strategies to manage field service for high-quality results. (200 pages)
ISBN: 1-55623-547-X

MANAGING FOR QUALITY
Integrating Quality and Business Strategy
V. Daniel Hunt
Maintaining a standard of quality doesn't have to cost a lot, but neglecting this standard can cost your company plenty. Hunt, author of the best-selling *Quality in America*, provides another excellent guide for achieving your quality goals—and effectively managing quality costs. (360 pages)
ISBN: 1-55623-544-5

INTEGRATED PRODUCTION AND INVENTORY MANAGEMENT
Revitalizing the Manufacturing Enterprise
Thomas E. Vollmann, William L. Berry, and D. Clay Whybark
Slash production and distribution costs by effectively monitoring inventory! This strategic guide explains the inventory control processes that strengthen the customer service function and improve purchasing forecasts and production schedules. (385 pages)
ISBN: 1-55623-604-2

Available in fine bookstores and libraries everywhere.

APICS
The Educational Society for Resource Management

Please send more information about...

❏ APICS Publications—More than 400 textbook and courseware items. *(#01041)*

❏ The APICS Certified in Integrated Resource Management (CIRM) process—A full curriculum and self-assessment system focusing on the functions and interrelationships of 13 areas of the business enterprise. *(#09016)*

❏ The APICS Certified in Production and Inventory Management (CPIM) process—A self-assessment system providing in-depth knowledge in the core areas of production and inventory management. *(#09002)*

❏ APICS Membership and Educational Programs—A wealth of opportunities, from 2 1/2-day workshops and courses to APICS' six-day all-encompassing international conference and exhibition. *(#82021)*

If you enjoyed this book, continue your learning through other APICS-sponsored educational opportunities.

Name:_____

Title: _____

Company:_____

Address:_____

City: _____

State: _____

ZIP:_____

Phone (w): _____

BUSINESS REPLY MAIL
FIRST-CLASS MAIL PERMIT NO 2858 FALLS CHURCH, VA

POSTAGE WILL BE PAID BY ADDRESSEE

ATTN: MARKETING DEPARTMENT
AMERICAN PRODUCTION AND INVENTORY
CONTROL SOCIETY INC
500 W ANNANDALE RD
FALLS CHURCH VA 22046-9701